Anonymous

Supplement to the alphabetical Catalogue of the Library of Parliament

Anonymous

Supplement to the alphabetical Catalogue of the Library of Parliament

ISBN/EAN: 9783337151911

Printed in Europe, USA, Canada, Australia, Japan

Cover: Foto ©Andreas Hilbeck / pixelio.de

More available books at **www.hansebooks.com**

SUPPLÉMENT

AU

CATALOGUE ALPHABÉTIQUE

DE LA

BIBLIOTHÈQUE DU PARLEMENT

CONTENANT TOUS LES LIVRES ET BROCHURES AJOUTÉS A LA BIBLIOTHÈQUE
DEPUIS LE 15 MARS 1887, JUSQU'AU 10 FÉVRIER 1888.

IMPRIMÉS PAR AUTORITÉ.

OTTAWA:
IMPRIMERIE MACLEAN, ROGER ET CIE, RUE WELLINGTON.
1888.

SUPPLEMENT

TO THE

ALPHABETICAL CATALOGUE

OF THE

LIBRARY OF PARLIAMENT

CONTAINING ALL BOOKS AND PAMPHLETS ADDED TO THE LIBRARY FROM
MARCH 15TH, 1887, UNTIL FEBRUARY 10TH, 1888.

PRINTED BY AUTHORITY.

OTTAWA:
PRINTED BY MACLEAN, ROGER & CO., WELLINGTON STREET.
1888.

Rules of both Houses of Parliament

RESPECTING THE

LIBRARY OF PARLIAMENT.

A proper Catalogue of the Books belonging to the Library shall be kept by the Librarians in whom the custody and responsibility thereof shall be vested; and who shall be required to report to the Houses through Mr. Speaker, at the opening of each Session, the actual state of the Library.

No person shall be entitled to resort to the Library during the session of Parliament except the Governor General, the Members of the Privy Council, and of the Senate and House of Commons, and the Officers of both Houses, and such other persons as may receive a written order of admission from the Speaker of either House. Members may personally introduce Strangers to the Library during the daytime, but not after the hour of seven o'clock, P.M.

During a Session of Parliament no books belonging to the Library shall be taken out of the building, except by the authority of the Speaker or upon receipts given by a member of either House.

During the recess of Parliament, the Library and Reading Room shall be open every day in each week, Sundays and Holidays excepted, from the hour of ten in the morning until three in the afternoon; and access to the Library shall be permitted to persons introduced by a member of the Legislature, or admitted at the discretion of the Librarian; subject to such regulations as may be deemed necessary for the security and preservation of the collection; but no one shall be allowed to take any book out of the Library except Members of the Legislature, and such others as may be authorized by the Speaker of either House.

During the recess of Parliament, no Member of either House not residing at the seat of Government shall have liberty to borrow or have in his possession at any one time more than three works, from the Library, or to retain the same for a longer period than one month.

No other person who may be privileged by card, by the Speaker of either House to borrow Books from the Library, shall be allowed to have in his possession more than two Books at any one time, or to retain the same longer than three weeks, and all such persons shall return the Books so taken when required by the Librarian.

No Books of reference, or Books of special cost and value may be removed from the seat of Government under any circumstances.

At the first meeting of the Joint Library Committee at every Session of Parliament, the Librarians shall report a list of the Books absent at the commencement of the Session, specifying the names of any persons who have retained the same in contravention of either of the foregoing Rules.

Règlements

CONCERNANT LA

BIBLIOTHÈQUE.

Un catalogue des livres de la Bibliothèque est tenu par les Bibliothécaires qui en ont la garde et la responsabilité; ils doivent faire rapport à la Chambre, par l'entremise de M. l'Orateur, à l'ouverture de chaque Session, de l'état dans lequel se trouve la Bibliothèque.

Aucune personne ne peut avoir accès à la bibliothèque, pendant les Sessions du Parlement, si ce n'est le Gouverneur-Général, les membres du Conseil Privé, ceux du Sénat et de la Chambre des Communes, les Officiers des deux Chambres, et toute autre personne qui obtient un billet d'admission de l'Orateur de l'une ou de l'autre Chambre. Les membres peuvent, en personne, introduire des étrangers dans la bibliothèque, pendant le jour, mais non après sept heures P.M.

Pendant les Sessions du Parlement aucun livre de la Bibliothèque ne peut être emporté de l'édifice excepté sur autorisation de l'Orateur, ou lorsqu'un membre de l'une ou de l'autre Chambre en donne un reçu.

Pendant la vacance du Parlement la Bibliothèque et la Chambre de Lecture sont ouvertes tous les jours de chaque semaine, excepté les dimanches et jours de fête, depuis dix heures du matin jusqu'à trois heures de l'après-midi; et la Bibliothèque sera ouverte aux personnes introduites par un membre de la Législature, ou admises à la discrétion du Bibliothécaire, sujettes aux règles qui sont jugées nécessaires pour la sûreté et la conservation des livres, mais il n'est permis à qui que ce soit, si ce n'est aux membres de la Législature et aux autres personnes ayant l'autorisation de l'Orateur de l'une ou de l'autre Chambre, d'emporter un livre hors de la Bibliothèque.

Durant les vacances du Parlement, aucun membre de l'une ou de l'autre Chambre, ne résidant pas au siège du gouvernement, n'aura le droit d'emprunter ou garder en sa possession plus de trois ouvrages à la fois; de plus, il ne devra pas les garder plus d'un mois en sa possession.

Aucune des personnes ayant le privilège,—sur la foi d'une carte du président de l'une ou de l'autre Chambre,—d'emprunter des livres à la Bibliothèque, ne pourra avoir en sa possession plus de deux ouvrages à la fois ou les garder plus de trois semaines, et toutes ces personnes devront remettre les livres ainsi empruntés, lorsqu'elles en seront requises.

Aucun livre de référence ou ouvrage de luxe et de prix ne pourra être emporté du siège du gouvernement pour aucune considération.

A chaque session du Parlement, les Bibliothécaires devront, à la première assemblée du comité mixte de la Bibliothèque, soumettre une liste de tous les livres qui n'ont pas été remis au commencement de la Session, en spécifiant les noms des personnes qui auront gardé ces livres contrairement aux règles qui précèdent.

In addition to the foregoing rules, the Joint Library Committee have agreed to the following new Rules, to which the attention of persons frequenting the Library, or making use of any books belonging thereto, is specially requested.

1. It is strictly forbidden to make any mark, by pencil or otherwise, in any book belonging to the Library, or to turn down leaves therein, or otherwise deface the same.

2. No person (other than a member of Parliament) is permitted to have access to any of the Galleries surrounding the Library, without the express permission of the Librarian, or unless accompanied by an officer of the Library.

3. No visitor shall be permitted to remain in the Library with his hat on; nor will smoking, or spitting on the floor or carpet be permitted, in any of the Library apartments.

4. No audible conversation will be allowed in the reading room; nor shall any person be permitted to partake of refreshments therein; and no dogs shall be allowed in the Library.

Outre les règles qui précèdent, le Comité de la bibliothèque a recommandé l'adoption des règles suivantes, dont toutes personnes fréquentant la bibliothèque ou faisant usage des livres qui la composent sont priées de prendre connaissance :

1. Il est strictement défendu de faire aucune marque, au crayon ou autrement, dans un livre appartenant à la Bibliothèque, d'en plier les feuilles ou de le défigurer d'aucune autre manière.

2. Personne, à l'exception des membres du Parlement, ne pourra monter dans les galeries sans la permission expresse du bibliothécaire, ou sans être accompagné de quelque employé de la Bibliothèque.

3. Aucun visiteur ne pourra garder son chapeau sur sa tête; personne ne pourra fumer, ni cracher sur le parquet ou le tapis d'aucune des chambres de la Bibliothèque.

4. On ne pourra converser à haute voix dans la chambre de lecture; on ne pourra non plus se permettre d'y manger. On ne laissera pas entrer de chiens dans la Bibliothèque.

REPORT

OF THE

JOINT LIBRARIANS OF PARLIAMENT.

REPORT OF THE JOINT LIBRARIANS OF PARLIAMENT.

Since the last Session the section devoted to United States Congressional Documents has been enriched by additions which extend the collection backward from 1854 to 1827. The Librarians hope to be able during the year to complete the series backward to 1820, the earliest period at which any such collections generally begin.

Two more alcoves of the Library have been placed at the disposal of members for the purpose of study and work, and the books have been more conveniently placed for reference.

The Canadian and American sections have received many valuable additions during the year. Among them, we may point out: *Champlain's Voyages*, 1613. Cotton Mather pamphlets on pre-historic America, very scarce. We have also been able to secure the following newspapers, which are perhaps the only copies existing, at least for several of them, bearing on the political troubles of 1837-8 : *The North American*, Swanton, Vt., 1839-41. *Mackenzie's Gazette*, New York and Rochester, 1838-40. *Le Patriote Canadien*, Burlington, 1839-40, published by M. Duvernay, after the suppression of La Minerve. *L'Aurore des Canada*, Montreal, 1838-9. *La Canadienne*, 1840. We have also bought in London a very fine collection of Canadian and American maps, published during the latter end of the eighteenth century.

Additions in considerable number have been made, partly by purchase and partly through the aid of the officer in charge of the distribution of Parliamentary documents, to the volumes of Hansard available for the use of members. The order of the Hansard Committee of last Session, to afford the Library an increase in the number of volumes annually sent to the Library, has been duly fulfilled by the officer in charge of the House of Commons printing. The Library is now fully provided with sufficient copies of the Debates since 1875, to stand the wear and tear of many Parliaments.

The Library has been duly provided with copies of all documents relating to the Fisheries question, and it will be seen, on reference to the Catalogue, that a special list or index of documents relating to the great international question has been prepared. This will probably be found very useful.

The various pamphlets bearing on our trade relations with the United States and England have been provided ; and a list of references to documents treating of Reciprocity, has also been prepared.

Considerable additions have been made to the Law section, the latest editions of the most useful text-books having been procured.

RAPPORT DES BIBLIOTHÉCAIRES CONJOINTS DU PARLEMENT

Depuis la dernière session, ils se sont efforcés de compléter la collection des documents du Congrès, en remontant de 1854 à 1827. Ils se flattent de pouvoir, pendant l'année prochaine, remplir le vide qui existe encore jusqu'à 1820, date au delà de laquelle ces documents sont maintenant introuvables.

Deux nouveaux compartiments de la bibliothèque ont été mis à la disposition des députés, pour leur permettre de travailler, et les livres de référence qui peuvent leur être utiles, se trouvent à proximité.

Les sections américaines et canadiennes se sont enrichies, pendant l'année, de plusieurs ouvrages remarquables ; entre autres, nous pouvons attirer l'attention sur les Voyages de Champlain, édition de 1813 ; une brochure très rare de Cotton Mather sur l'Amérique préhistorique ; dix volumes des Relations des Jésuites, *édition princeps*, etc.

Nous avons réussi à nous procurer les journaux canadiens suivants, tous très rares (quelques collections même sont uniques), et ayant tous rapport aux troubles de 1837-38 : *The North American*, publié à Swanton, Vermont, 1839-41 ; la *Mackenzie's Gazette*, publiée à New York et à Rochester, de 1838 à 1840 ; *Le Patriote Canadien*, fondé à Burlington par M. Duvernay, 1839-40, après la suppression de *La Minerve* ; *L'Aurore des Canadas*, 1838-39 ; *La Quotidienne*, 1839 ; *La Canadienne*, 1840, ces trois derniers publiés à Montréal.

Nous avons aussi acheté à Londres, une magnifique collection de cartes géographiques ayant rapport à l'Amérique et publiées dans la seconde moitié du 18e siècle.

La bibliothèque s'est aussi enrichie d'un nombre assez considérable des Rapports des débats officiels pour l'usage des députés, en partie par achat et en partie par l'intermédiaire de l'officier préposé à la distribution des documents parlementaires. L'ordre du comité des Débats, qui a recommandé, l'an dernier, d'augmenter le nombre des copies du rapport officiel des débats du Parlement, a été fidèlement suivi par celui qui est chargé de la distribution des impressions de la Chambre des Communes. La bibliothèque est maintenant amplement pourvue de débats officiels depuis 1875.

On trouvera à la bibliothèque tous les documents ayant rapport à la question des pêcheries et on verra, en référant à l'Index supplémentaire, qu'une liste spéciale des documents ayant rapport à cette grande question internationale a été préparée avec soin. Nous espérons que l'utilité d'une telle liste sera appréciée.

Les bibliothécaires se sont efforcés de réunir toutes les brochures publiées dernièrement sur nos relations commerciales avec les Etats-Unis et l'Angleterre ; ils y ont ajouté une liste des documents relatifs à la réciprocité.

La section des lois a été complétée et renferme maintenant les dernières éditions des ouvrages de droit.

The work on the Catalogue of Americana has been begun, as it is understood that the means for continuing a very essential work will be duly provided.

The annual catalogue of accessions has been delayed a little in order to include the latest publications. It will be distributed at an early date.

All of which is respectfully submitted.

A. D. De CELLES, *G. L.*
MARTIN J. GRIFFIN, *P. L.*

Les travaux préparatoires à la publication du catalogue américain ont été commencés, vu qu'il a été entendu que des mesures allaient être prises pour sa publication prochaine.

La distribution du catalogue annuel des additions à la bibliothèque sera retardée de quelques jours afin de nous permettre d'y inclure les dernières publications. Les membres du Parlement le recevront sous peu.

On trouvera, ci-joint, une liste des dons faits à la bibliothèque.

Le tout respectueusement soumis.

A. D. DeCELLES, *B.G.*
MARTIN J. GRIFFIN, *B.P.*

LIST OF DONATIONS TO THE LIBRARY OF PARLIAMENT FOR 1887.

N. F. Davin, Esq., M.P.:
: Ireland and the Empire—A speech.
: Home Rule for Ireland—A speech.

Hon. S. A. Green, Boston:
: Boston City Auditors' Report for 1885-6, 1886-7.
: Boston 7th Annual Report of the State Board of Health. And several pamphlets.

G. Johnson, Esq.:
: Official Register of the United States. 2 vols., 4to., 1885.

Andrew Russell, Esq., Ottawa:
: Bouchette's British Dominions in North America. 2 vols.
: —— —— Topographical Dictionary of Lower Canada.

Hon. J. S. D. Thompson, Minister of Justice:
: London (*official*) *Gazette* from 1854 to 1864. 42 vols.

G. W. Wicksteed, Esq., Q.C.:
: The Eton Latin Grammar. 8vo. L., 1885.

From Father Chiniquy:
: Fifty years in the Church of Rome. Cinquante ans dans l'Eglise de Rome.

The Dominion of Canada Rifle Association:
: Report of—for 1886.

The Law Society of Upper Canada:
: Catalogue of Library 1886.

The Corporation of the City of London, Eng.:
: Bronze medal commemorating the visit of the Colonial and Indian Representatives to London, in 1886.

The Royal Colonial Institute:
: Proceedings for 1886-7.

The Toronto University:
: Examination Papers, 1887.

The Government of Bahamas:
: Revised Laws to 1877 and for the years 1878, 1879, and 1880 to 1887.

The Government of British Columbia:
  Statutes, 1887. 4 copies.
  Sessional Papers, 1887. 4 copies.
  Journals, Leg. Assembly, 1827. 4 copies.
  Official Gazette, 1887.

The Government of the Cape of Good Hope:
  Votes and Proceedings, 1887.
  Annexures to Votes and Proceedings, 1887.
  Minutes of Legislative Council, 1887.
  Assembly Reports of Committees, 1887.
  Statistical Register for 1886.

The Dominion Government:
  Dom. Annual Register, H. J. Morgan, 1886.
  Statistical Abstract for 1886 (3 copies).
  Disallowance of Provincial Acts.
  Statutes: Journals: Votes and Proceedings and Debates for 1887. 6 copies.
  Official Gazette, 1887.

The Government of Hawaii:
  Annual Report of the Collector of Customs, 1886.
  Honolulu Almanac and Directory, 1887.
  Census of Hawaiian Islands, 1884.
  Laws of Hawaii for 1886.

The Government of Hong Kong:
  Blue Book, 1886.
  Sessional Papers, 1886-7.

The Imperial Government:
  Chronological Table and Index to Statutes, 10th Ed., 1887.
  Hansard. Vol. 311, 312, 313, 314, 315, 316, 317, 318, 319, 320 and 321.
  Parliamentary Blue Books.

The Government of India:
  Unrepealed General Acts of the Governor General in Council from 1834 to 1887. 8 vols.

The Government of Jamaica:
  Blue book for 1885-6.
  Handbook for 1887-8. 2 copies.
  Revised Statutes from 1680 to 1866.
  Laws for 1865, 1867 and 1873 to 1887. 17 vols.

The Government of New Brunswick:
 Laws, 1887.

The Government of Nova Scotia:
 Debates, 1887.
 Laws, 1887. 2 copies.
 Journals, 1887. 2 copies.
 Official Gazette, 1887.

The Government of New South Wales:
 Notes and Proceedings, Leg. Assembly, 1887.
 Journals Leg. Council, 1885-6. 4 vols., 1887, 1 vol.

The Government of New Zealand;
 Parliamentary Debates. Vol. 54, 55, 56 and 57.
 Journals Leg. Council, 1886.
  do H. of Representatives, 1886.
 Appendix do 1886. 4 vols.

The Government of Ontario:
 Sessional Papers, 1887, 21-50. 6 copies.
 Statutes for 1887.
 Journals Leg. Assembly, 1887.
 Annual Report Bureau of Industries, 1886. 2 copies.
 Annual Report Bureau of Agriculture, 1886. 2 vols.

The Government of Prince Edward Island:
 Statutes, 1886, 1887.
 Journals Leg. Council, 1886.
  do do Assembly, 1886.

The Quebec Government:
 Statutes, 1887. 4 copies Eng.
  do do 2 do Fr.
  do Report of Commission on Consolidation of. Part IV. 3 copies.
 Journals (Eng. and Fr.) Leg. Assembly, 1887. 6 copies of each.
  do Leg. Council for 1886 and 1887.

The Government of Queensland:
 Parliamentary Debates. Vol. 48, 49 and 50.

The Government of Tasmania:
 Statistics for 1885.
 Journals and Printed Papers, 1886. Vol. 7.

The United States Government :
  Report of Commissioner of Education, 1884-5.
    do of Educational Exhibits at New Orleans Exposition, 1884-5.
    do on under-valuation in Customs Entries. 2 vols., 1887.
    do of Commission of Fish and Fisheries, 1885 : 1887, 2 pts.
  Bulletin of the U. S. Fish Commission, 1886. Vol. 6.
  Report on Emigration and Immigration, 1887.
    do of Railway Commission for 1887.
  Customs Duties imposed by Foreign Nations on American Produce. 8 vol. Washington, 1887.
  Tri-Daily Meteorological Record, April, 1878.
  Atlantic Coasters Nautical Almanac, 1888.
  Cattle and Dairy Farming of the World, 1887.
  Forestry in Europe, 1887.
  Commercial Relations of U. S., 1884-1885.
  Proceedings International Monetary Conference at Paris in 1881.
  War of the Rebellion. Vol. 20.
  Register of the Dept. of Justice, 1886.
  Complete Army and Navy Register of the U. S., from 1776 to 1887.
  Congressional Record. Vol. 18, pts. 1, 2, 3.
  ——————————— Index to Vol. 18, pts. 1-3.
  Statutes at Large. Vol. 24.
  Land Law Decisions. Vol. 5.
  Postal Laws for 1887.
  Report of Attorney General, 1887.
  Michael, W. H. Congressional Directory.
  Report of Court of Claims. Vol. 22.
  ——— of Crops for December, 1887.
  Monthly Weather Review for Nov., 1887.
  Index Catalogue of the Library of the Surgeon General's Office. Vol. 8.
  Census, 1880. Vol. 12-18.
  Executive Documents, 1849-50. Vol. 8.
  Executive Documents, 1882-83. Vol. 7.
  Senate Miscellaneous Documents, 1883-4. Vol. 3.
  House   do   do   do   Vol. 1, 4, 6, 32 and 33.
    do Reports, 1883-4. Vol. 1, 2, 3, 4, 5, 7.
  Senate Miscellaneous Documents, 1884-5. Vol. 1, 5, 8.
    do Reports, 1884-5. Vol. 1, 2.
  House Miscellaneous Documents, 1884-85. Vol. 1, 2, 4, 5, 6, 7, 9, 10, 11, 12, 13, 14, 16, 17.
  House Reports, 1884-85. Vol. 1 and 4.

The United States Government :—Continued.
  Executive Documents, 1884-5. Vol. 5, 6, 7, 8, 9, 10, 12, 15, 16, 17, 18, 19, 20, 21, 22, 23, 24, 25, 26, 27, 28, 29, 30, 31, 32, 33, 34.
  Senate Miscellaneous Documents, 1885. Vol. 1 and 3.
  House   do   do   1885-6. Vol. 2, 4, 27.
  Executive Documents, 1885-6. Vol. 2.
  House Reports, 1885-6. Vol. 1, 2.
  Senate Journal, 1886-7.
  House   do   do
  McKee's Indices to Senate and House Reports to 1887.

The State of California :
  Report of the Bureau of Labour and Statistics for 1883-4 and 1886.
  Report on Condition of Labourers employed by contractors on the sea wall at San Francisco.
  Report on Advisability of Displacing Chinese Labour in Orchards, &c.

The State of Connecticut :
  Report of the Bureau of Labour and Statistics for 1885 and 1886.
  Senate Journal, 1887.
  House   "   1887.
  Legislative Documents, 1887. 2 vols.
  Law Reports. Vol. 54.
  Special Acts for 1887.
  Public Acts for 1887.

The State of Illinois :
  Report of the Bureau of Labour and Statistics for 1882, 1884 and 1886.

The State of Indiana :
  Annual Reports of the Bureau of Labour and Statistics for 1882, 1883, 1884, 1885 and 1886.

The State of Kansas :
  Report of the Bureau of Labour and Statistics for 1885 and 1887.
  Laws, 1887.
  Law Reports. Vol. 36.

The State of Louisiana :
  Annual Reports. Vol. 38.

The State of Maine :
  Maine Wills, 1640-1760.
  State Year Book, 1887.
  Insurance Reports, 1886 and 1887.
  State Board of Health, 1886.

The Ste of Maine :—Continued.
   Report on Cattle Disease, 1887.
   School Report, 1886.
   Report on Agriculture, 1884, 1885 and 1886.
      do   on Savings Banks and Trust Companies, 1887.
   Journal of the House, 1885.
      do   do   Senate, 1885.
   Acts and Resolves, 1887.
   Law Reports, 77 and 78.
   Legislative Documents, 1885. 2 vols.
      do   do   1886. 2 vols.

The State of Massachusetts :
   Acts, 1887.
   Manual of General Court, 1887.
   Law Reports. Vol. 144.
   Journal of the Senate, 1887.
      do   of the House, 1887.

The State of Michigan :
   Report of Bureau of Labour and Statistics for 1884, 1885, 1886 and 1887.
   Law Reports. Vols. 57, 58 and 59.
   Legislative Manual, 1887-8.
   Report of Auditor General, 1886.
   Insurance Report, 1887.
   Crop Reports, 1887.
   Report of Soldiers Home, 1887.
      do   of Committee on Life Assurance Companies.
      do   of Charges against M. H. Dakin.
      do   of Secretary of State relating to Farms.
      do   of State Prisons for 1885-6.
   Acts for 1897.
   Joint Documents, 1885. Vol. 1, 2, 3.

The State of Minnesota :
   Law Reports. Vol. 35.
   Executive Documents, 1886-7. 4 vols.
   Senate Journal, 1887.
   House   do   do
   General Laws   do
   Special   do   do

The State of Missouri :
   Report of Bureau of Labour and Statistics for 1886.
   Official History of the Great Strike of 1886.

The State of New Jersey:
   Supplement to Revision of Statutes, 1887.
   Legislative Documents. 3 vols. 1887.
   Senate Journal, 1887.
   Minutes of the Assembly, 1887.
   Laws for 1881.
   Equity Reports. Vol. 42.
   Digest of Decisions of the Courts. Vol. 3, 1887.

The State of New York:
   Law Reports. Vol. 49 and 52.
   Appeal Reports. Vol. 103-106.
   Laws from 1789-1796. Vol. 3.
         do   1797-1800. Vol. 4.
   Laws for 1801. Vol. 5.
   Regents of the University.
   Session Laws, 1887.
   State Museum Report, 39th.
      do Library Report.
   Sullivan's Campaign.
   Assembly Documents of 1886. Vol. 9.
   Chamber of Commerce Report for 1885-6 and 1886-7.
   Senate Journal, 1887.
      do Documents, 1887. 4 vols.
   Assembly Documents, 1887. 10 vols.
      do Journal, 1887. 2 vols.
   Manual for the use of the Legislature, 1887.
   Annual Report of the Agricultural Experiment Station for 1887.

The State of Pennsylvania:
   Legislative Documents, 1883 4. 2 vols.
         do   do   1885-6. 2 vols.
   Senate Journal, 1883 and 1885.
   House   do   do   do
   Executive Documents, 1885-6. 1 vol.
   Laws, 1887.
   Small's Legislative Handbook for 1871, 1873, 1874, 1878, 1879, 1881, 1883, 1885 and 1887.
   Reports of the second Geological Survey of the State. 42 vols.
      do of the Geological Survey for 1886. 2 vols.
      do of the Auditor General, 1886.
      do of Soldiers Orphans Institute, 1886.
      do of Inspector of Mines, 1886.

The State of Pennsylvania :—Continued.
    Reports of State Treasurer, 1886.
        do   of Public Charities, 1886.
        do   do   Instruction, 1886.
        do   of Fire and Marine Insurance, 1886.
        do   of Life Insurance, 1886.
        do   of Commissioner of Fisheries, 1886.
        do   of Adjutant General, 1886.
        do   of Banks and Savings Banks, 1886.
        do   of Internal Affairs. 2 vols, 1886.

The State of Vermont :
    Journals Senate, 1886.
        do   House, 1886.
    Compilation of the Election Laws, 1885.
    Laws of the Illegal Sale and use of Intoxicating Liquor, 1885.
    Biennial Report of the Fish Commission, 1885-6.

The State of Wisconsin :
    Report of the Bureau of Labour and Statistics, 1885-6.

The Government of Victoria :
    Acts for 1886.
    Debates. Vol. 51, 52 and 53.
    Votes and Proceedings Leg. Assembly, 1886. Vol. 1, 2, 3.

SUBJECT HEADINGS – DIVISIONS DE SUJETS.

	PAGE.
Agriculture	1
Anthropology and Zoology	2
Belles Lettres, English and Foreign	5
Belles Lettres Françaises	10
Bibliography	13
Botany	15
Brochures Françaises	117
Classics, Greek and Latin	20
Colonial	21
Commerce	21
Constitutional Law and History	21
Donations, List of	xii
Droit	25
Economie Politique	26
Education	26
Encyclopædias, etc	27
Engineering and Public Works (Génie Civil)	27
Essays—Selected from Leading Periodicals	123
Financial	29
Fine Arts (Beaux-Arts)	29
Fisheries Controversy. Official Documents relating to the	29
Genealogy and Heraldry	40
Geography and Travels	37
Geology	40
History, General	43
—— American	47
Law—Civil and Ecclesiastical	55
Librarians' (Joint) Report	ix
Mathematics	62
Medical Sciences	62
Military and Nautical Sciences	63
Music	65
Natural History	66
Natural Philosophy—Physique et Chimie	66
Painting, Engraving, etc	68
Pamphlets—English, Canadian and American	90
Parliamentary, Legislation, etc	68
Periodicals	127
Philology and Literary History	70
Philosophy	71
Political Economy	71
Politics	72
Politique	72
Railway Economy	74
Reciprocity—Official Documents (U.S.) relating to	75
Religion—Theology and History of Religions	76
Social Science	80
Sports and Games	81
Statistics	81
Travels in America	83
Useful Arts and Manufactures	86

Alphabetical Index of Authors and Subjects.

This Index refers to the pages of manuscript additions to the PRINTED CATALOGUE, by reference to which the full titles to the Books indicated will be found.

Index alphabétique des auteurs et des matières.

Cette table renvoie aux pages des additions manuscrites faites au CATALOGUE IMPRIMÉ où se trouvent les titres complets des ouvrages indiqués.

The names of authors are printed in SMALL CAPITALS. The titles of Works and of Works having no Author's name are printed in Roman Letters. Subjects are printed in *Italics*.

Les noms d'auteurs sont imprimés en PETITES CAPITALES ; les titres des ouvrages et les ouvrages anonymes sont en lettres romaines ; et les matières sont indiquées en caractères *italiques*.

	PAGE
ABBEY, C. J. The English Church and its bishops, 1700-1800.............	36
ABBOTT, H. L. System of Submarine Mines for the U. S.	686
ABBOTT, L. Henry Ward Beecher : a sketch of his career............	1229
A'BECKETT, T. Transfer of Land Statute............	90
ABERCROMBY, Hon. R. Weather changes from day to day (Int. S. S. 59)....	578
Academy Sketches, 1886	713
ACUNA, le P. C. d'. Voyages and Discoveries in South America	1352
ADAM, Sir C. E. Political State of Scotland in the last century	50
ADAMS, H. B. Study of History in American Colleges............	77
ADAMS, H. C. Public Debts............	50
———. Juridical Glossary............	59
ADAMS, J. Q. Letters on the Fisheries and the Mississippi............	16
AGASSIZ, L. Sa vie et sa correspondance	480
AGNEW, Hon. D. History of Pennsylvania, north of the Ohio............	1247
AGOSTINI, E. La France et le Canada............	1285
Agriculture. Annual Report of the Ontario Board for 1886............	660
——— ——— of the U. S. Commissioner, for 1886	660
——— ——— Agricultural Society of England, Journal of the Royal, for 1887	650

AGRICULTURE.

Agriculture. Annual Report of the Ontario Board for 1886.
——————————— Connecticut Board of, 1886.
——————— Agricultural Society of England, Journal of the Royal, for 1887.
American Short Horn Herd Book. Vols. 31 and 32.
Animal Castration. **Liautard, A.**
Annual Report of the U. S. Commissioner, for 1886.
Cattle and Dairy Farming of the World.
Herbages et prairies naturelles. **Boitel, Am.**
Maine Agricultural Reports for 1884-85-86.
Michigan Horticultural Society Report for 1886.
Mon Jardin : géologie, botanique, culture. **Since, A.**
Plantes vénéneuses. **Cornevin, C**

AITKEN, W. Science and practice of medicine. 7th ed	666
ALEXANDER, Mrs. Forging the Fetters	827
——— ——— Mona's choice............	827

	PAGE
ALEXANDER, C. B. New York Law of Insurance	104
ALEXANDER, Bishop W. St. Augustine's Holiday and other poems.	855
ALGER, J. G. New Paris Sketch Book	510
Alice, Princess. Scenes in the life of,—By E. C. Kenyon.	480
ALLAIN, l'abbé. La question d'enseignement en 1789	74
ALLARD, L. Les vie muettes	887
Allemagne (l') actuelle	391
ALLEN, A. V. G. Continuity of Christian Thought	44
ALLEN, Grant. The Beckoning Hand and other Stories	827
—————— In all shades (Picc. Nov. 177)	847
ALLEN, S. M. Old and New Republican Parties	158
ALLIES, T. W. The Throne of the Fisherman	31
ALLINSON (E. P.) and PENROSE, B. Philadelphia, 1681-1877	1247
American and Foreign Iron Trades. Statistics of	514
American Catholic Historical Researches	1182
American Catholic Historical Society of Philadelphia. Records of the.	1182
American Historical Association. Papers of the	1182
American Nautical Almanac for 1890	687
American Short Horn Herd Book. Vols. 31 and 32	659
American Society of Civil Engineers. Transactions	744
Ami (l') de la Religion (1814-42)	919
ANCKETILL, W. R. Adventure of Mick Calligbin, etc	827
ANDERSEN, H. C. Fairy tales and Stories. Translated by C. Siewers	896
ANDERSON, A. A. Twenty-five years in a waggon in the gold regions of Africa	564
ANDERSON, Dr. W. J. Two chapters' in the life of H. R. H. Edward, Duke of Kent	1412
Annual Register for 1886	308
ANQUEZ, L. Henri IV et l'Allemagne	424
ANSON, Sir W. R. Law of Contract. 4th ed	108
ANTHOINE, E. A travers nos écoles	84

ANTHROPOLOGY AND ZOOLOGY.

Bee-keeper's (The) Guide. **Cook, A. J.**
Birds (The) of Ontario. **McIlwraight, Thos**
Brachyura, Report on (Chall. Exp. Zool. Rep., v. 17). **Miers, E. J.**
Catalogue of Canadian Birds. **Chamberlain, M.**
—————— the birds of Kansas. **Goss, N S.**
Cephalodiscus Dodecalophus, Report of (Chall. Exp. Zool. Rep., v. 20.) **McIntosh, W. C.**
Cumacea, Report on (Chall. Exp. Zool. Rep. v. 19). **Sars, G. O.**
Hexactinellida, Report on (Chall. Exp. Zool. Rep., v. 21). **Schulze, Dr F E.**
Histoire générale des races humaines. **Quatrefages, A. de.**
Monaxonida, Report on (Chall. Exp. Zool. Rep. v. 20). **Ridley (S. O.) & Dendy, A.**
Nationalities of the United Kingdom. **Lubbock, Sir. J.**
Nemertea, Report on (Chall. Exp. Zool. Rep., v. 19). **Hubrecht, Dr. A. A.**

ANTHROPOLOGY AND ZOOLOGY—*Concluded.*   PAGE
  Pêche (la) et les poissons. **La Blanchère, H. de.**
  Phyllocarida, Report on (Chall. Exp. Zool. Rep. v. 19). **Sars, G O.**
  Physiognomonie (de la). **Delestre, J. B.**
  Pteropoda, Report on (Chall. Exp. Zool. Rep., v. 19). **Pelseneer, P.**
  Races (des) humaines. **Omalius d'Halloy, J. J. d'**
  Radiolaria, Report of the (Chall. Exp. Zool. Rep., v. 18). **Haeckel, E.**
  Systems of Consanguinity and Affinity of the Human Family. **Morgan, L. H.**
APPLETON's Cyclopedia of American biography........................ 1226
ARCHENHOLTZ, J. M. Von. History of the Free-Booters, or Buccaneers of America 1180
ARCHER, T. Gladstone and his contemporaries......................... 450
Archives des Affaires Etrangères. Inventaire analytique.............. 269
ARÈNE, Emm. Le dernier bandit....................................... 893
ARGYLL, Duke of. Scotland as it was and as it is.................... 397
ARISTOTLE. Politics and Economics. Translated by Walford............ 808
——————— Metaphysics. Translated by Rev. J. H. McMahon.............. 808
ARISTOPHANES. Comedies. Translated by W. J. Hickie.................. 807
Armée (l') et la démocratie.. 682
Armée (l') depuis le moyen-âge (l'Ancienne France).................. 410
ARMITAGE, T. R. Education and Employment of the Blind............... 87
ARMITAGE, W. Sketches of Church and State........................... 248
ARMOUR, E. D. Investigation of Titles............................... 93
ARMSTRONG, Rev. J. Life and Letters of Rev. Geo. Mortimer........... 1286
Arniston Memoirs. Three Centuries of a Scottish House............... 398
ARNOLD, T. J. Conspiracy and Protection Act, and Employers and Workmen Act... 87
ARNOULD, J. Marine Insurance. 6th ed................................ 112
ARON, J. Deux républiques sœurs: France et Etats-Unis............... 1230
Art, Masterpieces of Italian.. 712
Arts et métiers au moyen-âge. (L'Ancienne France)................... 410
Asbury, Bp. Francis. Life and times of. By W. P. Strickland........ 1196
ASHTON, Jno. Eighteenth Century Waifs............................... 828
Astor Library. Catalogue of the. Vol. 3............................. 905
ATKINSON, E. Margin of Profits...................................... 159
ATKINSON, W. N. and J. B. Explosions in coal mines.................. 764
AUBERT, F. Le Parlement de Paris (1314-1422)........................ 291
AUBERTIN, Chs. L'éloquence politique et parlementaire en France en 1789. 285
AUBINEAU, L. Epaves—récits et souvenirs............................. 887
AUDIAT, L. Brouage et Champlain (1578-1667)......................... 1272
Australasian Directory for 1887 525
AUSTIN, J. O. Genealogical Dictionary of Rhode Island............... 1226
AYTOUN, W. E. Lays of the Scottish Cavaliers........................ 856

		PAGE
BADEAU, A. Grant in peace from Appomattox to Mount McGregor		1230
——— ——— Military history of U. S. Grant. 1861-1865		1268
BADEN-Powell, G. State Aid		486
BAGENAL, P. H. Tory policy of Lord Salisbury		449
BAILLE, A. F. A Paraguayan treasure		828
BAILLON, H. Dictionnaire de botanique. Vol. 3		646
BAIREUTH, Margravine of. Memoirs, translated by H. R. H. Princess Christian		444
BAKER, G. L. C. History of the United States Secret Service		1218
BAKER, J. F. Federal Constitution		158
BAKER, Sir S. W. True tales for my Grandsons		828
BAKER, W. S. Character portraits of Washington		1221
BALDWIN, J. Elementary psychology and education		77
BALFOUR, F. H. Leaves from my Chinese Scrap book		557
BALL, J. Notes of a Naturalist in South America		608
BALL, Rt. Hon. J. T. Reformed Church of Ireland (1537-1886)		40
BALL, T. F. Queen Victoria, Scenes and Incidents of her life and reign		396
BALLANTYNE, R. M. Martin Rattler		828
——— ——— Red Rooney		828
——— ——— Big Otter		828
——— ——— Prairie Chief		828
Baltimore. The Chronicles of, by J. T. Scharf		1250
Baltimore Board of Trade Reports, 1886		524
Baltimore Council. Acts and Decrees of Third Council		252
BALZAC, H. de. Théorie de la démarche		879
——— ——— The Alkahest ; or, The House of Claës		879
——— ——— The Two Brothers		879
BANDELIER, A. F. Studies among the Sedentary Indians of New Mexico		1184
BAPST, G. Orfèvrerie française au XVIIIe siècle : les Germains		692
BARAT, L. Paris. Plage—rimes maritimes		887
BARBEY d'AUREVILLY, J. Les œuvres et les hommes		307
BARDOUX, A. La bourgeoisie française, 1789-1848		426
BARIL, le Comte V. L. L'empire du Brésil, monographie		1200
BARKER, A. E. J. On surgical operations		671
BARLOW, J. W. The Normans in South Europe		328
Barrow, Point. International Polar Expedition to		1392
BARTHÉLEMY. Correspondance politique (1792-1797)		269
BARTHÉLEMY, Ch. La guerre de 1870-71		434
BARTHOLEMEW, J. Gazetteer of the British Isles		511
——— ——— British Colonial Pocket Atlas		511

		PAGE
BARTRAM, W. Travels through North and South Caroline, Georgia, etc		1378
BASHKIRTSEFF, Marie. Journal de		898
BASSET, N. Guide du fabricant d'alcools et du distillateur		736
——— Guide du fabricant de sucre		737
BASTABLE, C. F. International Trade		518
BATBIE, A. Droit public et administratif, avec supplément		276
BATES, E. C. A year in the Great Republic		1372
BAUDONCOURT, J. de. Histoire populaire du Canada		1275
Bay of Fundy. Report of Trade of		524
BAZAN, E. P. Le Naturalismo		801
BEATTY, C. Two months' tour among the Indians of Pennsylvania		1198
BEAUDET, l'abbé L. Recensement de la ville de Québec, 1716		1273
BÉCHARD, F. Les deux Lucien		881
Becket, St. Thomas à. Life and Martyrdom. By Rev. J. Morris		35
BECQUE, H. Sardanapale—opéra		878
——— L'enfant prodigue—comédie		878
——— La Navette—comédie		878
——— Les honnêtes femmes—comédie		818
——— La Parisienne—comédie		878
——— Michel Pauper—drame		878
BEECHER, Henry Ward. Proverbs from Plymouth Pulpit. Selected by W. Drysdale		828
——————— A sketch of his career		1229
BÉGIN, l'abbé L. N. Chronologie de l'histoire du Canada		1274
BELKNAP, J. Discourse on the Discovery of America by Columbus		1167
BELL, B. Sketch of Lieut. Jno. Irving, of H. M. S. "Terror."		492
BELL, C. F. M. From Pharaoh to Fellah		560
BELL, Geo. Comment les monarchies finissent		411

BELLES LETTRES, ENGLISH.

    Adventure of Mick Callighin, etc. **Anckotill, W. R.**
    Alexia. **Price, E. C.**
    Allan Quatermain. **Haggard, H. R.**
    Allegra. **West, Mary.**
    Anchorage. **Field, Mrs. H.**
    André Cornélis. **Bourget, P.**
    Annals of a Sportsman. **Turgenieff, J.**
    April Hopes. **Howells, W. D.**
    Arthur Bonnicastle. **Holland, J. G.**
    Arthur Mervyn. **Brown, C. Brockden.**
    Autobiography of a Slander. **Lyall, E.**
    Baldine and other tales. **Edler. K. F.**
    Ballads of Books. **Matthews, B.**
    Bashkirtseff, Marie. Journal de.
    Bay-Path, The. **Holland, J. G.**
    Beckoning (The) Hand and other Stories. **Allen, Grant.**

BELLES LETTRES, ENGLI-II —*Continued.*

Bee (The) Man of Orn. **Stockton, F. R.**
Beyond the Seas. **Crawfurd, O.**
Big Otter. **Ballantyne, R. M.**
Bitter-Sweet—a poem. **Holland, J. G.**
Black, Wm. Novels. 17 vols.
Braddon, Miss. Complete Collection of Novels.
Bride of the Nile. **Ebers, Geo.**
Britta, a Shetland romance. **Temple, G.**
Brother Jonathan ; or, Thé New Englanders. **Neal, Jno**.
Brownies (The): their book. **Cox, P.**
Brownson, O. A. Complete works.
Buchholz (The) Family ; Sketches of German life. **Stinde, J.**
Buried Diamonds (Picc. Nov. 176). **Tytler, Sarah.**
Button's Inn. **Tourgee, A. W.**
Canada: a poem. **Gahan, J. J.**
Canadian Birthday Book. **",Seranus."**
Canadian Wild Flowers. **Johnson, Miss H. M.**
Canolles: Fortunes of a Partisan of '81. **Cooke, J. E.**
Captain Macdonald's Daughter. **Campbell, Arch.**
Captain Trafalgar. **Westall, W.**
Cavalier Lyrics: "For Church and Crown." **Ebsworth, J. W**
Histoire de la paroisse de Charlesbourg. **Trudelle, l'Abbe C.**
Chateau Bigot; its history and romance. **Lemoine, James M**
Children of Gibeon (Picc. Nov. 173). **Besant, W.**
Cid (The) ballads and other poems. **Gibson, J. Y.**
Clara Howard. **Brown, C. Brockden.**
Club (A) of one.
Cœruleans (The) : a vacation idyll. **Cunningham, H. S**
Colonel's (The) Money. **Lillie, L. C.**
Conspirateurs et policiers. **Tikhomirov, L.**
Constance ; a lay of the olden Time. **"Maple Leaf."**
Country (A) Gentleman and his family. **Oliphant, Mrs. M. O W**
Cowper, W. Concordance to poetical works of, by **Neve, J.**
Crime and Punishment: A Russian Novel. **Dostoyeffsky, F.**
Crowded out : and other sketches. **" Seranus."**
Crusade of the Excelsior. **Harte, Bret.**
Culture's Garland. **Field, Eug.**
Dawn. **Haggard, H. R.**
Dead Man's Rock : a romance. By **"Q."**
De Foe, D. Works 7 vols.
Diane de Breteuille—a love story. **Jerningham, H. E. H**
Dimitia Roudine. **Turgenieff, J.**
Disappeared (*Picc. Nov.* 178). **Tytler, Sarah.**
Dominion Day and other poems. **Dawson, Rev. Æ. McD**
Earth (The) trembled. **Roe, E. P.**
Edgar Huntly. **Brown, C. Brockden.**
Eighteenth Century Waifs. **Ashton, Jno.**
Emigrant (The) : a poem. **O'Grady, Standish.**
Enamarado (The) : a drama. **Hunter, D. J.**
En racontant : récits de voyages (traduits). **Gregory, J. W.**
Episodes in a life of adventure. **Oliphant, L.**
Essays. New Edition. **Helps, Sir A.**
Etudes religieuses, sociales, politiques et littéraires. **Tardivel, J. P.**
Evenings in the Library. **Stewart, Junr., G.**
Every-day Topics. **Holland, J. G.**
Evil (The) Genius (*Picc. Nov.* 174). **Collins, Wilkie.**

BELLES LETTRES, ENNLISH—*Continued.*

Excursion to the Holy Land of Thought. **Lacroix, H.**
Expédition autour de ma tente; **Chartrand (des Ecorres) Jos.**
Expiation : a novel of England and our Canadian Dominion. **Oppenheim, E. Phillips.**
Face to Face. **Grant, R.**
Fairy Tales and Stories. **Andersen, H. C.** Translated by C. Siewers.
Fatal Zero, a Homburg Diary, (*Picc. Nov.* 172). **Fitzgerald, P.**
Fathers and Sons. **Turgenieff, J.**
Fighting the Sea. **Rand, E. A.**
Fille (la) des Indiens rouges. **Chevalier, H. E.**
Fleur-de-Lys and other poems. **Weir, Arthur.**
Forging the Fetters. **Alexander, Mrs.**
Frau Whilhelmine. **Stinde, J.**
Frontier Stories. **Harte, Bret.**
Fur-clad Adventurers. **Mudge, Z. A.**
Garrison gossip gathered in Blankhampton. **Winter, J. S.**
Gates (The) between. **Phelps, E. S.**
Gate (A) of Flowers and other poems. **O'Hagan, Thos.**
Gaverocks (The). **Gould, S. Baring.**
Geraldine. A Souvenier of the St. Lawrence.
Glow Worm Tales. **Payn, J.**
Gold-Foil. **Holland, J. G.**
Half a century ; or, changes in Men and Manners. **Shand, A. J.**
Heir (The) of the Ages. **Payn, J.**
Henry Grattan and the Irish Volunteers. **Murphy, Rev. J. J.**
Holiday Tasks. **Payn, J.**
Home Again. **Macdonald, Geo.**
Hortus inclusus. Messages from the Wood to the Garden. **Ruskin, J.**
Hours of Childhood and other poems.
House (A) Party : a novel. "**Ouida.**"
Howe, Hon. Jos. Address delivered at the Howe Festival, 1871.
Hundred (A) Merry Tales—reproduced. **Hazlitt, W. C.**
Hundredth (The) Man. **Stockton, F. R.**
L'idiot. **Dostoievsky, Th.**
In all Shades (*Picc. Nov.* 177). **Allen, Grant.**
In and Around the Magdalen Islands. **Pope, A. M.**
In Divers Tones. **Roberts, C. G. D.**
In the Land of the Moose, the Bear and the Beaver. **Daunt, A.**
In the Wrong Paradise. **Lang, A.**
Invader (The) and other Stories. **Tolstoi, Cte. L.**
Irving (The) Club among the White Hills. **Glasier, Alfred.**
Ismay's Children. **Laffan, Miss.**
James Hepburn, Free Church Minister. **Veitch, S. F. F.**
Jane Talbot. **Brown, C. Brockden.**
Jess. **Haggard, H. R.**
Jill and Jack. **Dillwyn, E. A.**
Jones Family (The). **Holland, J. G.**
Joueur (le) et les nuits blanches. **Dostoievsky, Th.**
Julia Campbell. **Rowell, Mrs. J. H.**
Kaloolah. **Mayo, W. S.**
Kathrina : a poem. **Holland, J. G.**
Lapful (A) of Lyrics. **France, J.**
Laura Secord, the heroine of 1812. **Curzon, Sarah A.**
Lays of the Scottish Cavaliers. **Aytoun, W. E.**
Lessons in Life, by Timothy Titcomb. **Holland, J. G.**
Life, character and genius of Shakespeare. **Jones, Geo.**
Life and history of General Harrison. **Jones, Geo.**
Little Novels. **Collins, Wilkie.**

BELLES LETTRES, ENGLISH—*Continued.*
   Liza. **Turgenieff, J.**
   Locrine: a tragedy. **Swinburne, A. C.**
   Lord Floysham: a novel. **Walpole, F. G.**
   Loss and Gain. New ed. **Newman, Card.**
   "Loved I not Honour more!" **Rothwell, Annie.**
   Lyrical translations. **Parham, C. J.**
   Lyrics on Freedom, Love and Death. **Cameron, G. F.**
   Ma Confession. **Tolstoi, Cte. L.**
   Magnificent (A) Plebeian. **Magruder, Julia.**
   Malcolm: a story of Day Spring. **McKenzie, G. A.**
   Major & Minor. **Norris, W. E.**
   Martin Rattler. **Ballantyne, R. M.**
   Master of Tanagra (The). **Wildenbruch, E. von.**
   Memorials of Colcorton. **Knight, W.**
   Merry (The) Men and other tales. **Stevenson, R. L.**
   Millionaire (A) of Rough and Ready, and Devil's Ford. **Harte, Bret.**
   Miss Bayle's Romance; a story of to-day.
   Miss Gascoigne. **Riddell, Mrs. J. H.**
   Miss Gilbert's Career. **Holland, J. G.**
   Miss Jacobson's Chance. **Praed, Mrs. Campbell.**
   Mistress (The) of the Manse: a poem. **Holland, J. G.**
   Modern Men. By a Modern Maid.
   ——— (The) Vikings. **Boyesen, H. H.**
   Monarchs I have met. **Kingston, W. B.**
   Mona's Choice. **Alexander, Mrs.**
   Moore, S. Poems.
   Moral (The) Monitor: Essays. **Fiske, N.**
   Morgan, Mary. Poems and translations.
   Mother Carey's Chicken. **Fenn, G. M.**
   Moulin (le) sur la floss—traduction. **Eliot, George.**
   Mr. Absalom Billingslea and other Georgia Folk. **Johnston, R. M.**
   Mummer's (A) Wife. **Moore, Geo.**
   Mumu and the Diary of a Superfluous man. **Turgenieff, J.**
   Mystery (A). "**Caris Sima.**"
   Narka, the Nihilist. **O'Meara, Kathleen.**
   New history of Sandford and Merton. **Burnaby, F.**
   Nibelungenlied. Translated by Foster-Barham, Alfred G.
   Nibelungenlied. Traduit de l'allemand, par E. de Laveleye.
   Nicholas Minturn. **Holland, J. G.**
   North (The) American (Newspaper), Swanton, Vt.
   Nos grand'mères: discours. **Bourassa, Nap.**
   Novelist's (A) Note Book. **Murray, D. C.**
   Old Blazers Hero. **Murray, D. C.**
   Old (The) House at Sandwich. **Hatton, J.**
   Old (An) Woman's Story. **Rowe, Lizzie.**
   Only a Curate. **Egomet, E. G.**
   On the Eve. **Turgenieff, J.**
   On the Scent. **Majendie, Lady M.**
   Ormond. **Brown, C. B.**
   Our Radicals. **Burnaby, F.**
   Out of the Snow, and other stories. **Phillips, J. A.**
   Outsider (The). **Smart, H.**
   Pages from an old volume of life. **Holmes, O. W.**
   Perseverance Island. **Frazar, D.**
   The Phantom City: a volcanic romance. **Westall, W.**
   Plain Talks on familiar subjects. **Holland, J. G.**
   Poems of ten years, 1877-1886. **Knight, M. R.**

BELLES LETTRES, ENGLISH—*Continued.*

Possédés (Les) (Besi). **Dostoievsky, Th.**
Poulikouchka. **Tolstoi, Cte. L.**
Prairie Chief. **Ballantyne, R. M.**
Prince (A) of the Blood. **Payn, J.**
Princess (The) Casamassima. **James, H.**
Proverbs from Plymouth Pulpit. **Beecher, Henry Ward.**
La puissance des ténèbres: drame. **Tolstoi, Cte L.**
Pasco; a Cuban tale and other poems. **Manners, R R**
Recollections of Sedan. **Hewett. F. C.**
Red Rooney. **Ballantyne, R. M.**
Red Spider. **Gould, S. Baring.**
Representative Poems of Living Poets
Reveries of an Old Smoker. **Lewis, C. E.**
"Right (The) Honourable." **McCarthy (J.) and Praed, Mrs. C**
Ring (The) of Gyges. **Lisle, C. W.**
Romance of a Poor young man. **Feuillet, Oct**
——— ——— two Worlds. **Corelli. Marie.**
Rose (The) in Paradise. **Pyle, H.**
Sabina Zembra. **Black, Wm.**
St. Agustine's Holiday and other poems. **Alexander, Bishop W.**
Salad for the solitary and the social. **Saunders, F**
Scottish nationality and other papers. **Ker, Jno**
Sérapis: roman historique. **Ebers, Geo.**
Savenoaks. **Holland, J. G.**
Shakespeare, W. Works of. Victoria edition
——— ——— Index to the Works of. **O'Connor, E. M.**
Silence (The) of Dean Maitland. **Gray, M.**
Sir Hector's Watch. **Granville, Chs.**
Sketches in history and poetry. **Shairp, J. C.**
Smoke. **Turgenieff, J.**
Social Pressure. New ed. **Helps, Sir A.**
Some Modern Guides of English Thought. **Hutton, R. H**
Some Verdicts of History reviewed. **Stebbing, W**
Song (A) of Charity. **Cherriman, Prof.**
Spring Floods and a Lear of the Steppe. **Turgenieff, J.**
Springhaven, a Tale of the Great War. **Blackmore, R. D.**
Supplemental Nights to the Thousand and one Nights. **Burton, Sir R. F**
The Surgeon's Stories (from the Swedish). **Topelius, Z.**
Tchitchikoff's Journeys, or Dead Souls. **Gogol.**
Tecumseh and the Prophet of the West: a tragedy **Jones G.**
Thackeray, W. M. Collection of letters, 1847-1855
Titcomb's Letters. **Holland, J. G.**
Tony, the Maid. **Howard, B. W.**
Tour (The) of Doctor Syntax. **Combe, W.**
True tales for my Grandsons. **Baker, Sir S. W.**
Two chapters in the life of H. R. H. Edward, Duke of Kent. **Anderson, Dr. W J**
Two North country maids. **Wetheral, Mabel.**
Twok. **Griffin, W.**
Underwoods. **Stevenson, R. L.**
Unfortunate (An) Woman and Ass'ya. **Turgenieff, J.**
Vendetta! story of one forgotten. **Corelli, Marie.**
Virgin Soil. **Turgenieff, J.**
Waverly Anecdotes.
What to do. **Tolstoi, Cte. L.**
Wieland. **Brown, C. B,**
William and Annie: a tale. **Daniel, C. T.**
Win-on-ah; or, the Forest Light, and other poems **Ramsay, J. R.**

BELLES LETTRES, ENGLISH — *Concluded.*
   Witch's (The) Head. **Haggard, H. R**
   Woodlanders (The). **Hardy, T.**
   . Year (A) in Canada, and other poems. **Knight, Ann C.**

BELLES LETTRES FRANÇAISES.

   Affaire (l') Froideville. **Theuriet, A.**
   Agent (l') provocateur. **Revillon, T.**
   The Alkahest ; or, The House of Claës. **Balzac, H de**.
   Campaign in Kabylia. **Erckmann-Chartian**
   Alsacian (The) Schoolmaster. **Erckmann-Chatrian**.
   Amazone (l') bleue. **Pradel, G.**
   André le Justicier. **Oswald, F.**
   Assassinat de la ligne du Havre. **Oswald, F.**
   Autour du divorce, **" Gyp "**
   Bâton perdu (le). **Loyseau, Jean.**
   Bête (la). **Cherbuliez, V.**
   Blockade of Phalsbourg. **Erckmann-Chatrian.**
   By Order of the King. **Hugo, V.**
   Cabaret (le) du Puits sans vin. **Morin, L.**
   Calvaire (le). **Mirbeau, Oct**
   Candidat (le). **Claretie, J**
   Canne de M. Michelet (La). **Claretie, J.**
   Carmen (Translation). **Mérimée, Prosper.**
   Chateaubriand, Vte de. Œuvres complètes. 12 vols.
   Chenier, A. Poésies.
   Chicot. **Le Hounec, A.**
   Chimère. **Mouton, Eug.**
   Choses du Nord et du Midi. **Montégut, Em.**
   Choses vues. **Hugo, V.**
   Citizen Bonaparte, 1794-1815. **Erckmann-Chatrian.**
   Civils et Militaires. **Duraudeau, Em.**
   Clientes (les) du docteur Bernagius. **Biart, L.**
   Clipper (The) of the Clouds. **Verne, Jules.**
   Cloud and Sunshine. **Ohnet, G.**
   Club (le). **Cohen, F.**
   Comédie (la) du jour. **Milland, Alb**
   Comte (le) Kostia. **Cherbuliez, V.**
   Confessions of a Clarinet Player. **Erckmann-Chatrian**
   Conscript, The. **Erckmann-Chatrian.**
   Contre le Flot. **Claveau, A.**
   Corinne ou l'Italie. **Stael, Mme de**
   Country (The) in danger, 1792. **Erckmann-Chatrian.**
   Cousine (la) d'André. **Granfort, M. de.**
   Crime (le) de la 5ème Avenue. **Darcey, M.**
   Daniel Rock, the blacksmith. **Erckmann-Chatrian.**
   Dernier (le) Bandit **Arène, Emm.**
   Deux (les) Lucien. **Béchard, F.**
   Dos à dos. **Merouvel, Chs.**
   Drames (les) de la place de Grève. **Buffenoir, H.**
   Duchesse (la) Martin, comédie. **Meilhac, H.**
   Elévations poétiques et religieuses. **Jenna, Marie.**
   Encore Un. **Monselet.**
   Enfant (l') prodigue: comédie. **Becque, H.**
   Epaves : récits et souvenirs. **Aubinean, L.**
   Etudes familières de psychologie et de morale. **Bouillier, F.**
   Fils (le) de Porthos. **Mahalin, P.**
   Finesses (les) de Pinteau. **Leroy, Chs.**

BELLES LETTRES, FRANÇAISES—*Suite.*
  Fior d'Aliza. **Lamartine, A. de.**
  Francillon. **Dumas, A., fils.**
  Friend Fritz. Great Invasion, 1813-14. **Erckmann-Chatrian.**
  Gaietés (les) de l'année. **Grosclaude.**
  Gazul, Clara. Théâtre de. *Voir* **Mérimée, Prosper.**
  Girardin, Mme E. de. Poésies complètes.
  Goncourt, Edm. et J. de. Journal, 1851-61.
  History of a Crime. **Hugo, V.**
  Honnêtes (les) femmes : Comédie. **Becque, H.**
  Iceland (An) Fisherman. "**Loti, P.**"
  Illustrious (The) Dr. Matheus. **Erckmann-Chatrian.**
  Jeanne Avril. **Bonnières, R. de.**
  Jours (les) de Combat. **Hugues, C.**
  Jumeaux (les) de Lusignan. **Carpentier, Mlle E.**
  Les Misérables. (Translated into English). **Hugo, V.**
  Lettres à Babet **Boursault.**
  Lettres de ma chaumière. **Mirbeau, Oct.**
  Livre (le) de Caliban. **Bergerat, Em.**
  Madame Thérèse, or, the Volunteers of '92. **Erckmann-Chatrian.**
  Mal assortis. **Mouezy, A.**
  Man-Wolf, The. **Erckmann-Chatrian.**
  Marquis (les) de Saint-Lys.
  Mes moulins. **Bergerat, Em.**
  Michel Pauper: drame. **Becque, H.**
  Miss Eva **Deslys, C.**
  Moments de loisir. **Delbos, L.**
  Monde (le) où l'on vole. **Hosier-Grison.**
  Monstres (les) de Paris. **Mahalin, P.**
  Mont-Oriol. **Maupassant, G. de.**
  Moralité nouvelle du mauvais Riche et du Ladre.
  Moreau, Hegésippe. Œuvres complètes.
  My Brother Yves. "**Loti, P.**"
  Navette (la) : comédie. **Becque, H.**
  Née Michon. **Pène, H. de.**
  Ninety-three. **Hugo, V.**
  Noir et rose. **Ohnet, G.**
  Nord, contre Sud. **Verne, Jules.**
  North against South. **Verne, Jules.**
  Notre-Dame. (Translated into English). **Hugo, V.**
  Œuvre (l'). **Zola, Em.**
  Origine (l') du français. **Espagnolle, l'abbé J.**
  Poèmes barbares. **Leconte de Lisle.**
  Polish (The) Jew. **Erckmann-Chatrian.**
  Pradon. Œuvres de.
  Prisme (le) poésies diverses. **Prudhomme, Sully.**
  Paradis (Au) des Enfants. **Theuriet, A.**
  Paris—Plage : rimes maritimes. **Barat, L.**
  Parisienne (la) : comédie. **Becque, H.**
  Pécheur d'Islande. "**Loti, P.**"
  Poèmes antiques. **Leconte de Lisle.**
  Poèmes et récits. **Coppée, F.**
  Princesse. **Halevy, L.**
  Propos d'exil. "**Loti, P.**"
  Quand j'étais petit. **Biart, L.**
  Reboul, Jean. Poésies.
  Racine, Jean. Théâtre complet.
  Racot, A. Champagne Cornod.

Belles lettres, Françaises—*Fin*

   Roi (le) des Jacques. **Cassan, Mme.**
   Roi (le) Margot. **Perret, Paul.**
   Roman (le) d'un crime. **Tarbé, E.**
   Roman (le) d'un jésuite. **Beugny d'Hagerue, G. de.**
   Sardanapale: opéra. **Becque, H.**
   Souvenirs de la Place de la Roquette. **Grison, G.**
   Souvenirs et visions. **Vogue, E. M. de.**
   States (The) General. **Erckmann-Chatrian.**
   Stories of the Rhine. **Erckmann-Chatrian.**
   Survivants (les) de la Commune. **Chincholle, Chs.**
   Tales before Supper. Translated from Gautier and Merimée.
   Terre (la) de France. **Julliot, F. de.**
   Théâtre complet. **Dumas, A., Fils.**
   Théâtre de Clara Gazul. La Jaquerie, etc. **Merimée, Prosper.**
   Théorie de la démarche. **Balzac, H. de.**
   Things seen. **Hugo, V.**
   Toile (la) d'araignée. **Davyl, L.**
   Toilers of the Sea. **Hugo, V.**
   Toussaint Galabru. **Fabre, F.**
   Travers (A) l'âme et le monde. **Euchelli, C.**
   Trois femmes pour un mari: comédie. **Grenet-Dancourt, E.**
   Trop riche. **Geunevraye, A.**
   Two (The) Brothers. **Balzac, H. de.**
   Uncle Max. **Carey, Rosa H.**
   Une femme d'argent. **Malot, H.**
   Unisson (l'). **Duruy, G.**
   Victor de Laprade, sa vie et ses œuvres. **Biré, E.**
   Vies (les) Muettes. **Allard, L.**
   Vie parisienne, 1886. **Blavet, Em.**
   Vieux (le) General. **Chincholle, Chs.**
   Voyage au pays des singes. **Jacolliot, L.**
   Waterloo. **Erckmann-Chatrian.**
   Wild (The) Huntsman. **Erckmann-Chatrian.**
   Year One of the Republic. **Erckmann-Chatrian.**
   Zyte. **Malot, H.**

	PAGE
BELLESHEIM, Rev. A. History of the Catholic Church of Scotland	39
BELLOC, A. Les postes françaises	429
BENHAM, Rev. W. Dictionary of Religion	28
BENSON, A. C. William Laud, sometime Archbishop of Canterbury	493
BERGERAT, Em. Mes moulins	887
————— Le livre de Caliban	887
BERKELEY, H. Wealth and Welfare	485
BERLIOZ, H. Traité d'instrumentation et d'orchestration	721
BESANT, W. Children of Gibeon (Picc. Nov. 173)	847
BESSON, Mgr. Life and Works of F. F. X. de Mérode. (Translation)	495
BEUDANT. Travels in Hungary in 1818	522
BEUGNY D'HAGERUE, G. de. Le roman d'un jésuite	884
BEUST, F. F. Count von. Memoirs, written by himself	482
BIART, L. Quand j'étais petit	885
————— Les clientes du docteur Bernagius	885

BIBLIOGRAPHY.

Astor Library. Catalogue of the. Vol. 3.
Books, The Best. **Sonnenschein, W. S.**
Bibliography of Electricity and Magnetism, 1860-1883. **May, G.**
Bibliomania, or Book Madness. **Dibdin, T. F.**
Bibliotheca Americana. Vol. 16. **Sabin.**
Bibliographie historique de la Compagnie de Jésus. **Carayon le P. A.**
Foreign Office (English). Catalogue of the Library, 1885.
Iowa. Report of the State Librarian.
Peabody Institute, Catalogue of Library. Vol. 3.
Surgeon General's Office Library, U. S. Index Catalogue. Vol. 8.
Statistical Society. Catalogue of the Library of the. (1884).
————— Index to subject-matter of the Catalogue (1886).
Waltzemuller, M. H. Ses ouvrages et ses collaborateurs.

	PAGE
Bickersteth, R. (Bishop of Ripon). Life and Episcopate. By his Son	482
Bigelow, M. M. Index to Overruled Cases	205
————— On Estoppel	70
Biliotti, (E) et Cottret, l'abbé. L'île de Rhodes	322
Binet (A.) et Féré C. Le magnétisme animal	670
————— Animal Magnetism (Int. S. S. 60)	578

BIOGRAPHY.

Agassiz, L. Sa vie et sa correspondance.
Alice, Princess. Scenes in the Life of. By **Kenyon, E. C.**
Beust, F. F. Count von. Memoirs, written by himself.
Bickersteth, R. (Bishop of Ripon). Life and Episcopate. By his Son.
Bonpland, Biographie d'Aimé. **Brunel, Ad.**
Burton, Sir R. F.. Early, Private, and Public Life. By **Hitchman, F.**
Carlyle, Thomas. Correspondence between Goethe and
Celebrities of the Century Ed. by **Sanders, L. C.**
Cellini, B. Life of, translated by J. A. Symonds.
Chanzy, Le géneral, 1823-1883. **Chuquet, A.**
Colet, Jno. (Dean of St. Paul's). Life, by **Lupton, J. H.**
Darwin, Chs. Life and Letters. Ed. by his son Francis.
Dictionary of National Biography. Vols. 10, 11, 12. **Stephen, L.**
Doublet, Jean. Journal du Corsaire. Par **Breard, Chs.**
Emerson, R. W. Memoir of. By **Cabot, J. E.**
Epinay, La jeunesse de Mme. d'. **Perey (L.) & Maugras, G.**
Epinay, Dernières années de Mme d'. **Perey & Maugras.**
Fraser, Bishop Jas. A Memoir. By **Hughes, Thos.**
Frith, W. P. My Autobiography and Reminiscences.
Goethe. Correspondence with Carlyle.
Grimm, Melchior. Par **Scherer, E.**
Hamilton, Lady and Lord Nelson. By **Jeaffreson, J. C.**
Irving, Lieut. J. (H. M. S. "Terror"). Memorial Sketch, By **Bell, B.**
Jeanne d'Arc en face de l'église romaine. **Mourot, l'abbé V.**
Johnstone, Chevalier. Memoirs of the. (Translated).
Keats (Englishmen of Letters). **Colvin, S.**
Kennedy, D. (The Scottish Singer). Reminiscences of his Life.
Laud, William. Sometime Archbishop of Canterbury. **Benson, A. C.**
Lights of Two Centuries: biographies. **Hale, E. E.**
Ligne, Princesse de. Memoirs of. Edited by **Perey, L.**
Ligne, la Princesse Hélène de : Histoire. **Perey, L.**
Longfellow, H. W. Final Memorials of. By **Longfellow, S.**
Lytton, Rosina Lady. Life of, by Louisa Devey.

BIOGRAPHY—*Concluded*.
    Macaulay, Lord. Life and Letters. By **Trevelyan, G. O.** New ed.
    Maintenon, Mme de: d'après sa correspondance authentique. **Geffroy, A.**
    Marguerite d'Angoulême. By **Robinson,** A. Mary F. (*Em. Women Ser.*)
    Martineau, H. By **Miller,** Mrs. F. F. (*Em Women Ser.*)
    Maximimilien I, Souvenirs de ma vie. Traduits par Gaillard, J.
    Mérode. Life and Works of F. E. X. (Translation.) **Besson, Mgr.**
    Mohl, Julius and Mary. Letters and Recollections. By **Simpson, M. C. M.**
    Mon Père: avec les lettres du général Margueritte. **Margueritte, Paul.**
    Morley, S. Life of. By **Hodder, E.**
    Napier, Rt. Hon. Sir J. Life of, from his private correspondence. By **Ewald, A. C.**
    Nasmith, David. Memoirs of. By **Campbell, John.**
    Nos morts contemporains. 2e série. **Montegut, Em.**
    Ozanam. F. Sa vie et ses œuvers, par **Chauveau, P.**
    Paré, Ambroise. Par **Le Paulnier,** le Dr.
    Pen-portraits of literary women. **Cone (H. G.) and Gilder, (J. L.)**
    Personal Remembrances. **Pollock, Sir Fredk.**
    Peterborough, Earl of. Memoir by **Russell,** Col. F. S.
    Pole, Reg., Card. Ahbp. of Canterbury. An historical sketch by **Lee, F. G.**
    Portraits historiques. **Chantelauze, R.**
    Punshon, Rev. W. M. Life of. By **Macdonald, F. W.**
    Reade Chs Memoir by **Reade.** C. D. and Rev. Compton.
    Recamier, Madame. **M[ohl] Madame.**
    Recollections of forty years. **Lesseps, Ferd. de.**
    Rogers, S. Early life of: by **Clayden, P. W.**
    Rothschilds (The). The Financial Rulers of Nations. By **Reeves, J.**
    Scenes in the life of the Royal Family. **Kenyon, E. C.**
    Shakespeare, Life of. **Halliwell-Phillips, J. O.**
    Siddons, Mrs. By **Kennard,** Mrs. A. (*Em Women Ser.*)
    Simon, Jules. Sa vie et son œuvre. **Seché, L.**
    Soixante ans de Souvenirs. 2e partie. **Legouve, Ern.**
    Staël, Mme. de. By **Duffy Bella.** (*Em Women Ser.*)
    Struggles through life: various travels and adventures. **Harriott, Lt. John.**
    Studies in Naval History: Biographies. **Laughton, J. K.**
    Through the Long Day; or, Memorials of Half a Century. **Mackay, Dr. Chs.**
    Wesley, Susanna. By **Clarke, Eliza** (*Em. Women Ser.*)
    What I remember. **Trollope, T. A.**
    Ximenez, Life of Cardinal. **Hefele, C. J.**
    Yesterdays with Authors. **Fields, J. T.**

BIRÉ, E. Victor de Laprade, sa vie et ses œuvres 492
BISBEE (L. H.) and SIMONDS, J. C. Law of Produce Exchange 108
BISHOP. Fish and Men in the Maine Islands 1240
BLACK, H. C. Constitutional prohibition against obligation of contract 107
BLACK HAWK. Life of—dictated by himself 1188
BLACK, Wm. Novels. 17 vols 828
———— Sabina Zembra 828
BLACKBURN, Lord. Contract of Sale 92
BLACKMORE, R. D. Springhaven, a tale of the Great War 828
BLAINE, J. G. Political and other discussions 157
BLAKE, Hon. E. Election Campaign Speeches, 1886 130
BLANC, L. Questions d'aujourd'hui et de demain 392
BLANCHET, Hon. J. Discours sur l'autonomie des provinces 377

	PAGE
BLAVET, Em. (Parisis). La vie parisienne, 1886......	882
BLEEKER, Capt. L. Orderly Book of the Expedition under Gen. J. Clinton (1779)........	1263
BLYDEN, E. W. Christianity, Islam and the Negro Race.......	42
BOASE, C. W. History of Oxford. (Historic Towns Ser.)........	405
BOITEL, Am. Herbages et prairies naturelles.......	657
BONALD, le Vte de. Pensées sur divers sujets.......	67
BOND. Investment Tables.........	502
BONELLI, L H. de. Travels in Bolivia........	1357
BONHOMME, H. Louis XV et sa famille.......	426
BONNEFOUX et PARIS. Dictionnaire de marine.......	686
BONNEFOY, M. Histoire du bon vieux temps.......	410
BONNIÈRES, R. de. Jeanne Avril.......	881
BONTEMPS, G. Guide du Verrier	734
BONWICK, J. Romance of the Wool Trade.......	513
Books which have influenced me.......	803
BOSSUS (Mathæus). Opera varia.......	46
Boston Board of Health. Report for 1886	677

BOTANY.

Dictionnaire de botanique. Vol. 3. **Baillon, H.**
Forestry in Europe. U. S. Consular Reports.
Linnæus. Through the fields with—, by **Caddy, Mrs F.**
Physiology of plants. Lectures on the. **Sachs, J. Von.**
Report on Diatomaceæ, &c. (Chall. Exp. Bot. Rep., v. 2.) **Castracane, Cte. Abate F.**

BOUCHARD, Ch. Les auto-intoxications dans les maladies.......	674
BOUCHET, H. Le livre, illustration et reliure.......	692
BOUDET DE PARIS, D. M. La photographie sans appareils...	719
BOUILLIER, F. Etudes familières de psychologie et de morale.......	874
Bouquet, Col. Henry, and his campaigns of 1763 and 1764. By Rev. C. Cort.	1260
—— —— —— The Celebration on Bushy Run Battlefield, Aug. 6, 1883. By Rev. C. Cort.......	1260
BOURASSA, Nap. Nos grand'mères, discours.......	1411
BOURDALOUE. Sermons pour l'Avent	47
BOURDE, P. En Corse.......	541
BOURGET, P. André Cornélis.......	884
BOURNE, B. F. The Giants of Patagonia.......	1358
BOURSAULT. Lettres à Babet.......	871
BOUTMY, E. Développement de la Constitution en Angleterre.......	287
BOUTON, J. B. Roundabout to Moscow.......	546
BOUTWELL, G. S. The Lawyer, the Statesman and the Soldier.......	1229
BOWLES, Vice Adml. Pamphlets on Naval Subjects.......	688

	PAGE
BOWNE, Eliza S. Selections from the letters of "A Girl's life eighty years ago."	1228
BOYESEN, H. H. History of Norway	451
——— ——— The Modern Vikings	896
BRACHET, Aug. Morceaux choisis des écrivains du XVIe siècle	787
——— ——— Dictionnaire des doublets ou doubles formes	787
BRACKENRIDGE, H. M. Voyage to Buenos Ayes 1817-18	522
——— ——— ——— Views of Louisiana and the Missouri in 1811	1384
BRADDON, Miss. Complete Collection of Novels	82ʲ
BRADLEY, Mrs. M. Life and Christian experience of	1198
BRAULT, E. L'empire allemand à vòl d'oiseau	544
BRAZZA, S. de. Conférences et lettres sur les explorations	563
BREHM, A. E. Merveilles de la nature : l'homme et les animaux	606
BRESSON, A. Sept années d'explorations dans l'Amérique australe	1205
BRETT, T. Leading Cases in Equity	82
BRIGHAM, W. F. Guatemala, the land of the Quetzal	1361
BRINTON, D. G. Myths of the New World	309
——— ——— Grammar of the Cakchiquel language	794
——— ——— Religious sentiment : its source and aim	52
——— ——— The Books of Chilan Balam	1215
——— ——— Ancient Nahuatl Poetry	794
——— ——— Annals of the Cakchiquels	794
——— ——— Notes on the Floridian Peninsula	1256
British Columbia. Imperial Papers relative to	1406
British Magazine, 1760—1762	915
British Spy. Letters of the	1249
BROGLIE, duc de. Personal Recollections of the late, 1785-1820	431
BROOKS, E. S. The Story of the American Indian	1187
BROWN, C. Brockden. Wieland	829
——— ——— Arthur Mervyn	829
——— ——— Edgar Huntly	829
——— ——— Jane Talbot	829
——— ——— Ormond	829
——— ——— Clara Howard	829
BROWN, H. F. Venitian Studies	437
BROWN, Marie A. The Icelandic discoveries of America	1163
BROWN, S. R. History of Second War for Independence (1812-14)	1267
BROWNE, G. On Divorce	86
BROWNING, O. England and Napoleon in 1803	429
BROWNSON, O. A. Complete Works	829
BRUECK, H. History of the Catholic Church	23

	PAGE
BRUNEL. Ad. Biographie d'Aimé Bonpland........	482
BRYCE, W. A. History of Fort Wayne........	1258
BUCHANAN, R. A Look round literature........	794
BUCK, A. H. Reference Handbook of the Medical Sciences. Vols. 4, 5	665
Budget Speeches, Province of Ontario........	130
Buffalo Historical Society. Publications of........	1243
BUFFENOIR, H. Les drames de la place de Grève........	885
BULLEY, E. A. The First Lady in the Land........	396
BUNEL, H. Etablissements insalubres, incommodes et dangereux........	356
BUNYON, C. J. Fire Insurance........	104
BURCKHARDT, J. L. Travels in Egypt and India........	522
BURDETT. Official Intelligence for 1887........	500
BURGESS, Rev. W. Land, Labour, and Liquor........	486
BURKE, J. J. Letters to a Law Student........	133
BURKE, S. H. Historical portraits of the Tudor dynasty........	380
BURNABY, F. New history of Sandford and Merton........	829
———— Our Radicals........	829
BURNETT, J. C. Diseases of the veins........	672
BURNS, Rev. R. Life and times of. Edited by his son........	1286
BURRILL, A. M. On Assignments........	175
BURTON, Sir R. F. Supplemental Nights to the Thousand and One Nights.	888
———— Early, private and public life. By F. Hitchman........	483
BURWASH, N. The Epistle of St. Paul to the Romans........	17
BURY (Visct.) and HELLIER, G. L. Cycling (Badminton Lib.)........	724
BUSWELL, H. F. Law of Insanity........	117
BUTLER, A. J. Court life in Egypt........	560
BUTLER, W. F. Campaign of the Cataracts........	463
BUTTERFIELD. C. W. The Washington-Irvine Correspondence, 1781-83....	1221
CABOT, J. E. Memoir of Ralph W. Emerson........	487
CADDY, Mrs F. Through the fields with Linnæus........	646
CADET, F. L'éducation à Port-Royal........	74
CADWALADER, J. L. Opinions of Attorneys' General on International Law	19
CAILLIAUD, F. Travels in the Oasis of Thebes........	522
alifornia. By J. Royce (Amer. Com. Series)........	1258
ambridge University Calendar, 1886 and 1887........	78
CAMERON, G. F. Lyrics on Freedom, Love, and Death........	1410
CAMPBELL, Arch. Captain Macdonald's Daughter........	830
CAMPBELL, Sir G. The British Empire........	124
CAMPBELL, H. Prisoners of Poverty........	462
CAMPBELL, Jno. Memoirs of David Nasmith........	496

	PAGE
CAMPBELL, Rev. R. History of the Scotch Presbyterian Church of Montreal	1198
Canada. Voyage au—fait depuis l'an 1751 à 1761, par J. C. B.	1275
—— - Discours sur le	1282
—— — Nova Scotia, New Brunswick, Newfoundland, etc.	1404
Canadian Economics	486
Canadian Lawyer	137
Canadiens-Français. Conventions annuelles des—aux Etats-Unis	1276
CANIS. Histoire de la république française	434
CAPECELATRO, C. P. Alph. Histoire de Ste. Catherine de Sienne	25
CARAYON, le P. A. Bibliographie historique de la Compagnie de Jésus	899
CAREY, Rosa H. Uncle Max	831
"Caris Sima." A Mystery	1410
Carlyle, Thomas, Correspondance between Gœthe and	489
CARPENTIER, Mlle E. Les jumeaux de Lusignan	887
CARR, A. The Church and the Roman Empire	36
CARR, J. C. L'art en France	698
CARVER, T. G. Carriage of Goods by Sea	111
CASGRAIN, l'abbé H. R. Un Pèlerinage au pays d'Evangeline	1404
CASSAN, Mme. Le roi des Jacques	885
CASSINI, M. de. Voyage to Newfoundland and Sallee	1388
CASTEL, C. J. (l'abbé de St Pierre). Projet de taille tarifiée	422
CASTELLAN, A. L. Letters on Italy	522
CASTETS, Em. Mexique et Californie	1373
CASTLE, E. J. Law of Commerce in time of War	18
CASTONNETS des FOSSES, H. L'Inde française avant Dupleix	457
CASTRACANE, Cte Abate F. Report on Diatomaceæ, &c. (Chall. Exp. Bot. Rep. V. 2)	650
Cattle and Dairy Farming of the World	659
CAVANAGH, C. Money Securities, 2nd ed	106
CECCONI, Mgr Eug. Histoire du Concile du Vatican	28
Celebrities of the Century. Ed. by L. C. Sanders	474
Cellini, B. Life of—translated by J. A. Symonds	483
César. Opérations militaires. Par Léon Heuzey	681
CHAGNON, Rév. F. H. Annales de la paroisse de St. Jacques le Majeur (1772 à 1872)	1274
CHALAMET, Ant. Les Français au Canada	1272
CHALMERS (J.) and GILL, W. W. Pioneering in New Guinea	569
CHALMERS, G. Caledonia: historical and topographical	397
CHALMERS, M. D. Bills of Exchange	106
CHAMBERLAIN, Rt hon. J. Speeches on Home Rule	54

	PAGE
Chamberlain, M. Catalogue of Canadian Birds	639
Chambrun, A. de. Executive Power in the United States	157
Chandless, Wm. A visit to the Mormon Settlements at Utah	1199
Chantelauze, R. Portraits historiques	479
Chapleau, L'hon. J. A. Sa biographie et ses principaux discours	1286
Chapman, J. A. The French in the Alleghany Valley	1260
Chappe d'Auteroche, Jean. Voyage to California	1388
Charlton, W. H. Four months in North Ameria	1372
Charnay, D. The Ancient Cities of the New World	1373
Chartrand (des Ecorres) Jos. Expédition autour de ma tente	1411
Chassant (A) et Tausin H. Dictionnaire des devises	509
Chateaubriand, Vte de., Œuvres complètes. 12 vol	876
—————————— Lettres sur les voyages imaginaires de —, en Amérique, par M. de Mersennes	1367
Chateauvieux, F. L. de. Travels in Italy	522
Chatellux. Examen critique de ses voyages par Brissot de Warville	1378
Chaudordy, Cte de. La France à la suite de la guerre de 1870-71	434
Chauchetière, le P. C. Vie de la B. Catherine Tegakouita	1193
Chenier, A. Poésies	884
Cherbuliez, V. La bête	884
—————————— Le comte Kostia	884
Cherriman, Prof. A Song of Charity	1410
Chester, A. W. Powers, duties, and liabilities of Executive officers	66
Chester, G. J. Transatlantic Sketches	1351
Chevalerie (la) et les Croisades. (L'Ancienne France)	410
Chevalier, H. E. La fille des Indiens rouges	883
Chicago. Business Directory of	1257
——————— Board of Trade Reports	524
China. Overland journey from Maca to Canton	522
Chincholle, Chs. Les survivants de la Commune	434
—————————— Le vieux général	887
Chiniquy, Rév. C. Cinquante ans dans l'église de Rome	29
—————————— Fifty years in the Church of Rome	29
Chitty. Equity Index. Vol. 3. 4th ed	204
Choléra (le) n'est ni transmissible ni contagieux. Par un Rationaliste	675
Chotard, H. Le Pape Pie VII à Savone	31
Chuquet, A. Le général Chanzy, 1823-1883	483
Church of England. Year book for 1887	39
Church, A. J. Carthage : or, The Empire of Africa	304
Church (The) in the Colonies	40
Churchward, W. B. My Consulate in Samoa	570

	PAGE
CICERO. Book of Offices. Translated by C. R. Edmonds	820
Civil Engineers, (Institution of). Proceedings. Vols 87 to 90	743
CLARETIE, J. La Canne de M. Michelet	881
———— Le candidat	881
———— L'art et les artistes français	712
———— Camille et Lucile Desmoulins	427
CLARKE, Eliza. Susanna Wesley (Em. Wom. Ser.)	478
CLARKE, H. W. History of Tithes	246

CLASSICS : *Greek and Latin.*
    Aristophanes. Comedies. Translated by **Hickie, W. J.**
    Aristotle. Politics and Economics. Translated by **Walford.**
    ———— Metaphysics. Translated by **Riley, H. T.**
    Cicero. Book of Offices. Translated by **Edmonds, C. R.**
    Dionysius of Halicarnassus. Antiquitatum sive originum romanorum, libri XI.
    Hensius, D. De tragediæ constitutione liber. Et Aristotelis, de poetica.
    Herodotus. Historiæ libri IX et de vita Homeri libellus.
    Histoire (l') éthiopique : Amours de Théagenes et Chariclea. **Heliodore.**
    Homer. Iliad (The). Translated by **Buckley, T. A.**
    ———— Iliad and Odyssey. An introduction to the. **Jebb, J. R.**
    ———— Odyssey (The) done into English verse by **Morris, W.**
    ———— Odyssey (The). Translated by **Buckley, T. A.**
    Horace. Works of, translated by **Smart, E.**
    Livius. History of Rome. (Translation)
    Ovid. The Fasti. Tristia, &c Translated by **Riley, H. T.**
    ———— Metamorphoses (The). Translated by **Riley, H. T.**
    Pindar, Odes. Translated in prose by **Turner, D. W.** ; in verse by **Moore. A.**
    Quintilian. Institutes of Oratory. Translated by **Melby, J. S.**
    Sappho. Memoir, text, and a literal translation. By **Wharton, H T.**
    Tacitus. Works, Vol. 2.

CLAVEAU, A. Contre le Flot	882
Clay, Henry. Life of, by Carl Schurz	1229
CLERC, Alexis. Voyage au pays de petrole	1382
CLÉRY, R. de. Les avant-postes pendant le siége de Paris	434
CLINTON, Sir Henry. Correspondence with Earl Cornwallis	1263
———————— Letter to the Commrs. of Public Accounts	1263
CLODE, W. Law and Practice of Petition of Right	25
Club (A) of one	832
Cobden Club Papers. Vol. 4	488
COCHELET, Chs. Shipwreck of the "Sophia" on the Western coast of Africa	532
COCHRAN, W. Pen and Pencil in Asia Minor	549
COCHRANE, W. The Church and the Commonwealth	51
COHEN, F. Le club	887
COIGNET, Mme C. A gentleman of the olden time	424
———————— Un gentilhomme des temps passés	424
Colbert, Jules-Armand (marquis d'Ormoy). Une étude par P. Margry	425
Colet, Jno. (Dean of St. Paul's). Life, by J. H. Lupton	485

	PAGE
College (The) and the Church	81
COLLETTE, C. H. Life, times, and writings of Thomas Cranmer	36
COLLINS, Wilkie. The Evil Genius (*Picc.* Nov. 174)	847
——————— Little novels	832
Colonial Church Chronicle and Missionary Journal	40
COLONIAL conference. Proceedings of	124
Colonial Office List, 1887	27

COLONIAL.
    Australasian Directory.
    British Empire. **Campbell, Sir G.**
    Colonial Conference, Proceedings of.
    Colonial Office List, 1887.
    England and her Colonies.
    Indian Reservations. **Harrison, J. B.**
    Queensland Almanac and Directory.

COLVIN, S. Keats (English men of Letters)	479
COMBE, W. The tour of Doctor Syntax	857
COMBS, Capt. L. Col. Dudley's defeat opposite Fort Meiggs, 1813	1267

COMMERCE.
    American and Foreign Iron Trades, Statistics of.
    Baltimore Board of Trade Reports, 1886.
    Bay of Fundy, Report of Trade of.
    Canada Trade, Letters on. **Young, Hon. J.**
    Chicago Board of Trade Reports.
    Commerce, French Code of. **Mayer, S.**
    Commerce, Growth of. **Yeats, J.**
    United States Commercial Relations, 1880-1887.
    Industrial Ireland. **Dennis, R.**
    International Guide to British and Foreign Merchants and Manufacturers.
    International Trade. **Bastable, C. F.**
    Manufacturers of the United States, 1887.
    National Board of Trade Reports (U. S.), 1887.
    Natural Resources of U. S. **Patton, J. H.**
    Recent and Existing Commerce. **Yeats, J.**
    Shipping World Year Book, 1887.
    Trade Guilds of Europe.
    Wool and Manufactures of Wool.
    Wool Trade. **Bonwick, J.**
    Zollverein Papers, 1836-85.

CONDER, C. R. Altaic Hieroglyphs and Hittite Inscriptions	777
CONE, (H. G.) and GILDER, J. L. Pen-portraits of literary women	478
CONE, Mary. Life of Rufus Putnam	1260
Connecticut Board of Agriculture, 1886	660

CONSTITUTIONAL LAW, AND HISTORY.
    American State Constitutions. **Hitchcock, H.**
    Church and State. **Stimson, Rev. E. R.**
    Church and State. **Armitage. W.**
    Constitutional Conventions. **Jameson, J. A.**
    Debates in 1st Senate of United States. **Maclay, Wm.**

CONSTITUTIONAL LAW, AND HISTORY—*Concluded.* PAGE
   Executive Power in United States. **Chambrun, A. de.**
   Federal Constitution. **Baker, J. F.**
   How the Union was Carried. **McNeill, J. G. S.**
   Our Country. **Strong, J.**
   Political State of Scotland in the last century. **Adam, Sir C. E.**
   Principles of Government. **Kinnear, J. B.**
   Private Bill Legislation. **Macassey, L. L.**
   Republican Institutions. **Bannantyne, D. J.**

Contest (The) in America between Great Britain and France, 1757	1260
COOK, A. J. The bee-keeper's guide	643
COOK, W. W. Stock and stockholders	106
COOKE, C. K. Australian Defences. From paper's of Sir P. Scratchley	683
COOKE, J. E. Canolles: Fortunes of a Partisan of '81	832
COOKSON, Lt.-Col. Tiger-shooting in the Doon and Ulwar	725
COOPER, A. Diseases of the rectum	672
COPPÉE, F. Poèmes et récits	886
COQUELIN ainé et cadet. L'art de dire le monologue	806
——— cadet. Le rire	806
CORDOVA, Adml. Don. A. de. Voyage to the Strait of Magellan	522
CORELLI, Marie. Vendetta! Story of one forgotten	832
——————— A Romance of two Worlds	832
CORNELIUS, Rev. E. Tour in Virginia	522
CORNELL, W. M. History of Pennsylvania, up to the present time	1247
CORNWALLIS, Lord. Answer to Clinton's Narrative	1263
CORNEVIN, C. Des plantes vénéneuses	652
CORRA, Em. La bataille de Sedan, histoire complète	434
COSNEAU, E. Le connétable de Richemont, 1393-1458	424
COWPER, W. Concordance to poetical works of, by J. Neve	858
Cox, P. The Brownies: their book	832
Cox, S. S. Diversions of a diplomat in Turkey	546
CRAFTS, W. F. The Sabbath for man	51
Cramp, Rev. J. M. Life of, by Rev. T. A. Higgins	1198
CRAMP, W. B. Voyage to India and New South Wales	522
Cranmer, T. (Ahbp. of Canterbury). Life of, by C. H. Collette	36
CRAWFURD, O. Beyond the seas	833
CROCKFORD's Clerical Directory	39
CROZIER, J. B. Lord Randolph Churchill	449
CRUISE, F. R. Thomas à Kempis—scenes in which his life was spent	50
Cuisine (la) moderne	735
CUNNINGHAM, J. Law of Elections—3rd ed	40
CUNNINGHAM (Wm) of Craigend. Diary of, 1673 to 1680	398
CUNNINGHAM, H. S. The Cœruleans—a vacation idyll	833

	PAGE
CURRAN, J. J. Golden Jubilee of Fathers Dowd and Toupin	1196
Currency, Coinage and Banking Laws of the United States	176
CURZON, Sarah A. Laura Secord—the heroine of 1812	1410
CUTLER, Manasseh. Life and Correspondence	1227
CUTTS, E. L. Dictionary of the Church of England	36
Cyclopedia of Painters and Painting, Vol. 4	713
DABADIE, F. A travers l'Amérique du Sud	1354
DALE (C. W. M.) et LEHMANN, R. C. Digest of Overruled Cases	205
DALY, Mrs D. D. Digging, Squatting and Pioneering in South Australia	567
DANIEL, C. T. William and Annie, a tale	1410
DARAN, V. Le général Miramon : notes sur le Mexique	1216
DARCEY, M. Le crime de la 5ème Avenue	884
DARMESTETER. La vie des mots	787
DARWIN, Chs. Life and letters. Ed. by his son Francis	486
DAUDET, E. Souvenirs de la présidence du Maréchal de MacMahon	434
DAUNT, A. In the land of the Moose, the Bear and the Beaver	833
DAVENPORT, Mrs. Ride from Quebec to Lake St. John	1403
D'AVEZAC. Relation du voyage du Capitaine de Gonneville	1172
DAVIN, A. 50,000 milles dans l'océan Pacifique	527
DAVIS, A. Antiquities of Central America	1163
DAVIS, G. B. International Law	12
DAVIS, H. F. A. Building Societies	88
DAVIS, J. D. The Standard book-keeper	86
DAVIS, S. Notes of a tour of America, 1832 and 1833	1372
DAVISON, G. M. Traveller's Guide through the States and Canada	1364
DAVYL, L. La toile d'araignée	885
DAWSON, Rev. Æ. McD. Dominion Day and other poems	1408
DAWSON, G. F. Life and Services of Gen. John A. Logan	1229
DAWSON, G. M. Papers on Natural History and Geology	615
DAWSON, Jno. Practical Journalism	802
DAYMONAZ, B. Louis XVII vengé des impostures de P. Veuillot	427
Dead Man's Rock : a romance. By "Q"	833
DEANE, C. P. Drink and Licensing Laws	109
DEATH, Js. The Beer of the Bible	736
DEBRETT's House of Commons	51
Défense (la). Solutions courtes des principales objections contre la religion	46
DE FOE, D. Works. 7 vols	833
DELACROIX, F. Les suggestions hypnotiques, une lacune dans la loi	340
DELBIS, L. Moments de loisir	890
DELESTRE, J. B. De la physiognomonie	632

	PAGE
DELON, C. Les paysans : histoire d'un village avant la Révolution............	412
DENNIS, R. Industrial Ireland	509
DENOVAN, J. Was Moses Wrong ?..	19
DESDEVISES-DU-DEZERT. L'Amérique avant les Européens	1164
DESGODETS. Loix des batiments, suivant la coutume de Paris................	326
DESJARDINS, A. Les sentiments moraux au XVIe siècle..................	387
DESLYS, C. Miss Eva...	884
DESTREL, H. Le suffrage des femmes aux Etats-Unis..........	386
DEVEY, Louisa. Life of Rosina, Lady Lytton	434
DEWEY, T. H. Contracts for future delivery..	107
DE WITT, P. Les petits Jacobins ....,	428
DIBDIN, T. F. Bibliomania, or Book-Madness..............	900
DICEY, A. V. Letters on Unionist delusions............................	54
————— The Privy Council..	22
DIEULAFOY, Mme J. La Perse, la Chaldée et la Susiane	552
DILKE, Sir C. Present position of European politics (1887)................	445
—————. L'Europe en 1887...	392
DILLMONT, Thérèse de. Encyclopédie des ouvrages de dames................	735
DILLON, J. B. History of Indiana............................	1258
DILLWYN, E. A. Jill and Jack......	834
Dinwiddie (The) Papers, 1751-58. Records of Virginia History............	1249
Dionysius of Halicarnassus. Antiquitatum sive originum romanorum, libri XI...............................	810
DIXON, W. H. Free Russia..............................	547
DIXON, W. J. Law of Divorce........	86
DOMENECH, l'abbé E. La vérité sur le Livre des Sauvages...................	1180
Dominion of Canada Rifle Association Reports...............................	683
DONIOL, H. Participation de la France à l'établissement des Etats-Unis d'Amérique...	1263
DONKIN, Major. Military Collections and Remarks............................,	681
DORSEY, E. B. English and American Railroads......	508
DOS PASSOS, J. R. Inter-State Commerce Act.................................	176
——— ————— Stock-brokers and Exchanges.........................	108
DOSTOYEFFSKY, F. Crime and Punishment : A Russian Novel................	898
DOSTOIEVSKY, Th. Les Possédés (Besi).............................	898
——————— Le Joueur et les nuits blanches................	898
——————— L'idiot..	898
Doublet, Jean. Journal du Corsaire—par Chs. Bréard	486
DRAKE, S. A. The making of the Great West, 1512-1883.....................	1258
DRAKE, S. G. French and Indian Wars in New England................	1259

DROIT.

Antiquitatum romanorum jurisprudentiam illustrantium syntagma. **Heineccius, J. G.**
Bâtiments, (lois des) suivant la Coutume de Paris. **Desgodets.**
Commentaires sur l'acte de 1791. **Heney, H.**
Correspondance politique (1792-1797). **Barthelemy.**
Coustumes du gouvernement de Péronne, etc. **LeCaron, C.**
Développement de la Constitution en Angleterre. **Boutmy, E.**
Discours sur l'autonomie des provinces. **Blanchet, Hon. J.**
Droit (du) ancien et du droit nouveau. **Hugonin, Mgr.**
Droit des gens en temps de paix. **Twiss, Travers.**
Droit public et administratif, avec supplément. **Baibie, A.**
Elementa juris civilis secundum ordinem institutionum. **Heineccius, J. G.**
Elementa juris civilis secundum ordinem pandectarum. **Heineccius, J. G.**
Éloquence politique et parlementaire en France en 1789. **Aubertin, Chs.**
Érections des bénéfices, Traité des. **Laubry.**
Etablissements insalubres, incommodes et dangereux. **Bunel, H.**
Histoire du parlement de Normandie. **Floquet, A.**
Homme (l') criminel. **Lombroso, C.**
Hypnotisme (l') et les états analogues. **La Tourette, G. de.**
Instructions aux ambassadeurs de France avant la Révolution : Portugal.
Justice criminelle de France : Traité de la. **Jousse, M.**
Loi (la) sur les aliénés. Rapport sur. **Roussel, T.**
Ordo Historiæ juris civilis. **Martini, C. A. de.**
Parlement (le) de Paris (1314-1422). **Aubert, F.**
Plaidoyers et mémoires. **Mauleon, A. J. L. de.**
Procédure civile de Genève. **Taillandier, A.**
Questions constitutionnelles. **Laboulaye, E.**
Résumé du droit canadien. **Martel, J. Z.**
Suggestions hypnotiques. **Delacroix, P.**
Tribunal (le) international. **Kamarowsky, Ste. L.**

DRUMONT, E. La France juive devant l'opinion.............................	398
DU BLED, V. Histoire de la Monarchie de Juillet	432
Dublin University Calendar, 1887...	78
DUBUQUE, H. A. Les Canadiens-Français de Fall River.................	1276
DUCOUDRAY, G. Histoire sommaire de la civilisation.....................	392
DUFEY, P. J. S. Révolutions de l'Amérique méridionale.................	1200
DUMAS, A., fils. Théâtre complet	884
——— ——— Francillon...	884
DUMONCEL, Th. Elements of construction for Electro-Magnets.....	731
DUMONT, P. J. Narrative of thirty-four years slavery and travels in Africa.	522
DUNBAR, Mary F. P. The Queen's Birthday Book........................	397
DUNCAN. Tramway Manual	508
DUNN, H. Guatimala in 1827-8	1361
DUPIN, le baron Ch. Naval and Military Establishments of Gt. Britain......	522
——— ——— ——— Two Excursions to the Ports of Gt. Britain and Ireland.	522
DUPUY, P. Les Illustrations Canadiennes.....................................	1274
DURANDEAU, Em. Civils et Militaires..	881
DURRET, le Sieur. Voyage à Lima et aux Indes Occidentales (1707).........	1352
DURUY, G. L'unisson..	885
DURUY, V. L'Histoire des Grecs...	332

	PAGE
DUSSIEUX, L. Chateau de Versailles—histoire et description........	434
DUTRIPON, F. P. Concordantiæ Bibliorum Sacrorum...............................	16
EBERS, Geo. Bride of the Nile..	895
—————— Sérapis—roman historique...	895
EBSWORTH, J. W. Cavalier Lyrics : " For Church and Crown "...............	858
École (l') et la Science au moyen-âge. (L'Ancienne-France).................	410

ECONOMIE POLITIQUE.
    Alcool (l') et l'impot des boissons. **Hartmann, G.**
    Arabes pasteurs nomades. **Geoffroy, Aug**
    Etudes économiques et financières **Fournier, de Flaix, E.**
    Fer (le) et la houille. **Reybaud, L.**
    France (la) économique **Foville, A. de.**
    L'impot sur le revenu. **Guyot, Ives.**
    Laine (la). **Reybaud, L.**
    Lois naturelles de l'économie politique. **Molinari, G. de**
    Manieurs (les) d'argent **Vallee, O de**
    Monde (le) des prisons **Moreau, l'abbe G.**
    Postes (les) françaises, **Belloc, A.**
    Protection de l'enfance, Lois sur la. Rapport sur les. **Roussel, T.**
    Soie (la). **Reybaud, L.**
    Taille tarifiée. Projet de. **Castel, E. J.** (L'abbé de St. Pierre).
    Transport par les chemins de fer. **Hadley, A. T.**

EDDY, R. Universalism in America, 1636-1886....................................	1198
EDGCUMBE (Lady E.) and WOOD, Lady M. Four Months' Cruise in a Sailing Yacht...	546
EDGCUMBE, E. R. P. A holiday in Brazil and on the River Plate..............	1354
EDGELOW, G. Cure of hæmorrhoids and prolapsus	672
EDLER, K. E. Baldine and other tales............	896
Education, U. S. Commissioner of. Report for 1884-5............................	85

EDUCATION.
    A travers nos écoles. **Anthoine, E.**
    Book-keeper, The Standard. **Davis, J. D.**
    Cambridge University Calendar, 1887.
    College (The) and the Church.
    Dublin University Calendar, 1887.
    École (l') polytechnique, Histoire de. **Pinet, G.**
    Education (l') à Port-Royal. **Cadet, F.**
    Éducation (l') des femmes par les femmes. **Greard, Oct.**
    Education and Employment of the Blind. **Armitage, T. R.**
    Education, U.S. Commissioner of. Report for 1884-85.
    Educational list and directory of the United Kingdom. **Stephen, W.**
    Elementary psychology and education. **Baldwin, J.**
    German Elementary Schools and Training Colleges. **Perry, C. C.**
    Grandes (les) écoles de France. **O'Gagne M. d'**
    Grands (les) écrivains français. **Truan, H.**
    Lecture, l'art de la. 36e éd. **Legouve, Ern.**
    Lecture (la) en action. **Legouve, Ern.**
    McGill University Calendar, 1887-88.
    Maine. Superintendent of Common Schools Report for 1886.
    New (The) Education. **Palmer, G. H.**
    New York State University. Report of Regents for 1886.

EDUCATION.— *Concluded.* PAGE
    Nos filles et nos fils. **Legouve, Ern.**
    Oxford University Calendar 1887.
    Penmanship, Manual of. **Payson. Dunton & Scribner.**
    Petit traité de lecture. **Legouve, Ern.**
    Phillips' Exeter Lectures.
    Physical Culture. **Houghton, E. B.**
    Principles of the Art of Conversation. **Mahaffy, J. P.**
    Question (la) d'enseignement en 1789. **Allain, l'Abbe.**
    Science and Art Department of Great Britain Directory.
    Study of History in American Colleges. **Adams, H. B.**
    Schools (The) of Greater Britain. **Russell, Jno.**
    Toronto University. Fasti from 1850 to 1887. Compiled by **Loudon, W. J.** and **Maclean, W. F.**
    Toronto University. Year Book of the.
    Trois Rivières. Noces d'argent du Séminaire des (1885).

EDWARDES, Chs. Letters from Crete...... 545
EGAN, C. Status of the Jews in England...... 22
EGOMET, E. G. Only a Curate...... 834
ELIOT, George. Le moulin sur la floss—traduction...... 834
ELLIOTT, Chs. Trip to Canada and the Far North West, 1887...... 1403
ELLIS, Wm. Royal Jubilees of England...... 338
ELMES (J. J) and INGRAM, T. D. Law of Compensation...... 102
ELMES, W. Law of the Customs...... 109
EMDEN, A. Digest of Cases...... 204
Emerson, R. W. Memoir of, by J. E. Cabot...... 487
ENCHELLI, C. A travers l'âme et le monde...... 877
Encyclopédie des connaissances utiles...... 909
Encyclopædia Britannica. Vols. 21, 22...... 907
Encyclopædic Dictionary. Vols. 11, 12...... 792

ENCYCLOPÆDIAS, ETC.
    Ami (l') de la Religion (1814–42).
    British Magazine (1760–1762).
    Encyclopædia Britannica. Vols. 21, 22.
    Encyclopédie des connaissances utiles.
    Hazel's Annual Cyclopædia (1887),
    Royal Kalendar and Court Register for 1887.
    Westminster Magazine (1781).
    Year Book of Scientific and Learned Societies for 1887.

ENDICOTT, W. C. Immigration Laws...... 176

ENGINEERING AND PUBLIC WORKS.
    American Society of Civil Engineers. Transactions.
    Bridge Disasters in America. **Vose, G. L.**
    Civil Engineers (Institution of). Proceedings. Vols. 87 to 90.
    Engineers' Calculations, Manual of. **Smith, D. M. L.**
    Explosions in Coal Mines. **Atkinson, W. N. & J. B.**
    United States. Irrigation in the. Report. By **Minton, H. J.**

England A sketch of Old. By a New England Man...... 522
England and her Colonies...... 124

		PAGE
ERCKMANN-CHATRIAN.	Alsacian (The) Schoolmaster..................................	883
———————	Blockade of Phalsbourg..	883
———————	Campaign in Kabylia..	883
———————	Citizen Bonaparte, 1794-1815.................................	883
———————	Confessions of a Clarinet Player	883
———————	Conscript. The...	889
———————	Country (The) in danger, 1792	883
———————	Daniel Rock, the blacksmith..................................	883
———————	Friend Fritz. Great Invasion, 1813-14....................	883
———————	Illustrious (The) Dr Matheus..................................	883
———————	Madame Thérèse, or, The Volunteers of '92............	883
———————	Man-Wolf, The	883
———————	Polish (The) Jew...	883
———————	Stories of the Rhine..	883
———————	States (The) General...	883
———————	Waterloo...	883
———————	Wild (The) Huntsman..	883
———————	Year One of the Republic.....................................	883
ESPAGNOLLE, l'abbé J.	L'origine du français...	883
Ethnology. 3rd Annual Report of the U. S. Bureau of............................		1184
EVEREST, L. F. Insanity in Criminal Cases..		117
EVERETT, E. Discovery and Colonization of America...........................		1167
EVERSMANN & JAKOVLEW. Account of Bucharia..................................		522
EWELL, M. D. Medical Jurisprudence..		116
Exposition of New Orleans. Reports on Educational Exhibits.................		85
FABRE, F. Toussaint Galabru...		877
FABRE DE NAVACELLE H. Précis des guerres du second empire............		433
Fair Trade Papers.		518
FAIRBANKS, L. S. Massachusetts Laws of Marriage and Divorce............		85
Famous Breach of Promise Cases..		121
FAUNTHORPE, Rev. J. P. Geography of the British Colonies and Foreign Possessions...		511
FEATHERMAN, A. Social history of the races of mankind.......................		305
FEATHERSTONHAUGH, G. W. On the Treaty of Washington (1842)...........		14
FEILD, Bhp. E. Journal of a Visitation in Newfoundland (1849).............		40
FENN, G. M. Mother Carey's Chicken..		835
FERNOW, B. Documents relating to the early history of Rhode Island.......		1212
FERRAZ. Histoire de la philosophie en France au XIXe siècle..................		57
———— Traditionalisme et ultramontanisme..		57
———— Socialisme, naturalisme et positivisme.....................................		57

	PAGE
FERRAZ. Spiritualisme et libéralisme	57
FEUILLET, Oct. Romance of a poor young man	884
FIELD, Eug. Culture's Garland	835
FIELD, Mrs. H. Anchorage	835
FIELDS, J. T. Yesterdays with Authors	478
Financial Reform Almanac for 1857 and 1888	499

FINANCIAL.
Bank of England. **Rogers, J. E. T.**
Bankers' Calculations. **Pownall, G. H.**
Bankers Magazine, vol. 21.
Bond Investment Tables.
Budget Speeches of Ontario.
Burdett's Official Intelligence for 1887.
Business Directory of New York City. **Wilson's.**
Coins, Moneys, Weights, &c. **Nelson-Smith, W.**
Counting-House Guide. **Younger, R. R.**
Financial Reform Almanac for 1887.
From Poverty to Competence. Graduated Taxations. **Washburn, C. A.**
Great Strike of 1886, Official History of.
Import Duties, U. S., 1887. **Heyl.**
Margin of Profits. **Atkinson, E.**
Public Debts. **Adams, H. C.**
Silver Pound. **Horton, S. D.**
Sketch of American Finances. **Kearney, J. W.**
Stock and Stock-holders. **Cook, W. W.**
Sugar Bounties, **Smart, Wm.**
Sutro Tunnel Company. **Sutro, T.**

FINCH, G. B. Law of Contract	107

FINE ARTS.
Anatomie appliquée aux beaux-arts. Traité d'. **Rochet, Chs.**
Art (l') en France. **Carr, J. C.**
Art (l') japonais. **Gonse, L.**
Glass-Painting. **Miller, F.**
Handbook of Pottery and the Precious Metals. **Wheatly, H. B.**
Livre (le), illustration et reliure. **Bouchet, H.**
Orfèvrerie française au XVIIIe siècle : les Germains. **Bapst, G.**
Pottery-Painting. **Miller, F.**

FIORE, Pasquale. Droit pénal international et l'extradition	272
FISHER, A. Voyage of discovery to the Arctic Regions	522
FISHER, G. P. History of the Christian Church	28
FISHER, Pearl. Britain's Queen, a story and a memorial	396
Fisheries, Report on question of the (1871)	526

FISHERIES CONTROVERSY.—INDEX TO BRITISH AND AMERICAN OFFICIAL DOCUMENTS RELATING TO THE,—

1783. DEFINITIVE TREATY of Peace and Friendship between Great Britain and the United States of America (Article No. 3.) 3rd September, 1783.

[*Ref.* Eng. State Papers, vol. 1, pt. 1, p. 781. "Public Treaties of the U. S. in 1873," p. 267. U. S. Senate Docs. No. 37—41st Cong., 3rd Sess.]

FISHERIES CONTROVERSY—*Continued.*

1791. COD AND WHALE FISHERIES. Report of the Hon. Thomas Jefferson on the subject of the Cod and Whale Fisheries, made to the House of Representatives. 1st February, 1791.
[*Ref.* House Mis. Docs. No. 32—42nd Cong., 2nd Sess., vol. 1.]

1794. TREATY between Great Britain and the United States of America, relating to Amity, Commerce, Navigation and Claims. London, 19th November, 1794.
[*Ref.* Eng. State Papers, vol. 1, p. 784. Vol. 5, p. 9. Vol. 20, p. 847.]

1806. CONVENTION between Great Britain and the United States—(Commerce and Navigation). London, 31st December, 1806.
[*Ref* English State Papers, vol. 1, p. 1190.]

1814. TREATY between Great Britain and the United States. (Peace, Amity, Boundary, Slaves) &c. Ghent, 24th December, 1814.
[*Ref.* Eng. State Papers, vol. 2, p. 357.]

1815. NEGOTIATIONS ON THE FISHERIES in 1815—Secretary J. Q. Adams—Letters during the negociations at Ghent, respecting the Fisheries of Newfoundland. Washington, 1822.
[*Ref.* Adams—"Fisheries and the Mississippi."]

1817. BOUNDARY COMMISSIONERS. Decision of under Article 4 of Treaty of Ghent of 1814 (Islands in Bay of Passamaquoddy and Island of Grand Manan, Bay of Fundy.) New York 24th November, 1817.
[*Ref.* Eng. State Papers, vol. 5, p. 199.]

1818. CONVENTION between Great Britain and the United States of America—(Commerce, Boundary, Slaves and Newfoundland Fishery.) London, 20th October, 1818.
[*Ref.* Eng. State Papers, vol. 6, p. 3, and vol. 20, p. 428. Hertslet's, vol. 2, p. 392, Public Treaties of the United States in 1873—p. 298. U. S. Senate Doc. No. 36—41s. Cong., 3rd Sess., vol. 2, p. 350.]

1819 ACT OF THE BRITISH PARLIAMENT to enable His Majesty to make regulations with respect to the taking and curing of fish on certain parts of the coasts of Newfoundland and Labrador and His Majesty's other possessions in North America, according to a convention made between His Majesty and the United States of America on the 20th October, 1818.
[*Ref.* 59. Geo. 3rd, cap. 38, 14th June, 1819; also Hertslets, vol. 4, p. 480.]

1822. DECISION—Commissioners under Article 4 of the Treaty of Ghent of 1814 (Water Boundaries). Utica, 18th June, 1822.
[*Ref.* Eng. State Papers, vol. 9, p. 791.]

1827. CONVENTION between Great Britain and the United States of America (Territory, North-West Coast of America). London, 6th August, 1827.
[*Ref.* Eng. State Papers, vol. 14, p. 975.]

1832. MESSAGE ON THE FISHERIES—Pres. A. Jackson—Transmitting reports relative to the regulations of England, France and the Netherlands respecting Fisheries. 6th February, 1832.
[*Ref.* House Ex. Docs. No. 99. 22nd Cong., 1st Sess., vol. 3.]

1851. CANADIAN RIVERS AND FISHERIES, Message on—President M. Fillmore—Regarding the free navigation of the St. Lawrence, St. John and other large rivers, and the free enjoyment of the British North American Fisheries by the citizens of the United States. 15th December, 1851.
[*Ref.* Senate Ex. Doc. No. 8, 32nd Congress, 1st Session, vol 4.]

1852. PRINCIPAL FISHERIES OF THE AMERICAN SEAS, Report on the—by Lorenzo Sabine—Report on the principal Fisheries of the American seas, made 6th December, 1852. Codfishing of France, Spain, Newfoundland, Nova Scotia, Labrador and Plymouth Colony, from 1620 to 1693.
[*Ref.* U.S. Senate Doc. No. 32—32nd Cong., 2nd Sess., vol. 5, p. 181. U.S. House Ex. Doc. No. 23—32nd Cong., 2nd Sess., vol. 3. U.S. House Mis. Doc. No. 32—42nd Cong., 2nd Sess., vol. 1.]

1852. BRITISH AMERICAN FISHERIES, Message on—Pres. M. Fillmore—Transmitting report of the Secretary of State, with testimony and documents furnishing information in regard to the fisheries on the coasts of the British Provinces in North America. 2nd August, 1852.
[*Ref.* Senate Ex. Doc. No. 100—32nd Cong, 1st Sess. Vol. 10.]

Fisheries Controversy—*Continued.*

1852. Message on the Fisheries. Pres. M. Fillmore. Transmitting a report of the Secretary of State, and accompanying documents in reference to the fisheries on the British North American coasts and the protection of American Fishermen, 9th August, 1852.
[*Ref.* House Ex. Doc. No. 120—32nd Cong., 1st Sess., vol. 12.]

1853. Finances and the Fisheries, Report on the—Secretary Thomas Cormier—On the state of the finances. Receipts and Expenditures, Estimates, Public Debt, Mint., Survey of the Coast, Lighthouse and Custom House Establishments, Public Buildings, Exportations and Importations; with a report and accompanying documents on the fisheries and controversies arising therefrom, 15th January, 1853.
[*Ref.* House Ex. Doc. No. 23—32nd Cong., 2nd Sess., vol. 3.]

1853. Fisheries and Commercial Reciprocity, Message on the—President M. Fillmore—Transmitting a report on the subject of the fisheries and commercial Reciprocity with Canada, 7th February, 1853.
[*Ref.* House Ex. Doc. No. 40—32nd Cong., 2nd Sess., vol. 4.]

1853. Florida Fisheries—Message on the—Pres. M. Fillmore—Transmitting report of the Secretary of State and accompanying documents respecting the enjoyment of the fisheries on the coasts of Florida by British subjects, 19th February, 1853.
[*Ref.* Senate Ex. Doc. No. 45—32nd Cong., 2nd Sess., vol. 7.]

1853. Message on the Fisheries—Pres. M. Fillmore—Secretary of State, Edmund Everett transmits the correspondence between American and English Officials, relative to the fisheries on the coast of British North America, 28th February, 1853.
[*Ref.* Senate Ex. Doc. No. 53—33rd Cong., Special Sess.]

1854. Fishing Bounty and Reciprocity—Reso'ution on—Legislature of the State of Maine favoring certain modifications of the navigation laws, allowance of county to vessels, and reciprocal trade with the British North American colonies, 19th April, 1854.
Ref. House Mis. Doc. No. 67—33rd Cong., 1st Sess., vol. I.

1854. Treaty between Great Britain and the United States of America, relative to Fisheries, Commerce and Navigation, signed at Washington, 5th June, 1854.
[*Ref.* Hertslets, vol. 9, p. 998. Eng. State Papers, vol. 44, p. 25. "Public Treaties of the U. S. in 1873," p. 329. U. S. Senate Doc. No. 36—41st Cong., 3rd Sess., vol. 12, p. 383.]

1854. Act of the British Parliament for the execution of the Treaty of 5th June, 1854.
[*Ref.* 18 Vict., c. 3. Hertslets, vol. 10, p. 653.]

1854. Act of Congress of the United States of America, to carry into effect the Treaty of 5th June, 1854, chap 269. 5th August, 1854.
[*Ref.* Hertslets, vol. 10, p. 647.]

1855. Act of Congress of the United States of America to amend the Act of 5th August, 1854 (chap. 269), to carry into effect the Treaty of 5th June, 1854, chap 144. 2nd March, 1855.
[*Ref.* Hertslets, vol. 10, p. 655.]

1861. Message on the Fisheries—Pres. A. Lincoln—Correspondence with the British Minister relative to the appointment of a joint commission to enquire concerning practices destructive of the fisheries adjacent to the North Eastern coast and Islands of North America. 19th July, 1861.
[*Ref.* Senate Doc. No. 4. 37th Cong., 1st Sess.]

1866. Fishery Grounds near British Provinces—Message on the—President Andrew Johnson transmits information in regard to the rights and interests of American citizens in the fishing grounds adjacent to the British Provinces. 13th April, 1866.
[*Ref.* House Ex. Doc. 88. 39th Cong., 1st Sess., vol. 12.]

1866. Commercial Relation with Canada—Report on—Secretary Hugh McCulloch—Transmitting statements showing the trade of the Provinces of British North America especially Canada in 1854 and 1865 (the value being estimated in gold), and what proportion of said trade was with the United States. A summary of tariff legislation in Canada since 1854. American Commerce on the canals of Canada, and by the St. Lawrence River, and general information of the commercial relations between the United States and British America. 12th June, 1866.
[*Ref.* House Ex. Doc. No. 128. 39th Cong., 1st Sess., vol. 12.]

Fisheries Controversy – *Continued.*

1867. Message on the Fisheries—Pres. A. Johnson—Transmitting information regarding the practicability of establishing equal reciprocal relations between the United States and the British North American Provinces; and the actual condition of the question of the fisheries. 19th February, 1867.
[*Ref.* Senate Ex. Doc. No. 30—39th Cong., 2nd Sess., vol. 2.]

1867-8. Russian America, Message relative to—Pres. A. Johnson—Transmitting correspondence relative to Russian America.
[*Ref.* House Ex. Doc. No. 177—40th Cong., 2nd Sess., vol. 13.]

1868. Canadian Fisheries, Letter on—Sec. H. McCulloch—Transmitting a communication from G. W. Brega containing additional information relating to the Canadian fisheries and the regulations of the Canadian Government in regard to granting licences to foreign vessels to fish within their waters. 25th May, 1868.
[*Ref.* House Ex. Doc No. 295—40th Cong., 2nd Sess., vol 17.]

1869. Colonial Trade and Fisheries, Report on the—Sec'y. H. McCulloch—Transmitting a report of Mr. E. H. Derby upon the colonial trade and the fisheries of the coast of the British Provinces, with the accompanying papers 8th February, 1869.
[*Ref.* House Ex. Doc. 75—40th Cong., 3rd Sess., vol. 9.]

1870. Message on the Fisheries—Pres. U. S. Grant—Transmitting a report relative to fisheries in the British waters. 6th April, 1870
[*Ref.* House Ex. Doc. No. 239—41st Cong., 2nd Sess., vol. 11.]

1871. Treaty of Washington—signed 8th May, 1871
[*Ref.* Eng. Com'rs. Papers, 1871, vol 70, p. 45; Eng. State Papers, vol. 61, p. 40; Hertslets, vol. 13, p. 970; U.S. Senate Doc No. 36—41st Cong., 3rd Sess., vol. 2, p. 413.]

1871. Rules and Regulations adopted by the Commission under Article 12 of the Treaty between the United States of America and Great Britain, signed at Washington, 3rd May, 1871. 26th September, 1871.
[*Ref.* Hertslets, vol. 13, p. 1000.]

1872. Act of the Government of Canada to carry into effect the Treaty between Great Britain and the United States of America (signed at Washington, 8th May, 1871) relating to the fisheries. 14th June, 1872.
[*Ref.* Statutes of Canada, 35 Vict., cap. 2; Hertslets, vol. 13, p. 1257.]

1872. Act of the Government of Prince Edward Island to carry into effect the provisions of the Treaty between Great Britain and the United States of America, of 8th May, 1871, relating to the fisheries. 29th June, 1872.
[*Ref.* P.E.I. Statutes, 35 Vict., cap. 2; Hertslets, vol. 13, p. 1259.]

1872. Act of the British Parliament, to carry into effect the Treaty between Her Majesty and the United States of America (of 8th May, 1871), so far as related to the fisheries. 6th August, 1872.
[*Ref.* Imperial Statutes, 35 and 36 Vict., cap. 45; Hertslets, vol. 13, p. 1005.]

1872. Cod and Whale Fisheries, Report on the—Report of the Hon. Thomas Jefferson on the subject of the cod and whale fisheries, made to the House of Representatives 1st February, 1791 Also a report by Lorenzo Sabine on the principal fisheries of the American seas, made 6th December, 1852. Cod fishery of France, Spain, Newfoundland, Nova Scotia, Labrador, Plymouth Colony, from 1620 to 1692. The Herring Fishery. 8th January, 1872.
[*Ref.* House Mis. Doc. No. 32—42nd Cong., 2nd Sess., vol. 1.]

1872. Correspondence with the British Government in connection with the appointment of the Joint High Commission and the Treaty of Washington.
[*Ref.* Imper'l Comm. Papers, 1872. Vol. 43, pp 125, 143, 147.]

1872 Coast Fisheries—Statutes of Newfoundland relating to the—in 1872.
[*Ref* Hertslets. Vol. 14, p. 1239.]

1873. Treaty of Washington—Report of the Committee on Foreign Affairs of the U. S. House of Representatives on the Bill to carry into effect the provisions of the—1st February, 1873.
[*Ref.* House Report No. 52—42nd Cong., 3rd Sess., Vol. 1.

FISHERIES CONTROVERSY—*Continued*.

 1873. CORRESPONDENCE with the British Government in connection with the appointment of the Joint High Commission and the Treaty of Washington.
  [*Ref.* Imper'l. Comm. Papers, 1873. Vol. 49, p. 71.]

 1873. FURTHER CORRESPONDENCE with the Government of Canada. Prince Edward Island and Newfoundland respecting the Treaty of Washington, and the Canadian Pacific Railway.
  [*Ref.* Imp'l. Comm. Papers, 1873. Vol. 49, pp. 83, 109.]

 1873. ADDITIONAL ARTICLE TO THE TREATY OF WASHINGTON—signed 18th January, 1873.
  [*Ref.* Imperial Com'ns Papers, 1873. Vol. 74, p. 1; Hertslets. Vol. 14, p. 681.]

 1873. ACT OF CONGRESS of the United States of America, to carry into effect the provisions of the Treaty between the United States and Great Britain, signed at Washington, 8th May, 1871, relating to the fisheries, 25th February, 1873.
  [*Ref.* U. S. Statutes at large. Vol. 17, part 1, p. 482; being 42nd Cong., 3rd Sess. chap. 213; Hertslets vol. 14, p. 682.]

 1873 PROTOCOL of Conference between Great Britain and the United States of America, relative to Articles 18 to 25 and Article 30 of the Treaty of Washington, of 8th May 1871 (Fisheries) signed at Washington, 7th June, 1873.
  [*Ref.* Hertslets, vol. 14, p. 684; Eng. State Papers, vol. 63, p. 39; Imp. Comm. Papers 1873. Vol. 74, p. 5.]

 1873. ACT OF THE GOVERNMENT OF NEWFOUNDLAND to carry into effect the Treaty of Washington of 8th May, 1871, relating to fisheries. 5th May, 1873.
  [*Ref.* Statutes of Newfoundland. 36 Vict., chap. 37; Hertslets, vol. 14, p. 841.] This Act was repealed by an Act dated 29th April, 1874.

 1874. ACT OF THE LEGISLATURE OF NEWFOUNDLAND, to carry into effect the provisions of the Treaty of Washington so far as they relate to that colony (Fisheries) passed 28th March, 1874. Assented to 12th May, 1874.
  [*Ref.* Statutes of Newfoundland, 37 Vict., chap. 2; Hertslets, vol. 14, p. 1232.]

 1874. PROTOCOL of a Conference between Great Britain and the United States of America relative to the Newfoundland Fisheries. Washington, 28th May, 1874.
  [*Ref.* Hertslets, vol. 14, p. 1181; Eng. State Papers, vol. 65, p. 1283.]

 1874 PROCLAMATION of the President of the United States of America, respecting fisheries. 20th 28th May, 1874.
  [*Ref.* Hertslets, Vol. 14, p. 1183; Eng. State Papers, vol 65, p. 1284.]

 1877. RESOLUTION OF THE VERMONT LEGISLATURE—relating to the Fisheries—Instructing the Senators and requesting the Representatives of the State of Vermont to use all proper efforts for legislation for the protection of fisheries in waters within the jurisdiction in part of different States and the British Provinces of North America. 15th January, 1877.
  [*Ref.* Senate Mis. Doc. No. 28. 44th Cong., 2nd Sess., vol. 1.]

 1877. AWARD of the British, United States and Belgian Commissioners appointed under the Treaty of 8th May, 1871, to award the amount of compensation, if any, to be paid by the United States Government to the British Government in respect of the North American Fisheries. Halifax, 23rd November, 1877.
  [*Ref.* Hertslets, Vol. 14. p. 1185.]

 1878. HALIFAX FISHERIES COMMISSION—Correspondence respecting the—
  [*Ref.* Imp'l Commons Papers, 1878. Vol. 80, p. 1.]

 1878-9. HALIFAX FISHERIES COMMISSION—Correspondence respecting the Award of the—
  [*Ref.* Imp'l Comm. Papers, 1878-9. Vol. 77, pp. 35 59.]

 1878. AWARD OF THE FISHERIES COMMISSION—Report of the Committee on Foreign Relations on the Message of the President, together with the letter of the Secretary of State, and the papers transmitted therewith relating to the—to accompany S. Bill No. 1328. 28th May, 1878.
  [*Ref.* Senate Report No. 439—45th Cong., 2nd Sess., vol. 2]

 1878. MESSAGE ON THE FISHERIES—Pres. R. B. Hayes—Transmitting information relative to the appointment of a third commissioner under the 23rd Article of the Treaty of Washington, 19th and 21st March, 1878.
  [*Ref.* Senate Ex. Doc. No. 44—45th Cong., 2nd Sess., vol. 2.]

Fisheries Controversy —*Continued*

1878. AWARD OF THE FISHERY COMMISSION—Message on the—President R. B. Hayes. Transmitting the award of the Fishery Commission. Documents and proceedings of the Halifax Commission of 1877, under the Treaty of Washington, 8th May, 1871.—18th May, 1878.
[*Ref.* House Ex. Doc. No 89—45th Cong., 2nd Sess , vol. 18, 19, 20.]

1878 AWARD OF FISHERY COMMISSION - Report on—M Hamlin—Favourable to paying to the Canadian Government the award fixed upon by the above commission, if the British Government declare such award lawfully due. 28th May, 1878
[*Ref.* Senate Report No. 439—45th Cong., 2nd Sess., vol. 2.]

1879. PROPAGATION OF SALT WATER FISH—Report on the—Rep. Acklen. Favorable to the United States possessing paramount authority over the open sea and its fisheries, below low water mark. Hon. R. L. T. Beale, as minority of committee dissents, 4th June, 1879.
[*Ref.* House Report No. 7—46th Cong , 1st Sess., vol 1.]

1880. PROPAGATION OF SALT WATER FISH—Report on the—Rep. Beale—Adverse to any legislation on the subject by Congress. Jurisdiction of State authority sufficient to protect the interests involved. Hon. Jos. H. Acklen as a minority of committee dissents from the views of the majority; holding that the United States possesses paramount authority over the open sea and its fisheries below low water mark, and recommends the passage of substitute for House Bills 1355 and 1858. 9th January, 1880.
[*Ref.* House Report No 85—46th Cong., 2nd Sess., vol 1.]

1880. REPORT ON THE FISHERIES—Rep. W. W. Rice—Favorable to a resolution requesting the President to take such measures as will secure indemnity to our citizens for the damages sustained by them from past unlawful violence committed against them by the inhabitants of Newfoundland, and to procure the early abrogation of the Articles in the Treaty of 1871, relating to the Fisheries. 28th April, 1880.
[*Ref.* House Report No. 1275—46th Cong , 2nd Sess , vol. 4.]

1880. FISHERY PROVISIONS OF THE TREATY OF WASHINGTON, Report on the—Rep. S. S Cox—Favorable to House Bill No. 6453, relating to certain provisions of the Treaty of Washington Treaty right to inshore fishing. Fishermen of the United States driven by unlawful force from the fishing grounds; local legislation of Newfoundland the pretended justification. Bill is intended to provide the best remedy now possible for wrongs inflicted. Favors imposition of duties on fish-oil and fish produced by the Dominion fisheries, including Prince Edward Island and Newfoundland. 9th June, 1880.
[*Ref.* House Report No. 1746 - 46th Cong., 2nd Sess., vol. 15]

1881 DUTY ON FRESH WATER FISH, Report on - Rep. Conger—Session too near close to expect present action. No special recommendations made. Review of fresh water fisheries. Capital invested. Duty on fresh water fish caught in American waters and exported to Canada one cent per pound. No duty on fresh water fish imported into the United States. Injustice to our fresh water fisheries 3rd March, 1881.
[*Ref.* House Report No. 338—46th Cong., 3rd Sess., vol 1.]

1882 TERMINATION OF THE TREATY OF WASHINGTON—Report of the Committee on Foreign Affairs of the House of Representatives on H.R. 99, relating to the termination of certain provisions of the treaty with Great Britain of 1871, concerning the fisheries. 4th February, 1882.
[*Ref.* House Report No. 235 - 47th Cong., 1st Sess., vol 1.]

1883. TERMINATION OF THE TREATY OF WASHINGTON—Notification of the United States Government of the termination on the 2nd July, 1885, of Articles 18 to 25 and Article 30 of the Treaty with Great Britain of 8th May, 1871 (Canada and Newfoundland Fisheries). London, 2nd July, 1883.
[*Ref.* Hertslets, vol. 15, p. 841.]

1884 PROTECTION OF FISH AND FISHERIES on the Atlantic coasts—Report of the Committee on Foreign Relations on Senate Bill No. 155, entitled a Bill for the—24th March, 1884:
[*Ref.* Senate Report No. 365—48th Cong., 1st Sess., vol. 3.]

FIS   INDEX.

FISHERIES CONTROVERSY—*Continued.*

1886. STATISTICS OF U S. VESSEL FISHERIES—Senate Bill No. 2287—For securing statistics of the extent and value of the vessel fisheries of the United States. 29th April, 1886.
[*Ref.* Senate Bill No 2287—49th Cong., 2nd Sess]

1886. THE MACKEREL FISHERY—Hearings, before the Senate Committee on Fisheries, of parties interested in the Bill (H.R. 5538) relating to the importing and landing of mackerel caught during the spawning season. 1st June, 1886.

1886. FREEDOM OF COMMERCIAL INTERCOURSE—Report from the Committee on Commerce of the House of Representatives on the Bill (H.R. 9210) relating to—17th July, 1886.
[*Ref.* House Reports No. 3361—49th Cong., 1st Sess.]

1886. PROTECTION OF FUR SEAL AND SEA OTTER (Alaska).
[*Ref.* Report of the Governor of Alaska for the fiscal year 1886, p 47.]

1986 RIGHTS OF AMERICAN FISHERMEN in British North American waters—Message from President Grover Cleveland, transmitting a letter from the Secretary of State accompanied by the correspondence relating to the—8th December, 1886.
[*Ref.* House Ex. Doc. No. 19—49th Cong., 2nd Sess.; vol. of Am. Fishery Papers 1886-87.]

1887 NORTH AMERICAN FISHERIES.—Mr. Belmont.—Report of the Committee on Foreign Affairs, to which were referred the President's message of 8th December, 1886 (House Ex. Doc. No. 19) and the reply of the Secretary of the Treasury on 10th January, 1887 (House Ex. Doc. No. 78) to the resolution of the House adopted on 14th December, 1886, and House Bill 10241.
[*Ref* House Report No. 3,648—49th Cong., 2nd Sess.]

1887. LIST OF NEW ENGLAND FISHING VESSELS which have been inconvenienced in their fishery operations by the Canadian authorities during the past season. Communication of Spencer F. Baird with a report of R. E. Earl, in charge of the Division of Fisheries of the United States Commission of Fish and Fisheries. 5th February, 1887.
[*Ref.* Senate Mis. Doc. No 54—49 Cong., 2nd Sess.: vol. of Am. Fishery Papers. 1886-7.]

1887. REVISED LIST OF VESSELS involved in the Fisheries Controversy with the Canadian authorities.
[*Ref.* Senate Ex. Doc. No. 55—49th Cong., 2nd Sess.; vol. of Am. Fishery Papers, 1886-7.

1887. RIGHTS OF AMERICAN FISHERMEN IN THE WATERS OF BRITISH NORTH AMERICA—Message from President Grover Cleveland transmitting Report from the Secretary of State with accompanying correspondence between the Government of the United States and Great Britain, concerning the—supplementary to correspondence already communicated to Congress, 8th December, 1886. 8th February, 1887.
[*Ref* House Ex. Doc. No. 153—49 Cong., 2nd Sess.: vol. of Am. Fishery Papers 1886-7.]

1887. DEFENSE OF AMERICAN FISHING INTERESTS. Report of the Committee on Foreign Affairs of the House of Representatives on bill S. 3,173. ' An Act to authorise the President of the United States to protect and defend the rights of American fishing vessels, American fishermen, American trading and other vessels, in certain cases, and for other purposes " and (H. R. 10,786) "A bill to protect American vessels against unwarrantable and unlawful discrimination in the ports of British North America. 16th February, 1887.
To which is appended the following, viz:—A. Report from Committee on Foreign Affairs (No. 3648)—B. Letter of the Hon. Daniel Manning, Secretary of the Treasury.—C. Revised list of vessels seized, detained or warned off from Canadian Coasts—D. Article 29 of the Treaty of 1871.
[*Ref.* House Report No. 4087—49th Cong., 2nd Sess ; vol. of Am. Fishery Papers, 1886-7.]

1887. REPLY OF THE SECRETARY OF THE TREASURY (Daniel Manning), to the resolution of the House of Representatives of the 14th December, 1886, relating to American Fisheries (in Pam. form). 10th Jan'y, 1887.
[*Ref.* also vol. of Am. Fishery Papers, 1886-87.]

1887. RIGHTS OF U S. FISHERMEN. Resolution submitted to the Senate by Mr. Gorman, relative to the rights of United States fishermen. Ordered to be printed. 18th January, 1887.
[*Ref.* Senate Mis. Doc. No. 33 - 49th Cong., 2nd Sess.; vol. of Am. Fishery Papers, 1886-7.]

1887. DEFENSE OF AMERICAN FISHERY INTERESTS. Report of the Committee on Foreign Affairs to the Senate on Bill S. 3173, "An Act to authorize the President of the United States to protect and defend the rights of American fishing vessels, American fishermen, American trading and other vessels in certain cases and for other purposes."

FISHERIES CONTROVERSY — *Concluded.*
    To which is appended the testimony taken by a sub-committee (consisting of Senators Edmunds, Frye and Saulsbury of the Committee on Foreign Affairs, relative to American Fishery interests.
    [*Ref.* Senate Report No. 1683—49th Cong., 2nd Sess.; vol. of Am. Fishery Papers, 1886-7.]
    1887. DEFENSE OF AMERICAN FISHERY INTERESTS.   Report of Mr. Edmunds, Mr. Frye and Mr. Morgan, managers on the part of the Senate, on the disagreeing votes of the two Houses on the amendment of the House of Representatives to the bill (S. 3173), to authorize the President of the United States " to protect and defend the rights of American fishing vessels, American fishermen, American trading and other vessels, in certain cases and for other purposes."
    [*Ref.* Senate Report No. 1981—49th Cong , 2nd Sess.; vol. of Am. Fishery Papers, 1886-7.]

	PAGE
FISKE, N. The Moral Monitor : Essays	835
FITZGERALD, P. Royal Dukes and Princesses of the family of George III.	394
——————— Fatal Zero, a Homburg diary, (*Picc. Nov.* 17½)	847
FITZ-PATRICK, T. An Autumn Cruise in the Ægean	545
FLAMMARION, C. Astronomie populaire	584
——————— Les terres du ciel	584
——————— Histoire du ciel	584
——————— Mes voyages aériens	584
——————— Les mondes imaginaires	584
——————— Les merveilles célestes	584
FLOQUET, A. Histoire du parlement de Normandie	291
FONVIELLE, W. de. Mort de faim—étude sur les nouveaux jeûneurs	573
——————— La mesure du mètre: dangers des savants qui l'ont déterminée	535
FORBES, Anna. Insulinde: Experiences in the Eastern Archipelago	569
FORBIN, Cte. L. N. P. A. de. Travels in the Levant in 1817-18	522
——————— Travels in Egypt in 1817-18	522
——————— Recollections of Sicily	522
Foreign Office (English). Catalogue of the Library, 1885	905
Forestry in Europe. U. S. Consular Reports	648
FORSTER, T. H. A voyage in a Convict Ship to Tasmania	40
FORNERON, H. Louise de Kéroualle, Duchess of Portsmouth	383
——————— Histoire des émigrés pendant la Révolution	427
FOUQUE, O. Les révolutionnaires de la musique	721
FOURNIER, Ed. Paris capitale	434
FOURNIER, de FLAIX, E. Etudes économiques et financières	418
FOVILLE, A. de. La France économique	407
FOWLER (J. C.; and Lewis, D. Law of Collieries	114
France, l'Ancienne	410
FRANCE, H. L'armée de John Bull	682
" France, J." A lapful of Lyrics	1410

	PAGE
FRANKLIN, A. L'annonce et la réclame ; les cris de Paris..................	434
——— ——— Les soins do la toilette ; le savoir vivre...................... ...	434
FRANKLIN, Jos. History of the United States of America (1784)............	1217
Fraser, Bishop Jas. A Memoir. By Thos. Hughes............................	488
FRAZAR, D. Perseverance Island...	835
FREEMAN, E. A. Exeter (Hist. Towns Ser.).....	404
FREMINVILLE, Chev. de la Poix de. Voyage to the North Pole........	522
FREMONT, J. B. Souvenirs of my time.	1229
FREMONT, J. C. Memoirs of my life: a retrospect of fifty years...............	1229
FREY, A. R. Sobriquets and Nicknames..............	803
FRIEDLANDER, H. Views in Italy, 1815-16.........	522
FRIGNET (E.) et CARRY, E. Les Etats du Nord-Ouest de l'Amérique..........	1257
FRITH, W. P. My Autobiography and Reminiscences........................	489
FROMENT, A. La mobilisation et la préparation à la guerre..................	682
FROUDE, J. A. The English in the West Indies..............................	1360
FUSTER, Chs. Essais de critique................................	801
GAHAN, J. J. Canada: a poem...	1410
GALLENGA, A. Italy present and future..	436
GARÇON, A. Histoire du canal de Panama.....................................	1361
GARIEL, C. M. Electricité : application aux sciences........................	590
GARNIER, Jos. Traité complet d'arithmétique..................................	599
GARRETT, Rev. C. Loving Counsels : Sermons and Addresses...............	50
GAUTHIER, l'abbé L. O. Histoire du Canada..................................	1273
GAUTIER, H. Pendant le seize mai..	434
GAUTIER, L. La poésie liturgique au moyen-âge..............................	799
GAUTIER, Théop. L'Orient...	526
——— ——— Portraits contemporains..	801
——— ——— Histoire du romantisme..	801
Gazul, Clara. Théâtre de. Voir Merimée, Prosper	
GEFFROY, A. Mme de Maintenon d'après sa correspondance authentique....	494
GENNEVRAYE, A. Trop riche..	882
GENTY, l'abbé A. E. Histoire de la Norville.................................	433
GEOFFROY, Aug. Arabes pasteurs nomades....,..............	416

GEOGRAPHY AND TRAVELS.

Adventures among the Kalmucs. **Michailow.**
Autumn Cruise in the Ægean. **Fitz-Patrick. T.**
Athos : or, the Mountain of the Monks. **Riley, A.**
Au pays du Rhin. **Weiss, J. J.**
Autour du Concile : croquis et souvenirs. **Yriarte, Ch.**
Balkan (The) Peninsula **Laveleye, Em. de.**
Boy travellers on the Congo. **Knox, T. W.**
British Colonial Pocket Atlas. **Brrtholomew, J.**
Bucharia, Account of. **Eversmann & Jakovlew.**

GEOGRAPHY AND TRAVELS—*Continued.*

Classical Excursion from Rome to Arpino. **Kellsall, Chs.**
China: travels and investigations in the " Middle Kingdom." **Wilson, J. H.**
China : Overland journey from Macao to Canton.
Conférences et lettres sur les explorations. **Brazza, S. de.**
Côte (la) barbaresque et le Sahara. **Luborminki, le Prince J.**
Court life in Egypt. **Butler, A. J.**
Crescent (The) and the Cross. **Warburton, E.**
Digging. Squatting and Pioneering in South Australia. **Daly, Mrs. D. D.**
Diners artistiques et littéraires de Paris. **Lepage, A.**
Diversions of a diplomat in Turkey. **Cox, S. S.**
Dix mois autour du monde. **Lieussou, G.**
Ecosse (l') jadis et aujourd'hui. **Lafond, Cte. L.**
Empire (l') allemand à vol d'oiseau. **Brault, F.**
En Corse. **Bourde, P.**
England, a sketch of Old. By a New England Man.
Eothen. **Kinglake, A W.**
Expedition to Kokand. **Nazaroff, P.**
Famous travels and travellers. **Verne, Jules.**
50,000 milles dans l'océan Pacifique. **Davin, A.**
Four Months' Cruise in a Sailing Yacht. **Edgcumbe (Lady E.) and Wood, Lady M.**
Free Russia **Dixon, W. H.**
From Pharaoh to Fellah. **Bell, C. F. M.**
Gazetteer of the British Isles. **Bartholomew, J.**
Géographie générale. **Gregoire, L.**
Geography of the British Colonies and Foreign Possessions. **Fanulhorpe, Rev. J. P.**
Great Explorers of the 19th Century. **Verne, Jules.**
Great Navigators of the 18th Century.   do
Greece and the Ionian Islands. 1821. **Muller, Dr. C.**
Haifa : or, Life in Modern Palestine. **Oliphant, L.**
Historical Geography of the British Colonies. **Lucas, C P.**
Ice Pack and Tundra, account of the search for the "Jeannette." **Gilder, W. H.**
Insulinde : Experiences in the Eastern Archipelago. **Forbes, Anna.**
Journal of a tour into Missouri and Arkansaw. **Schoolcraft, H R.**
Journey through the North of Germany, Denmark, etc. **Hallberg, Baron von.**
Journey through Africa. **Mahomed Misrah.**
Journey through Turcomania and China. **Mouravlew, Capt.**
Leaves from my Chinese Scrap book. **Balfour, F. H.**
Letters from Crete. **Edwardes, Chs.**
Letters from Europe (during 1801 and 1802)   By a Native of Pennsylvania.
Letters on Italy. **Castellan, A. L.**
My Consulate in Samoa. **Churchward, W. B.**
My Winter on the Nile. **Warner, C. D.**
Narrative of Thirty-four Years Slavery and Travels in Africa. **Dumont, P. J.**
Naval and Military Establishments of Great Britain. **Dupin, le baron Ch.**
Navigations, Voyages, Traffiques, etc   Vols 3, 4, 5. **Hakluyt, R.**
New Paris Sketch Book   **Alger, J. G.**
Notes sur Rome et l'Italie. **Toste. L.**
Nouvelle géographie universelle. Vol. 12. **Reclus, E.**
Orient (L'). **Gautier, Théop.**
Our Hundred Days in Europe. **Holmes, O. W.**
Pen and Pencil in Asia Minor. **Cochran, W.**
Perse (la) la Chaldée et la Susiane. **Dieulafoy, Mme J.**
Petermanns Mittheilungen, 1886–87.
Picturesque New Guinea. **Lindt, J. W.**
Pioneering in New Guinea. **Chalmer, (J.) and Hill, W. W.**
Progress of Arctic Discovery. **Hayes, I. J.**
Promenades in Constantinople and on the Bosphorus. **Pertusier, Chs.**

GEOGRAPHY AND TRAVELS—Continued.

Recollections of Sicily. **Forbin, Cte. L. N-P. A. de.**
Romantic Spain ; a Record of Personal Experiences. **O'Shea, J. A.**
Roundabout to Moscow. **Bouton, J. B.**
Run away from the Dutch : Adventures in Borneo. **Perelaer, M. T. H.**
Saône (The), a Summer Voyage. **Hamerton, P. G.**
Scott, Alex. Captivity of, among the Arabs of Africa.
Shipwreck of the "Sophia" on the Western coast of Africa. **Cochelet, Chs.**
Société (La) de Londres. **Vasili, Cte. P.**
———————— Paris. **Vasili, Cte. P.**
———————— Rome. **Vasili, Cte. P.**
———————— Vienne. **Vasili, Cte. P.**
Solomon (The) Islands and their natives. **Guppy, H. B.**
Story of the Niger. **Richardson, R.**
Tenerife and its six satellites. **Stone, O. M.**
Terre d'Irlande. **Moore, Geo.**
Three years of Arctic Service (1881-84). **Greely, Lieut. A W.**
Tour (A) in both hemispheres. **Vetromille, Eug.**
Tour (A) to Quebec in 1819. **Silliman, B.**
Travels, Sport, and Politics. **Huntly, Marquis of.**
———— in Brazil, 1815-17. **Maximilian de Wied Newwied.**
———— on foot through Ceylon. **Haafner, J.**
———— on the Continent and in England. **Niemeyer, Dr. A. H.**
———— in Egypt, 1818-19. **Montule E. de.**
———— in Egypt in 1817-18. **Forbin, Cte. L. N. P. A. de.**
———— in Egypt and India. **Buckhardt, J. L.**
———— in Egypt and the Lybian desert. **Scholz.**
———— in Greece. **Pouqueville.**
———— in Hungary in 1818. **Beudant.**
———— in Italy. **Chateauvieux, F. L. de.**
———— in the Levant in 1817-18. **Forbin, Cte L. N. P. A. de.**
———— in Lower Canada **Sansou, Jos.**
———— in Montenegro. **Sommières, L. C. V. de.**
———— through Portugal and Spain during the Peninsula War. **Graham, W.**
———— in Scotland. **Necker de Saussure.**
———— in Sicily, 1819. **Gourbillon, M.**
———— in Southern Epirus. **Pouqueville.**
———— in Switzerland. **Simond, L.**
———— in the Oasis of Thebes. **Cailliaud, F.**
———— in Tunisia. **Graham (A) and Ashbee, H. F.**
Turquie (La) inconnue. **Hugonnet, L.**
Twenty-five years in a waggon in the gold regions of Africa. **Anderson, A. A.**
Two Excursions to the Ports of Great Britain and Ireland. **Dupin, le baron Chs.**
Ulysses : or, Scenes and Studies in many lands. **Palgrave, W. G.**
Views in Italy, 1815-16. **Friedlander, H.**
Voyage to Buenos Ayres, 1817-18. **Brackenridge, H. M.**
———— along the Eastern Coast of Africa. **Prior, J.**
———— To North America and West Indies. **Montulé, E. de.**
———— of discovery to the Arctic Regions. **Fisher, A.**
———— from France to Conchin-China. **Rey, Captain.**
———— au Groënland. **Mesange, le P. Pierre de.**
———— to the Hebrides. **Necker de Saussure.**
———— to Hudson's Bay in 1812. **McKeevor, T.**
———— on the Indian Seas **Prior, J.**
———— to India and New South Wales. **Cramp, W. B.**
———— to the Strait of Magellan. **Cordova, Adml. Don. A. de.**
———— to the North Pole. **Fremluville, Chev. de la Poix de.**
———— to the South Sea and to Behring's Straits. **Kotzebue, O.**

GEO INDEX

GEOGRAPHY AND TRAVELS—*Continued.* PAGE
  Voyage in the West Indies. **Waller, J. A.**
  Voyages autour du monde depuis Christophe Colomb.
  ——— round the World, 1816-1819. **Roquefeuil, C. de.**

GEOLOGY, ETC.
  British Mining, 2nd edition. **Hunt, R.**
  Mineral Physiology and Physiography. **Hunt, T. S.**
  Origin of Mountain Ranges. **Reade, T. M.**

GENEALOGY, HERALDRY, ETC.
  America Heraldica: Arms, Crests, and Mottoes. **Vermont, E. de.**
  British Roll of Honour: Orders of Chivalry. **Simmonds, P. L.**
  Dictionnaire des devises. **Chassant (A) et Tausin, H.**
  Great historic families of Scotland. **Taylor, J.**
  Heraldry, English and Foreign. **Jenkins, R. C.**
  Insignia of the Orders of British Knighthood. **Hunter, J.**

GEORGE III. The Jubilee of 394
——— ——— The Jubilee of, by T. Preston. 394
Geraldine. A Souvenir of the St. Lawrence............................... 859
GIBBS, W. A. Fifty years in fifty minutes................................... 396
GIBSON, J. Y. The Cid ballads and other poems 897
GILDER, W. H. Ice Pack and Tundra, account of the search for the Jeannette 532
GILL, R. Free Trade... 518
GILMAN, A. Rome from the earliest times................................ 304
——— ——— Saracens, The 304
GILMORE, J. R. The Rear-Guard of the Revolution................. 1265
——— ——— John Sevier, as a Commonwealth builder............. 1265
GIRARDIN, Mme E. de. Poésies complètes 878
GISORS, le Cte de (1732-1758). Par Camille Rousset............ 426
Gladstone and his Contemporaries.. 450
GLASIER, Alfred. The Irving Club among the White Hills..... 1410
Goethe. Correspondence with Carlyle...................................... 489
GOGOL. Tchitchikoff's journeys, or Dead Souls 898
GONCOURT, Edm. et J. de. Journal 1851-61........................... 884
GONSE, L. L'art japonais.. 692
Good (The) Hermione, a story for jubilee year. By Aunt Belinda........ 396
GOODWIN, W. L. Text-book of chemistry for students of medicine......... 595
GORDON, J. E. H. Electric lighting.. 590
GORDON, W. History of the Independence of the United States........... 1262
GOSS, N. S. Catalogue of the birds of Kansas......................... 639
GOSSELIN, l'abbé D. Tablettes chronologiques de l'histoire du Canada...... 1274
——— ——— Histoire populaire de l'église du Canada............. 1196
GOULD, R. F. History of Free Masonry.................................... 469
GOULD, S. Baring. Germany (Story of the Nations)................ 304

	PAGE
GOULD, S. Baring. Red Spider	836
——— ——— The Gaverocks	836
GOURBILLON, M. Travels in Sicily, 1819	522
GOURDON de GENOUILLAC, H. Paris à travers les siècles	434
GRAHAM, W. Travels through Portugal and Spain during the Peninsular War	522
GRAHAM (A) and ASHBEE, H. S. Travels in Tunisia	561
GRAHAM, W. Social Problems	489
GRANDFORT, Manoël de. La cousine d'André	885
GRANT, R. Face to Face	836
Grant, U. S. Memoirs of, vs. the Record of the Army of the Potomac, by C. McClellan	1268
——— ——— Grant in Peace. By Adam Badeau	1230
GRANVILLE, Chs. Sir Hector's Watch	836
GRAVIER, G. Nouvelle étude sur La Salle	1252
GRAY, A. The merchandise Marks Act, 1887	114
GRAY, J. C. Restraints on alienation	91
GRAY, M. The Silence of Dean Maitland	836
GRÉARD, Oct. L'éducation des femmes par les femmes	75
Great Strike of 1886. Official History of	489
GREELY, Lieut. A W. Three years of Arctic Service (1881-84)	532
Greely Relief Expedition, Proceedings of Court of Enquiry	243
GREENE, G. W. The German Element in the war of American Independence	1264
GREENOUGH, H. Letters to his brother Henry	1229
Greenwich Observatory. Astronomical observations, 1885. 4 Vols	584
GREER, E. Land Law (Ireland) Act, 1887	98
GREG, P. History of the United States	1219
GRÉGOIRE, L. Géographie générale	511
GREGORY, J. W. En racontant : récits de voyages (traduits)	1409
GRENET-DANCOURT, E. Trois femmes pour un mari ; comédie	878
GRIFFIN, W. Twok	1410
GRIFFIS, W. E. Biographical Sketch of Com. M. C. Perry	1229
Grimm, Melchior. Par E. Scherer	490
GRINNELL, C. E. Law of Deceit	83
GRISON, G. Souvenirs de la Place de la Roquette	887
GROSCLAUDE. Les gaietés de l'année	852
Gugy, Col. A. Pamphlets on the Case of	133
GUIZOT, M. et Mme. Le temps passé : Mélanges de critique et de morale	800
GUNTON, G. Wealth and Progress	485
GUPPY, H. B. The Solomon Islands and their natives	569

	PAGE
GUYOT, Ives. L'impôt sur le revenu	422
" Gyp." Autour du divorce..	882
HAAFNER, J. Travels on foot through Ceylon	522
HADLEY, A. T. Transport par les chemins de fer..	429
HAECKEL, E. Report of the Radiolaria (Chall. Exp. Zool. Rep. V. 18).......	635
HAGGARD, H. R. Jess..	837
———————— Dawn	837
———————— The Witch's Head	837
———————— Allan Quartermain..	837
HAKLUYT, R. Navigations, Voyages, Traffiques, etc. Vols. 3, 4, 5............	521
HALE, E. E. Franklin in France..	1220
———————— Lights of Two Centuries : biographies	475
HALE, J. P. First White settlements West of the Alleghanies (1748).......	1246
HALÉVY, L. Princesse...	886
HALLBERG, Baron von. Journey through the North of Germany, Denmark, etc..	522
HALLIWELL-PHILLIPS, J. O. Life of Shakespeare....................................	500
HAMEL, l'abbé T. E. Le premier Cardinal canadien. Souvenir de 1886......	1196
HAMERTON, P. G. The Saône, a summer voyage..	540
Hamilton, Lady and Lord Nelson. By J. C. Jeaffreson.............................	490
HAMILTON, Archbp. John. Catechism of 1552...	39
HAMMICK, J. T. Marriage Laws of England and Colonies......................	86
HAMONT, T. Lally-Tollendal : La fin d'un empire français aux Indes.......	457
Harden, Ben. His times and contemporaries ; by L. P. Little	1229
Harding, Rev. H. Life and Times ; by Rev. J. Davis...............................	1198
HARDY, T. The Woodlanders...	837
HARPER, J. C. Inter-State Commerce..	176
HARRIOTT, Lt. John. Struggles through life : various travels and adventures.	495
HARRIS, S. The Self-Revelation of God	44
HARRIS, S. F. Criminal Law, 4th ed..	76
HARRISON, J. B. Indian Reservations...	161
HARTE, Bret. A millionaire of Rough and Ready, and Devil's Ford.........	837
———————— Frontier Stories..	837
———————— Crusade of the Excelsior..	837
HARTMANN, G. L'alcool et l'impôt des boissons..	422
HARVEY, H. History of the Shawnee Indians..	1157
HASTINGS, E. J. Statistical Atlas..	511
HATTON, J. The Old House at Sandwich...	837
HAWEIS, H. R. Christ and Christianity..	17
HAWS, Samuel. Military Journal for 1775..	1262

	PAGE
HAYEM, G. Leçons de thérapeutique	671
HAYES, I. J. Progress of Arctic Discovery	532
HAZELL'S Annual Cyclopædia, 1887	908
HAZLITT, W. C. A hundred merry tales—reproduced	837
HEALEY, WHEELER and JENKINS. Joint Stock Companies	102
HEARD, A. F. The Russian Church and Russian Dissent	30
HECKEWELDER, Rev. J. History of the Indian Nations of Pennsylvania	1187
HEFELE, C. J. Life of Cardinal Ximenez	506
HEILPRIN, A. Geographical and Geological distribution of Animals (Int. S. S. 58)	578
HEINECCIUS, J. G. Elementa juris civilis secundum ordinem institutionum.	262
————— Antiquitatum romanarum jurisprudentiam illustrantium syntagma	262
————— Elementa juris civilis secundum ordinem pandectarum	262
HEINSIUS, D. De tragœdiæ constitutione liber. Et Aristotelis, de poetica	808
HELIODORE. L'histoire éthiopique : Amours de Théagenes et Chariclea	811
HELPS, Sir A. Social Pressure. New edition	837
————— Essays. New edition	837
Hendricks, Thos. A. Life and character of—Memorial Address	1224
HENEY, H. Commentaires sur l'acte de 1791	374
Henri IV et l'Allemagne d'après Jacques Bongars	424
————— et Louis XIII. Etude sur le XVIIe siècle (L'Ancienne France)	410
HÉRISSON, Cte. d'. The Black Cabinet	427
HERMANT, A. Le cavalier Miserey, 21e chasseurs	885
HERODOTUS. Historiæ libri IX et de vita Homeri libellus	811
HEUZEY, L. Opérations militaires de Jules César	681
HEWETT, F. C. Recollections of Sedan	1410
HEYD, W. Histoire du commerce du Levant au moyen âge	424
HEYL, U. S. Import Duties, 1887	521
HIGGINS, Rev. T. A. Life of John M. Cramp, D.D.	1198
HIGH, J. L. On Receivers. 2nd ed.	79
HILLYARD, M. B. The New South	528
HILTS, J. H. Experiences of a Backwoods preacher	51
Historical Researches in Western Pennsylvania	1182

HISTORY, GENERAL.
    Alexander's Empire. **Mahaffy, J. P.**
    Allemagne (l') à la fin du Moyen-Age. **Janssen, J.**
    Ancient Egypt (Story of the Nations). **Rawlinson, G.**
    Annonce (l') et la réclame ; les cris de Paris. **Franklin, A.**
    Annual Register for 1886.
    Antiquités de la ville de Paris, Histoire des. **Sauval, H.**
    Armée (l'),—depuis le moyen-âge. (*L'Ancienne France*).
    Arniston Memoirs. Three Centuries of a Scotish House. **Omond, G. W. T.**

HISTORY, GENERAL—*Continued.*

Arts et métiers au moyen-âge. (*L'Ancienne France.*)
Avant-postes (les) pendant le siège de Paris. **Cléry, R. de.**
Baireuth, Margravine of. Memoirs, translated by H. R. H. Princess Christian.
Bastille, La prise de la. **Lecocq, G.**
Bataille (la) de Sédan, histoire complète. **Corra, Em.**
Black (The) Cabinet. **Hérisson, Comte d'.**
Boers in South Africa, History of the. **Theal, G. Mc.**
Bourgoisie (la) française, 1789-1848. **Bardoux, A.**
Bristol (*Historic Towns*). **Hunt, Wm.**
Britain's Queen, a story and a Memorial **Fisher, Pearl.**
Brunswick (The) Accession. **Thornton, P. M.**
Caledonia : historical and topographical. **Chalmers, G.**
Camille et Lucile Desmoulins. **Clarette, J**
Campaign of the Cataracts. **Butler, W. F.**
Campaign of Sedan. **Hooper, G.**
Carthage ; or, the Empire of Africa. **Church, A. J.**
Château de Versailles—histoire et description. **Dussieux, L.**
Chevalerie (la) et les croisades. (*L'Ancienne France.*)
Chute de la Royauté. **Sorel, A.**
Colbert, Jules Armand (marquis d'Ormoy) Une étude par **Margry, P.**
Comédie (la) française pendant les deux sièges (1870-71). **Thierry, E.**
Comment les monarchies finissent. **Bell, Geo.**
Connétable (le) de Richemont. 1393-1458. **Cosneau, E.**
Correspondance diplomatique par Zeller, J. **Pellicier, G.**
—— —— inédite. Marie-Antoinette, par d'**Hunolstein**, le Cte. P. V.
—— —— pendant les premières années de la Restauration. Vols. 5, 6. **Remusat, M. de**
Corsaires (les) barbaresques et la marine de Soliman le Grand. **La Gravière, J. de.**
Court of the Emperor Justinian. **Procopius.**
Courte histoire de Napoléon I. **Seeley, J. R.**
Course (The) of Empire. **Wheeler, C. G.**
Criminal history of the English Government. **Regnault, E.**
Cunningham (Wm.) of Craigend. Diary of, 1673 to 1680.
Dalmatia, the Quarnero and Istria. **Jackson, T. G.**
Diplomatie francaise du XVIe siècle. **Zeller, J.**
Ecole (l') et la Science au moyen-âge. (*L'Ancienne France.*)
England under the Angevin Kings. **Norgate, Kate.**
—— and France in India. **Rapson, E. J.**
—— and Napoleon in 1803. **Browning, O.**
England's Jubilees. **Hudson, E. H.**
Exeter (His. Towns. Ser.) **Freeman, E. A.**
Fifty years in fifty minutes. **Gibbs, W. A.**
First (The) Lady in the Land. **Bailey, E. A.**
First year of a Silken Reign, (1837-38). **Tuer (A. W.) and Fagan, C. F.**
Français et Allemands. **Londay, D de.**
Français (les) à Madagascar. **Hue, F.**
France, l'Ancienne.
France (la) à la suite de la guerre de 1870-71. **Chaudordy, Cte. de.**
France (la) martyre. **Lermina, J.**
French Court and Society. **Jackson, Lady.**
Gentleman (A) of the olden time. **Coignet, Mme. C.**
George III ; The Jubilee of. By **Preston, T.**
Germany (Story of the Nations). **Gould, S. Baring.**
Gisors, le Cte. de (1732-1758). Par **Rousset, Camille.**
Good (The) Hermione, a story for jubilee year. By Aunt Belinda.
Greek life and thought. **Mahaffy, J. P.**
Greater England. **Hodgetts, J. F.**
Guerre (la) de 1870. **Leclercq, Em.**

HISTORY, GENERAL—*Continued.*

 Guerre (la) de 1870-71. **Barthélemy, Ch.**
 Hampton Court Palace in Tudor Times. **Law, E.**
 Henri IV et l'Allemagne d'après Jacques Bongars. **Anquez, L.**
 Henri IV., et Louis XIII. Etude sur le XVIIe siècle. (*L'Ancienne France.*)
 Her Majesty, Her Ancestors and Her Family. **Ritchie, A. F.**
 Histoire du bon vieux temps. **Bonnefoy, M.**
 ——— de la guerre de Crimée, 2e édition. **Rousset, C.**
 ——— des émigrés pendant la Révolution. **Forneron, H.**
 ——— des Grecs. **Duruy, V.**
 ——— du commerce du Levant au moyen-âge. **Heyd, W.**
 ——— de la Monarchie de Juillet. **Du Bled, V.**
 ——— de la Norville. **Genty, l'abbé, A. F.**
 ——— de la république française. **Canis.**
 Historians of the Church of York. (Rolls Chron.)
 Historical basis of modern Europe (1760-1815). **Weir, A.**
 Historical portraits of the Tudor dynasty. **Burke, S. H.**
 Historiens (les) fantaisistes—M. Thiers. **Martel, Cte. de.**
 History of the Commune of 1871. **Lissagaray.**
 ——— of England in the 18th Century. Vols. 3, 4, 5, 6. **Lecky, W. E H.**
 ——— of the Irish People. **O'Conor, W. A.**
 ——— of Norway. **Boyesen, H. H.**
 ——— of Our Own Times down to end of 1886. **McCarthy, Justin.**
 ——— of Oxford. **Boase, C. W.**
 ——— of the Rebellion, 1745. **Home, Jno.**
 Icelandic Sagas retating to British Iles (Rolls Chron.)
 Imposture (l') des Naundorff. **Veuillot, P.**
 Inde (l') française avant Dupleix. **Castonnets des Fosses, H.**
 Industrie (l') et l'art décoratif. (*L'Ancienne France.*)
 Invasion of the Crimea. Vols. 7 and 8. **Kinglake, A.W.**
 Ireland. (Story of the Nations) **Lawless, Hon. Emily.**
 Ireland since the Union. **McCarthy, J. H.**
 Irish (The) in Australia. **Hogan, J. F.**
 Italy, present and future. **Gallenga, A.**
 Jews (The) in ancient, mediæval and modern times. **Hosmer, J. K.**
 Jubilate An offering for 1887. **Tupper. M. F.**
 Jubilee Date Book.
 Jubilee Echoes. **Morton, Mrs. G. E.**
 Jubilee Memoir of Her Majesty Queen Victoria. **Walford, E.**
 Jubilee of Queen Victoria, 1887—Works on.
 ——————————— Hymns for the year.
 ——————————— Special illustrated numbers of periodicals.
 Lally-Tollendal : La fin d'un empire français aux Indes **Hamont, T.**
 Legends and Superstitions of Ireland. **Wilde, Lady** (Speranza).
 Les Volontaires, 1791-1794. **Rousset, C.**
 Life and Reign of Queen Victoria. **Leslie, Emma.**
 Life and Reign of Victoria, Queen and Empress. **Moore, Emily J.**
 Life and times of Queen Victoria. **Wilson, R.**
 Lismore Papers. Second Series Vols. 1, 2.
 Literæ Cantuarienses (Rolls Chronicles).
 Livre (le) et les arts qui s'y rattachent. **Louisy, P.** (*L'Ancienne France*).
 Lord Randolph Churchill. **Crozier, J. B.**
 Lorraine (la) illustrée.
 Louis XIV à Strasbourg—politique de la France en Alsace. **Legrelle, A.**
 Louis XVII vengé des impostures de P. Veuillot. **Daymonas, B.**
 Louis XVII La survivance du Roi-Martyr. Par un ami de la Vérité.
 Louise de Kéroualle, Duchess of Portsmouth. **Forneron, H.**
 Mary, Queen of Scots. Letters of, translated by W. Turnbull.

HISTORY, GENERAL—*Continued.*

Mes petits papiers (1860-1870). **Pessard, H.**
Misères (les) de l'Anjou aux XVe et XVIe siècles. **Joubert, A.**
Myths of the New World. **Brinton, D. G**
Napoléon Bonaparte et ses détracteurs. Par le prince **Napoléon** (Jérôme).
Normans (The) in South Europe. **Barlow, J. M**
Œuvres (les) et les hommes. **Barbey d'Aurevilley, J.**
On the track of Ulysses. **Stillman, W. J.**
" Our Gracious Queen " **Walton, Mrs. O. F.**
Our Queen.
Our Sovereign Lady : a book for Her people.
Paris à travers les siècles. **Gourdon de Genouillac, H.**
Paris capitale. **Fournier, Ed.**
Paris Police. **Virmaitre, Chs.**
Paysans (les) : histoire d'un village avant la Révolution. **Delon, C.**
Pendant le seize mai. **Gautier, H.**
Personal Recollections of the late, **Broglie**, duc de. 1785-1820.
Petits (les) Jacobins. **De Witt, P.**
Précis des guerres du second empire. **Fabre de Navacelle, H.**
Prince Alexander : Reminiscences of his reign in Bulgaria. **Koch, A.**
Profils vendéens. "**Sylvanecte.**"
Punch's (Mr.) Victoria Era.
Queen's (The) Birthday Book. **Dunbar, Mary F. P.**
Queen (The) her early life and reign. **Valentine, L.**
Queen Victoria, Reign of. A survey of fifty years. **Ward, T. H.**
———— Scenes and Incidents of her life and reign. **Ball, T. F.**
Recollections of a minister to France (1869-1877). **Washburne, E. B.**
Records of Service and Campaigning. **Munro, Surg. Gen.**
Reigns of Stephen, Henry II and Richard I. (Rolls Chron.)
Revolutions (The) of 1848-49. **Maurice, C. E.**
Revolutions politiques de Florence (1177-1530). **Thomas, G.**
Rhodes in Ancient Times. **Torr, C.**
Rhodes, l'ile de. **Billotti (E) et Cottret, l'abbe.**
Roger de Wendover. Vol 1. (Rolls' Chronicles).
Rome from the Earliest Times. **Gilman, A.**
Rome, its Princes and People. Vol. 3 **Silvagni, D.**
Royal Dukes and Princesses of the Family of George III. **Fitzgerald, P.**
Royal Jubilees of England. **Ellis, Wm.**
Russie (la) sous les tzars **Stepniak**
St. Petersburg and London in the years 1852-64. **Vitzthum von Eckstædt, Ct. C. F.**
Saracens, (The). **Gilman, A.**
Scotland as it was and as it is. **Argyll, Duke of.**
Short History of England. **Ransome, C.**
Sketches of some distinguished Anglo-Indians **Laurie, Col. W. F. R.**
Social History of the Races of Mankind. **Featherman, A.**
Soins (les) de la toilette. (*Vie privée d'autrefois*). **Franklin, A.**
Souvenirs de la présidence du Maréchal de MacMahon. **Daudet, E.**
Statues (les) de Paris. **Marmottan, P.**
Story (The) of England (*Rolls' Chron*). **Robert (Manning) of Brunne.**
Story of the Life of Queen Victoria. **Tulloch, M. M.**
Théatre (le) et la Musique jusqu'en 1789 (*L'Ancienne France*).
Tours in Scotland (1747, 1750, 1760). **Pococke, R.**
Two Royal Lives : The Crown Prince and Princess of Germany. **Roberts, Dorothea.**
Un fils de Colbert. (Marquis d'Ormoy). **Margry, P.**
Un gentilhomme des temps passés. **Colquet, Mme. C.**
Universal History compiled from original authors.
Variétés révolutionnaires. **Pellet, M.**
Venetian Studies. **Brown, H. F.**

HISTORY, GENERAL—*Concluded.*
  Victoria, as Maiden, Mother and Monarch. **Kirton, J. W.**
  ——— Queen, Jubilee of. Celebration at St. John's, N.B.
  ——— Queen and Empress. **Pike, G. Holden.**
  ——— R. I. Her life and reign. **Macaulay, Dr.**
  Victorian Triumphs: a jubilee bead roll. **Press, W. H.**
  Victorian half century. A Jubilee Book. **Yonge, C. M.**
  Voyageurs (les) canadiens à l'expédition du Soudan. **Labat, G. P.**
  Wars of the Emperor Justinian, History of the. **Procopius.**
  William the Third. **Torriano, W. H.**
  Windsor Castle. Jubilee Edition. **Loftie, W. J.**

HISTORY AND BIOGRAPHY, AMERICAN.

  American Ancestry. **Hughes, T, P.**
  ——— Catholic Historical Researches.
  ——— Catholic Historical Society of Philadelphia. Records of the.
  ——— Historical Association. Papers of the.
  ——— Indian. The story of the. **Brooks, E. S.**
  Amérique (l') avant les Européens. **Desdevises du Dezert.**
  André: Life and carreer of Major John. **Sargent, W.**
  Annales de la paroisse de St. Jacques le Majeur (1772 à 1872.) **Chagnon, Rév. F. H.**
  Anticipation; a political pamphlet (1778). **Tickell, R.**
  Antiquities of Central America. **Davis, A.**
  Appleton's Cyclopedia of American Biography.
  Army and Navy of America from the French and Indian War to Florida War (1755-1835). **Neff, J. K.**
  Asbury, Bp. Francis. Life and times of. **Strickland, W. P.**
  Baltimore. The Chronicles of, by **Scharf, J. T.**
  Beecher, Henry Ward: a sketch of his career. **Abbott, L.**
  Ben Hardin: his times and contemporaries. **Little, L. P.**
  Biographical memoir of Williams, Rev. Jno. **Williams, S. W.**
  Black Hawk. Life of—dictated by himself.
  Books (The) of Chilan Balam. **Brinton, D. G.**
  Bouquet, Col. Henry, and his campaigns of 1763 and 1764. By **Cort, Rev. E.**
  Boutwell. G. S. The Lawyer, the Statesman and the Soldier.
  Bradley, Mrs. M. Life and Christian experience of.
  Brésil, l'empire du, monographie. **Baril, le Comte V. L.**
  British (The) Lion Roused. **Ogden, Jas.**
  British Spy. Letters of the.
  Brouage et Champlain (1578-1667). **Audiat, L.**
  Buffalo Historical Society. Publications of.
  Burns, Rev. R. Life and times of. Edited by his son.
  California. By **Boyce, J.** (*Amer. Comm. Series.*)
  Campaigns against the Six-Nations of Indians (1779). **Sullivan, Maj Gen. Jno.**
  Canada. Voyage au—fait depuis l'an 1751 à 1761, par. **J. C. B.**
  Canadiens-Français Conventions annuelles des—aux Etats-Unis.
  Canadiens-Français (les) de Fall River. **Dubuque, H. A.**
  Capture and Burning of Fort Massachussetts (1746) **Norton, Rev. J.**
  Celebration on Bushy Run Battlefield, Aug 6, 1883. **Cort. Rev. C.**
  Chapleau, L'hon. J. A. Sa biographie et ses principaux discours.
  Character portraits of Washington. **Baker, W. S.**
  Chicago. Business Directory of.
  Chief Joseph (Nez Percé), his pursuit and capture. **Howard, O. O.**
  Chronologie de l histoire du Canada. **Begin, l'abbe L. N.**
  Clay, Henry. Life of, by **Schurz, Carl.**
  Clinton, Sir Henry. Correspondence with Earl Cornwallis.
  Colonisation et agriculture au Canada. **Passy, L.**
  Conewago: a historical sketch. **Reily, John I.**

HISTORY AND BIOGRAPHY, AMERICAN—*Continued.*
    Connecticut. (*Amer. Comm. Series.*) **Johnston, A.**
    Contest (The) in America between Great Britain and France, 1757.
    Conversion of Fitzgerald and Clark executed at St. John's, N.B., 1789. **Milton, Rev. Mr**
    Cornwallis, Lord. Answer to Clinton's Narrative.
    Cramp, Rev. J. M. Life of, by **Higgins, Rev. T. A.**
    Cutler, Manasseh. Life and Correspondence.
    Deux républiques sœurs: France et Etats-Unis. **Aron, J.**
    Dinwiddie (The) Papers, 1751-58. Records of Virginia History.
    Discovery of America by Columbus, Discourse on the. **Belknap, J.**
    Discovery and Colonization of America. **Everett, E.**
    Documents relating to the early history of Rhode Island. **Fernow, B.**
    Dudley's (Col.) defeat opposite Fort Meigs, 1813. **Combs, Capt. L.**
    Ecclesiastical history of Newfoundland. **Howley, Rev. M. F.**
    Esquimaux, les grands. **Petitot, R. P. E.**
    Etats (les) du Nord-Ouest de l'Amérique. **Frignet, E., et Carry, E.**
    Ethnology; 3rd Annual Report of the U. S. Bureau of.
    Fate (The) of Madame La Tour. **Paddock, Mrs. A. G.**
    First White Settlements West of the Alleghanies (1748). **Hale, J. P.**
    Fish and Men in the Maine Islands. **Bishop.**
    Forest life and forest trees of Maine **Springer, J. S.**
    Four years with General Lee. **Taylor, W. H.**
    France (la) et le Canada. **Agostini, E.**
    Franklin in France. **Hale, E. E.**
    Français (les) au Canada. **Chalamet, Ant.**
    Fremont, J. B. Souvenirs of my time.
    Fremont, J. C. Memoirs of my life: a retrospect of fifty years.
    French and Indian Wars in New England. **Drake, S. G.**
    French (The) in the Alleghany Valley. **Chapman, J. A.**
    Genealogical Dictionary of Rhode Island. **Austin, J. O.**
    German (The) Element in the war of American Independence. **Greene, G. W.**
    Golden Jubilee of Fathers Dowd and Toupin. **Curran, J. J.**
    Gospel (The) in the British Colonies up to 1728. **Humphreys, D.**
    Grant in peace from Appomattox to Mount McGregor. **Badeau, A.**
    Grant, U. S. Memoirs of, vs. the Record of the Army of the Potomac. **McClellan, C.**
    Great (The) Conspiracy: its origin and history. **Logan, Gen. J. A.**
    Great West, 1512-1883. The making of the. **Drake, S. A.**
    Greenough, H. Letters to his brother Henry.
    Half-hours with American history. **Morris, Chs.**
    Harding, Rev. H. Life and Times. **Davis, Rev. J.**
    Hendricks, Thos. A. Life and Character of—Memorial Address.
    Histoire du Canada. **Gauthier, l'abbé L. O.**
    ——— populaire de l'église du Canada. **Gosselin, l'abbé D.**
    ——— populaire du Canada. **Baudoncourt, J. de.**
    Historical Researches in Western Pennsylvania.
    History of Canada. **Kingsford, W.**
    ——— of Cumberland (Md). **Lowdermilk, W. H.**
    ——— of Hernando de Soto and Florida. **Shipp, B.**
    ——— of Indiana. **Dillon, J. B.**
    ——— of Kentucky. **Smith, Z. F.**
    ——— of Pennsylvania, north of the Ohio. **Agnew. Hon. D.**
    ——— of Pennsylvania, up to the present time. **Cornell, W. M.**
    ——— of Second War for Independence (1812-14). **Brown, S. R.**
    ——— of the Confederate States Navy. **Scharp, J. T.**
    ——— of the 18th Regiment Connecticut Volunteers. **Walker, Rev. W. C.**
    ——— of the Free-Booters, or Buccaneers of America. **Archenholtz, J. W. Von.**
    ——— of the Independence of the United States. **Gordon, W.**
    ——— of the Indian Nations of Pennsylvania. **Heckewelder, Rev. J.**

HISTORY AND BIOGRAPHY, AMERICAN – *Continued.*

History of the Negro troops in the American Rebellion. **Williams G. W.**
——— of the Scotch Presbyterian Church of Montreal. **Campbell, Rev. R.**
——— of the Shawnee Indians. **Harvey, H.**
——— of the United States. **Greg, P.**
——— of the United States of America (1784). **Franklin, Jos.**
——— of the United States of America. **Shaffener, T. P.**
——— of the United States Secret Service. **Baker, G. L. C.**
Icelandic Discoveries of America. **Brown, Marie A.**
Illustrations (les) canadiennes. **Dupuy, P.**
Indians of Pennsylvania: Two months among the. **Beatty, C.**
John Sevier, as a Commonwealth builder. **Gilmore, J. R.**
Journal of military operations (1776-84). **Krafft, J. C. P. von.**
Journal of the journeys to the Ohio country (1788-89). **May. Col. Jno.**
Knickerbocker's History of New York. **Irving, Washington.**
La Salle. Nouvelles études sur **Gravier, G.**
Laval, Mgr. de. Esquisse biographique, par **Tetu, l'abbe H.**
Leatherwood (The) God. **Tanneyhill, R. H.**
Letter to the Comnrs. of Public Accounts. **Clinton, Sir H.**
Lincoln, Abraham. Reminiscences of, By distinguished Men of his time.
Livingstone, Mrs. E. Memoir of By **Hunt, L. L.**
Livre des Sauvages. La vérité sur le. **Domenech, l'abbe E.**
Logan, Gen. J. A. Life and Services of By **Dawson, G. F.**
Loyalists. Claim of the American—reviewed.
Maine Wills (1640-1760). Edited by **Sargent, W. M.**
Mandements. lettres pastorales, des évêques du Canada.
Massachusetts. Transactions of the, Historical Society of.
Medical Sketches of the war of 1812-14. **Mann, J.**
Mémoire concernant les grèves du Sault au Matelot.
Mémoire sur les biens des Jésuites en Canada.
Memoirs of U. S. Grant *vs* the Record of the Army of the Potomac. **McClellan, C.**
Memorials of a half-century. **Hubbard, Bela.**
Methodist Church of Canada. Minutes of Annual Conferences.
Micmac Indians in Nova Scotia and P. E. Island. **Rand, S. T.**
Military Journal for 1775. **Haws, Samuel.**
Military Journal for 1758. **Lyon, Lemuel.**
Military Journal, 1775-79. **McDonald, Capt. Alex.**
Military Monitor and American Register, 1812-14.
Miramon, le Gén. M. Etude historique, par **Daran, V.**
Monographie des Dènè Dinjié. **Petitot, R. P. E.**
——————— Esquimaux Tchiglet du Mackenzie. **Petitot, R. P. E.**
Montreal. The first Catholic cemeteries of,—and a Guide.
Mortimer, Rev G. Life and Letters of. By **Armstrong, Rev. J.**
Narrative and Critical History of America. Vols. 5 & 6 **Winsor, J.**
Nerinckx, Life of Rev. Charles **Maes, Rev C. P.**
Newfoundland, its trade and fishery **Williams, Capt. G.**
New York Historical Society's Collections, Vol. 15.
Notes on the Floridian Peninsula. **Brinton, D. G.**
Nova Scotia Baronets, and the British American Association.
Orderly Book of the Expedition under Gen. J. Clinton. **Bleeker, Capt. L.**
Origine Touranienne des Américains Tupis-Caribes.
Parent, Rev. A. Life of.
Participation de la France a l'establissement des Etats-Unis d'Amérique. **Doniol, H.**
Pemaquid under the Colony of New York. **Hough, F. B.**
Pennsylvania Magazine of History and Biography.
Perry, Biographical Sketch of Com. M C. **Griffis, W. E.**
Phillips, Cath. Memoirs of the life of.
Pocahontas and her descendants. By **Robertson, W. & Brock, R. A.**

HISTORY AND BIOGRAPHY, AMERICAN—*Concluded.*
Poetic (The) Globe. **Moon, C. E.**
Public (The) Men of the Revolution. **Sullivan, W.**
Rufus Putnam, Life of. **Cone, Mary.**
Random Recollections. **Stanton, H. B.**
Rear-Guard (The) of the Revolution. **Gilmore, J. R.**
Recensement de la ville de Québec (1716). **Beaudet, l'abbé L.**
Recollections of Eminent Men. **Whipple, E. P.**
Recollections of the American Revolution. **Post, L. M.**
Relation du voyage du Captaine de Gonneville. **D'Avezac.**
Reminiscences of Abraham Lincoln. **Rice, A. T.**
Revolutions de l'Amérique méridionale. **Duffey, P. J. S.**
Rhode Island. Genealogical Dictionary of. By **Austin, J. O.**
Saint Sulpice. Memoirs in behalf of the Seminary of at Montreal.
Sedentary Indians of New Mexico. **Bandelier, A. F.**
Selections from the Letters of " A Girl's Life Eighty Years Ago." **Bowne, Eliza S.**
Sept années d'explorations dans l'Amérique australe. **Bresson, A.**
Sermon preached at St Paul's London, on the taking of Quebec. **Townley, Rev. J.**
Semmes, Capt. R. Service Afloat : or the Career of the " Sumpter " and the " Alabama."
Sherman, Gen. W. T. and his Campaigns : a biography. By **Cols. S. M. Bowman** and **Irwin,**
Shiloh, or the Tennessee Campaign of 1862.
Spanish Settlements in America, 1762.
Sillery. Vie de de l'illustre serviteur de Dieu, Noël Brûlart de.
Tablettes chronologiques de l'histoire du Canada. **Gosselin, l'abbé D.**
Taschereau, Mgr. Le Premier Cardinal Canadien. Par le **Rev. T. E. Hamel.**
Tegakouita, la B. Cath. Sa vie. Par le **Chauchetière, P. Cl.**
Timberlake, Lieut. H. Memoirs of.
Tories (The) or Loyalists in America. **Myers, T. B.**
" Twentieth (The) Connecticut." A Regimental History. **Storrs, J. W.**
United States. Secret service during the Civil War.
Universalism in America, 1666-1886. **Eddy, R.**
Vestiges of the Mayas. **Le Plongeon, A.**
Visit to the American Churches in 1834. **Reed, (Dr. A.) and Matheson, Jas.**
Visit (A) to the Mormon Settlements at Utah. **Chandless, Wm.**
Vue de la colonie espagnole au Mississippi (1803).
War. History of the late, 1812-14. **Perkins, S.**
Washington-Irvine Correspondence, 1781-83. **Butterfield, C. W.**
Waymouth's Voyage to the Coast of Maine, 1605. **Rosier.**
Wayne (Fort) History of. By **Bryce, W. A.**
Weed, Thurlow. Life of, by **Barnes, T. W.**
Welcome (A) to Albert, Prince of Wales, and other poems. **Sherwood, H.**
Wesleyan Methodist Church of Canada. Annual Conferences of.
Williams, Life of Thomas. chief of the Caughnawaga Indians. **Williams, Rev. E.**

	PAGE
HITCHCOCK, H. The American State Constitution	159
HITCHMAN, F. Life, Travels, and Explorations of R. F. Burton	483
HODDER. E. Life of Samuel Morley	496
HODGETTS, J. F. Greater England	409
HOGAN, J. F. The Irish in Australia	471
HOGIER-GRISON. Le monde où l'on vole	885
HOLLAND, J. G. Arthur Bonnicastle	838
—————— Bay-Path, The.	838
—————— Bitter-Sweet—a poem	859
—————— Every-day Topics	838

		PAGE
HOLLAND, J. G.	Gold-Foil	838
———————	Jones Family, The	838
———————	Kathrina—a poem	859
———————	Lessons in Life, by Timothy Titcomb	838
———————	Miss Gilbert's Career	838
———————	Mistress (The) of the Manse—a poem	859
———————	Nicholas Minturn	838
———————	Plain Talks on familiar subjects	838
———————	Sevenoaks	838
———————	Titcomb's Letters	838
HOLMES, A. B.	The Electric light popularly explained	731
HOLMES, O. W.	Pages from an old volume of life	838
———————	Our Hundred days in Europe	535
HOME, Jno.	History of the Rebellion, 1745	399
HOMER.	The Iliad. Translated by T. A. Buckley	814
———	The Odyssey. Translated by T. A. Buckley	814
———	The Odyssey done into English verse by W. Morris	813
———	An introduction to the Iliad and Odyssey by R. C. Jebb	813
HONEYMAN, Rev. D.	Giants and Pigmies	617
HOOK, W. F.	Church Dictionary, 14th ed	28
HOOPER, G.	Campaign of Sedan	434
HOOTON, C.	St. Louis' Isle, or Texiana	1386
HORACE.	Works of, translated by C. Smart	821
HORTON, S. D.	The Silver Pound	496
HOSMER, J. K.	The Jews in ancient, mediæval and modern times	304
HOSPITALIER, E.	Principales applications de l'électricité	590
HOUGH, F. B.	Pemaquid under the Colony of New York	1240
HOUGHTON, E. B.	Physical Culture	85
Hours of Childhood and other poems		1410
HOWARD, B. W.	Tony, the Maid	838
HOWARD, O. O.	Chief Joseph (Nez Percé), his pursuit and capture	1188
HOWE, Hon. Jos.	Address delivered at the Howe Festival, 1871	1412
HOWELLS, W. D.	Modern Italian Poets	797
———————	April Hopes	838
HOWLEY, Rev. M. F.	Ecclesiastical history of Newfoundland	1198
HOWSE, J.	Grammar of the Cree Language : the Chippeway dialect	794
HUBBARD, Bela.	Memorials of a half-century	1257
HUBRECHT, Dr A. A.	Report on Nemertea (Chall. Exp. Zool. Rep. v. 19)	635
HUDSON, E. H.	England's Jubilees	396
HUDSON, T. S.	A Scamper through America	1372
HUE, F.	Les Français à Madagascar	469

	PAGE
HUGHES, Thos. Memoir of Bishop James Fraser	488
HUGHES, T. P. American Ancestry	1226
HUGO, V. Choses vues	877
———— Things seen	877
———— History of a Crime	877
———— Toilers of the Sea	878
———— Notre-Dame (Translated into English)	878
———— Les Misérables, (Translated into English)	878
———— By Order of the King	878
———— Ninety-three	878
HUGONIN, Mgr. Du droit ancien et du droit nouveau	366
HUGONNET, L. La Turquie inconnue	545
HUGUES, C. Les jours de Combat	877
HUMPHREY, F. S. Manual of type-writing	732
HUMPHREYS, D. The Gospel in the British Colonies up to 1728	1196
HUNOLSTEIN, le Cte P. V. d'. Correspondance inédite de Marie-Antoinette	426
HUNT, R. British Mining, 2e édition	625
HUNT, T. S. Mineral Physiology and Physiography	624
———— A new basis for Chemistry	593
HUNT, W. Then and now : Fifty years of newspaper work	802
HUNT, Wm. Bristol (Historic Towns)	405
HUNTER, D. J. The Enamarado, a drama	1411
HUNTER, J. Insignia of the Orders of British Knighthood	508
HUNTER, J. H. Ontario Insurance Act	104
HUNTLY, Marquis of. Travels, Sport, and Politics	545
Huron District, map of (1843) By D. McDonald	1398
HUTH, A. H. Marriage of near kin	464
HUTTON, R. H. Some modern Guides of English Thought	839
HYDE, J. N. Diseases of the Skin	672
ICELANDIC Sagas relating to British Isles (Rolls' Chron.)	337
Imperial Hansard. Vols	50
Imperial White Books	50
" Inchiquin," The Jesuits letters during a late residence in the United States	1379
INDERWICK, F. A. Divorce and Matrimonial Causes Act	85
INDIANA, History of	1258
Industrie (l') et l'art décoratif. (L'Ancienne France)	410
INGRAM. Irish Union	51
Instructions aux ambassadeurs de France avant la Révolution : Portugal	269
International Guide to British and Foreign Merchants and Manufacturers	525

	PAGE
Inter-State Act and Rules...	176
————- Commerce. Law...	111
Iowa. Report of the State Librarian...	905
IRISH, H. C. American Corporation Cases..	229
Irish Law Reports. Vols. 17 and 18...	219
Irish (The) Problem...	54
Irish State Trials (1844)...	241
Irving, Lieut. J. (H. M. S. " Terror.") Memorial sketch, by B. Bell..........	492
IRVING, Washington. Knickerbocker's History of New York....................	1245
ISHAM, C. The Fishery Question..	159
Italian Art. Masterpieces of..	712
JACKSON, Lady. French Court and Society..	426
JACKSON, T. G. Dalmatia, the Quarnero and Istria.....................................	444
JACOB, Jules. Le jeu de l'épée..	724
JACOBSON, A. Higher Ground...	489
JACOLLIOT, L. Voyage au pays des singes	882
JAMES, H. The Princess Casamassima..	840
JAMESON, J. A. Constitutional Conventions...	158
JAMIESON. Supplement to Scottish Dictionary.......................................	791
JANET, P. La science politique dans ses rapports avec la morale.............	385
JANSSEN, J. L'Allemagne à la fin du Moyen-Age...................................	442
JAY, J. The Fishery dispute—a letter..	526
JEAFFRESON, J. C. Lady Hamilton and Lord Nelson.................................	490
JEBB, R. C. An introduction to the Iliad and Odyssey...............................	813
JENKINS, R. C. Heraldry, English and Foreign.....................................	508
JENNA, Marie. Elévations poétiques et religieuses....................................	882
JERNINGHAM, H. E. H. Diane de Breteuille—a love story......................	840
JOHNSON, Miss H. M. Canadian Wild Flowers......................................	1410
JOHNSTON, A. Connecticut. (American Commonwealths).........................	1219
JOHNSTON, R. M. Mr. Absalom Billingslea and other Georgia Folk..........	840
JOHNSTONE, Chevalier. Memoirs of the—Translated................................	492
JONES, Rev. C. The Welsh Pulpit of to-day..	49
JONES, Geo. Tecumseh and the Prophet of the West—a tragedy.............	840
——— ——— Life and history of General Harrison.....................................	840
——— ——— Life, character and genius of Shakespeare	840
JONES, L. A. Index to Legal Periodicals	58
JONES, W. H. Federal Taxes and State Expenses...................................	159
JOUBERT, A. Les Misères de l'Anjou aux XVe et XVIe siècles...............	424
JOUIN, H. Maîtres contemporains..	712
JOUSSE, M. Traité de la justice criminelle de France...............................	304

	PAGE
Joyce, J. W. Handbook of Convocations	249
Jubilee of Queen Victoria, 1887—Works on	396
—————————— Hymns for the year	396
—————————— Special illustrated numbers of periodicals.	397
Jubilee Date Book	396
Jullien, Ad. Richard Wagner, sa vie et ses œuvres	721
Julliot, F. de La terre de France	884
Justice Department (U. S.) Register of the	161
KAMAROWSKY, Cte. L. Le tribunal international	267
Kearny, J. W. Sketch of American Finances	498
Keats, J. By Sidney Colvin (Eng. Men of Letters)	479
Kebbel, T. E. Agricultural labourer	471
Kellog, A. H. Abraham, Joseph and Moses in Egypt	18
Kellsall, Chs. Classical Excursion from Rome to Arpino	522
Kelso, S. J. Notes on the Saguenay	1403
Kennard, Mrs. A. Mrs. Siddons (Em. Women Series)	478
Kennedy, D. (The Scottish Singer). Reminiscences of his life	493
Kenyon, E. C. Scenes in the life of the Royal Family	396
—————— Scenes in the life of the Princess Alice	480
Ker, Jno. Scottish nationality and other papers	841
Kerr, W. H. S. Shores and Alps of Alaska	1392
Kinglake, A. W. Eothen	551
—————— Invasion of the Crimea. Vols. 7 and 8	448
Kinnear, J. B. Principles of Government	23
Kingsford, W. History of Canada Vol. 1	1274
Kingston, W. B. Monarchs I have met	841
Kirton, J. W. True Royalty : Victoria as Maiden, Mother and Monarch..	396
Knight, Ann C. A year in Canada, and other poems	1410
Knight, M. R. Poems of ten years, 1877-1886	1410
Knight, W. Memorials of Coleorton	841
Knox, T. W. Boy travellers on the Congo	563
Koch, A. Prince Alexander : Reminiscences of his reign in Bulgaria	449
Koettschau, C. The Coming Franco German war	683
—————— Les forces respectives de la France et de l'Allemagne	683
Kotzebue, O. Voyage to the South Sea and to Behring's Straits	522
Krafft, J. C. P. von. Journal of military operations (1776-84)	1244
LABAT, Gaston P. Les voyageurs canadiens à l'expédition du Soudan....	463
La Blanchère, H. de. La pêche et les poissons	640
Laboulaye, C. Dictionnaire des arts et manufactures. 6e éd	723
—————— Economie des machines et des manufactures	728

	PAGE
LABOULAYE, C. Traité de cinématique	580
——— Questions constitutionnelles	279
LACROIX, H. Excursion to the Holy Land of Thought	1410
LAFFAN, Miss. Ismay's Children	841
LAFFITTE, P. La Parole	805
LAFOND, Cte L. L'Ecosse jadis et aujourd'hui	537
LA GRAVÈRE, J. de. Les corsaires barbaresques et la marine de Soliman le Grand	329
LAMARTINE, A. de. Fior d'Aliza	877
LAMBERT, L. A. Tactics of Infidels	45
LAMBERT DE SAINTE-CROIX, Alex. De Paris à San Francisco	1372
LAMI, E. O. Dictionnaire de l'industrie. Vols. 6 et 7	7-6
LANG, A. In the Wrong Paradise	841
LANGLEY, S. P. The New Astronomy	582
LANMAN, C. Biographical Annals	161
LA PORTE, J. P. A. de. Hygiène de la table	668
Laprade, V. de. Sa vie et ses œuvres, par E. Biré	492
LARROUMET, G. La Comédie de Molière	800
LASSERRE, H. Les Saints Évangiles, traduction nouvelle	11
——— L'organisation normale du suffrage universel	386
LA TOURETTE, G. de. L'hypnotisme et les états analogues	340
LAUBRY. Traité des érections des bénéfices	370
LAUD, Abbp. of Canterbury. A study by A. C. Benson	493
LAUGHLIN, J. L. Political Economy	484
LAUGHTON, J. K. Studies in Naval history: Biographies	477
LAUNAY, A. Nos missionnaires: La Société des missions Etrangères	42
LAURIE, Col. W. F. B. Sketches of some distinguished Anglo-Indians	461
Laval, Mgr de. Esquisse biographique, par l'abbé H. Têtu	1192
LAVELEYE, Em. de. The Balkan Peninsula	545
Law Times Reports. Vol. 55	215
LAW, E. Hampton Court Palace in Tudor Times	402

LAW, CIVIL AND ECCLESIASTICAL.

American Corporation Cases. **Irish, H. C.**
Anglo-Indian Codes. **Stokes, W.**
Appeal Cases. **Ramsay's.**
Appeals from Justices. **Trotter, J. G.**
Assignments. **Burrill, A. M.**
Baltimore Council. Decrees of 3rd Council.
Banking Law. **Walker, J. D.**
Bankruptcy and Bills of Sale, Law of. **Lee (L. T.) & Wace, H.**
Bills of Exchange. **Chalmers. M. D.**
Building Cases, Digest of. **Roscoe, E. S.**
Building Societies. **Davis, H. F. A.**
Canadian Lawyer.

LAW, CIVIL AND ECCLESIASTICAL.—*Continued.*

Carriage of Goods by Sea. **Carver, T. G.**
Central Law Journal, vol. 24.
Clubs, Law relating to. **Wertheimer, J.**
Collieries, Law of. **Fowler & Lewis.**
Commerce in time of War, Law of. **Castle, E. J.**
Common Law, 10th Ed. **Smith, J. W.**
Compensation, Law of. **Elmes & Ingram.**
Compensation, Law of, 5th Ed. **Lloyd, E.**
Conspiracy and Protection Act, and Employers and Workmen Act. **Arnold, T. J.**
Constitutional Prohibitions against Obligation of Contracts. **Black, H. C.**
Contract, Law of. **Finch, G B.**
Contract of Affreightment in Charter-parties. **Scrutton, T. E.**
Contract of Sale. **Blackburn, Lord.**
Contracts. **Pollock, F.**
Contracts for future delivery. **Dewey, T H.**
Contracts, Law of. **Anson, Sir W. R.**
Corrupt Practices at Elections. **Mattinsons (M. W.) & Macaskie, S. C.**
Corrupt Practices Prevention Act, 1883. **Wheelhouse, Sir Wm.**
Criminal Law, 4th Ed. **Harris, S. F.**
Criminal Law, Digest of. **Stephen, Sir J. F.**
Currency Coinage and Banking Laws (U. S)
Customs, Laws of the. **Elmes, W.**
Deceit, Law of. **Grinnell C. E.**
Digest of Cases. **Emden, A.**
Divorce. **Browne, G.**
Divorce. **Dixon, W. J.**
Divorce and Matrimonial Causes Acts. **Inderwick, F. A.**
Divorce, Law of. **Lloyd, A. P.**
Divorce Practice. **Oakley, T. W. H.**
Dower, Law of. **Scribner, C. H.**
Drink and Licensing Laws. **Deane, C. P.**
Elections, Law of, 3rd Ed. **Cunningham.**
Employers and Employed, Law of. **Spens (W. C.), Younger, R. T.**
English Land Laws. **Moss, S.**
Equity Index, vol. 3, 4th Ed. **Chitty's.**
Equity, Leading Cases in. **White & Tudor.**
Estoppel. **Bigelow, M. M.**
Evidence, Digest of. **Stephen, Sir J F.**
Famous Breach of Promise Cases.
Fire Insurance **Bunyan, C J.**
Greely Relief Expedition. Proceedings of Court of Enquiry of.
Handbook of Convocations. **Joyce, J. W.**
Husband and Wife, 3rd Ed. **Macqueen, J. F.**
Husband and Wife, Law of. **Thicknesse, R.**
Immigration Laws. **Endicott, W. C.**
Index to Legal Periodicals. **Jones, L. A.**
Index to Overruled Cases. **Bigelow, M. M.**
Informations, Mandamus and Quo Warranto. **Short, J.**
Insanity as a defence to crime. **Lawson, J D.**
Insanity in Criminal Cases. **Everest, L. F.**
Insanity, Law of. **Buswell.**
International Law. **Davis, G. B.**
International Law. **Levi, L.**
International Law, Opinions on. **Cadwalader, J L.**
Inter-State Act and Rules.
Inter-State Commerce. **Harper, J. C.**
Inter-State Commerce Act. **Dos Passos J R.**

LAW INDEX.

LAW, CIVIL AND ECCLESIASTICAL—*Continued*.
    Inter-State Commerce Law.
    Investigations of Titles. **Armour, E. D.**
    Irish Law Reports. Vols. 17 and 18.
    Irish State Trials, 1844.
    Joint Stock Companies. **Henley (C. E. H.), Wheeler (P. F) & Jenkins, C. E. E.**
    Juridical Glossary. **Adams, H. C.**
    Land Laws. **Pollock, F.**
    Land Law (Ireland) Act, 1887. **Greer, E.**
    Law Magazine, 10:11.
    Law of Nations, new edition. **Twiss, T.**
    Law Quarterly Review, 1885-6-7.
    Law Times, vols. 81, 82. U. S. Reports, v. 55.
    Laws (1887), Prince Edward Island.
    Leading Cases in Equity. **Brett, F.**
    Legal News, 1886.
    Law of Legitimacy. **Robertson, E.**
    Letters to a Law Student. **Burke, J. J.**
    Light, Digest of Law of. **Roscoe, E. S.**
    Light on the Law-Inter-State Commerce.
    Mandamus. **Wood, H. G.**
    Manitoba Statutes, 1886.
    Marine Insurance, 6th edition. **Arnould, J.**
    Marriage and Divorce. **Stewart, D.**
    Marriage indissoluble and Divorce unscriptural.
    Marriage and Legitimacy, Law of. **Weightman, H.**
    Marriage Law of England and Colonies. **Hammick, J. T.**
    Marriages, Compendium of. **Lognn's.**
    Massachusetts Laws of Marriage and Divorce. **Fairbanks, L. S.**
    Medical Jurisprudence. **Ewell, M. D.**
    Mercantile Agreements. **Wood, J D.**
    Mercantile and Maritime Law. **Tudor, O. D.**
    Merchandise Marks Act, 1887. **Gray, A.**
    Mines and Minerals. Law of. **MacSwinney, R. F.**
    Money Securities, 2nd edition. **Cavanaugh, C.**
    Montreal Law Reports, Q. B. (12).
    National Bank Act, Digest of. **Pratt.**
    New Brunswick Reports, v. 24. **Freeman.**
    New York Law of Insurance. **Alexander, C. B.**
    Ontario Insurance Act. **Hunter, J. H.**
    Ontario Law Reports, vols. 11, 12.
    Overruled Cases, Digest of. **Dale and Lehmann.**
    Pamphlets in Case of **Gugy, Col. A.**
    Petition of Right, Law and Practice of. **Clode, W.**
    Powers, Duties and Liabilities of Executive Officers. **Chester, A. W.**
    Practice Reports (Ontario), vol. 11.
    Printers, Publishers and Newspapers, Law of. **Powell, A.**
    Private Roman Law. **Muirhead, J.**
    Proceedings *In Rem*. **Waples, R.**
    Produce Exchange, Law of. **Bisbee and Simonds.**
    Prohibitory Legislation in United States. **McCarthy, J.**
    Quarantine Laws, United States.
    Quebec Law Reports. Vol. 12.
    Railway and Corporation Law Journal.
    Receivers, 2nd Ed. **High, J. L.**
    Restraints on alienation. **Gray, J. C.**
    Rules of Law Courts in Canada and United States.
    Slander and Libel, Digest of. 2nd Ed. **Odgers, W. B.**

LAW INDEX.

LAW, CIVIL AND ECCLESIASTICAL—*Continued.* PAGE
   Steamboat Inspection (U. S.) Laws.
   Stock-brokers and Exchanges. **Dos Passos, J. R**
   Test Act Reporter.
   Tithes, History of. **Clarke, H. W.**
   Tramway Manual. **Duncan's.**
   Transfer of Land Statute. **A'Beckett, T.**
   Treasury Decisions (U. S) Synopsis of.
   Treaty of Washington, 1842. **Featherstonhaugh, G. W.**
   Tower, Trial of Capt. W. H.
   United States Statutes at Large. Vol. 24.
   Vessels and Voyages, as regulated by Federal Statutes. **Wynkoop, R.**
   Weekly Notes, 1886.
   Witnesses, Law of. **Rapalje, S.**

LAWLESS, Hon. Emily. Ireland. (Story of the Nations) 304
LAWSON, J. D. Insanity as a defence to crime 118
LAXTON. Builder's Price Book (1887) 708
LAYARD, Mrs G. Through the West Indies 1360
LEA, H. C. History of the Inquisition of the Middle Ages 32
LEAY, W. Columbia, New Grenada, Equatorial South America 1358
LE CARON, C. Coustumes du gouvernement de Péronne, etc 296
LECHLER, G. The Apostolic and Post-Apostolic Times 22
LECKY, W. E. H. History of England in the 18th Century. Vols. 3, 4, 5, 6 392
LECLERCQ, Em. La guerre de 1870 434
LECONTE DE LISLE. Poèmes antiques 885
———— ———— Poèmes barbares 885
LECOY DE LA MARCHE, A. La chaire française au moyen-âge 33
LECOCQ, G. La prise de la Bastille 426
LEE, Gen. R. E. Four years with,—by W. H. Taylor 1229
LEE (L. T.) and WACE, H. Laws of Bankruptcy and Bills of Sale 90
LEFEVRE, Rt. hon. G. Shaw. Peel and O'Connell 51
LEGOUVÉ, Ern. Nos filles et nos fils 75
———— ———— L'art de la lecture. 36e éd 806
———— ———— Petit traité de lecture 806
———— ———— La lecture en action 806
———— ———— Comédies en un acte 879
———— ———— Soixante ans de Souvenirs. 2e partie 800
———— ———— Conférences parisiennes 879
LEGRELLE, A. Louis XIV et Strasbourg—politique de la France en Alsace 425
LE HOUNEC, A. Chicot 884
LELOIR, L. L'art de dire—extraits commentés 801
LEMOINE, James M. Chateau Bigot : its history and romance 1411
LEMAITRE, J. Les contemporains—études et portraits. 3e série 801
Leo XIII. Life of, by Rev. B. O'Reilly 31
———— ————, by John Oldcastle 31

	PAGE
LEPAGE, A. Dîners artistiques et littéraires de Paris............................	539
LE PAULMIER, Dr. Ambroise Paré d'après de nouveaux documents..........	497
LE PLONGEON, A. Vestiges of the Mayas..	1163
LEBMINA, J. La France martyre..	434
LEROY, Chs. Les finesses de Pinteau...	856
LEROY, le P. M. D. Evolution des espèces organiques........................	611
LESCUBE, M. de. Les femmes philosophes.......................................	800
——————— Etude sur Beaumarchais..	800
LESLIE, Emma. Life and Reign of Queen Victoria.............................	396
LESSEPS, Ferd. de. Recollections of forty years	494
Letters from Europe during (1801 and 1802). By a Native of Pennsylvania.	541
Letters from Ireland..	54
LEVI, L. International law..	7
LEVIN, Dr M. La nivrose. Etude chimique et thérapeutique................	668
LEWIS, C. E. Reveries of an Old Smoker.......................................	1410
LIAUTARD, A. Animal Castration..	659
Liberal Year Book, 1887 and 1888..	532
LIEUSSOU, G. Dix mois autour du monde......................................	527
Light on the Law. Inter-State Commerce	176
Ligne, la Princesse Hélène de. Histoire de L. Perey.........................	494
——————————— Memoirs of. Edited by L. Perey.............	494
LILLIE, L. C. The Colonel's Money...	842
Lincoln, Abraham. Reminiscences of — by distinguished Men of his time.	1229
LINDSAY, J. A. Climatic treatment of Consumption.........................	672
LINDT, J. W. Picturesque New Guinea...	569
Linnœus. Through the fields with—, by Mrs. F. Caddy....................	616
LISLE, C. W. The Ring of Gyges..	842
Lismore Papers. Second Series. Vols. 1, 2....................................	401
LISSAGARAY. History of the Commune of 1871. (Translation)............	434
Literæ Cantuarienses. (Roll's Chronicles)	337
LITTLE, A. W. Reasons for being a Churchman..............................	36
LITTLE, L. P. Ben Hardin, his times and contemporaries..................	1229
Liverpool Literary and Philosophical Society. Poceedings. Vols. 39, 40. ...	911
Livingston, Mrs. E. Memoir of—, by L. L. Hunt.............................	1227
LIVIUS. History of Rome. (Translation).......................................	822
Livre (le) et les arts qui s'y rattachent (L'Ancienne France)..............	410
LLOYD, A. P. Law of Divorce..	86
LLOYD, E. Law of Compensation. 5th ed......................................	102
LOCKYER, J. N. Chemistry of the Sun...	588
LOFTIE, W. J. Windsor Castle. Jubilee Edition..............................	402
LOGAN's Compendium of the laws of Mariage.................................	85

	PAGE
LOGAN, D. D. Obstinate diseases of the Skin.	672
LOGAN, Gen. J. A. The Great Conspiracy: its origin and history	1268
———— ———— Life and Services of—, by G. F Dawson	1229
LOMBROSO, C. L'homme criminel	340
London Board of Trade Journal	509
LONGFELLOW, H. W. Final Memorials of—, by S. Longfellow	494
London Post Office Directory, 1887	404
LONLAY, D. de. Français et Allemands	434
Lorraine (la) illustrée.	433
"LOTI, P." Pêcheur d'Islande	884
———— ———— An Iceland Fisherman	884
———— ———— My Brother Yves	884
———— ———— Propos d'exil	884
(Louis XVII) La survivance du Roi-Martyr. Par un ami de la Vérité	427
LOUISY, P. Le livre et les arts qui s'y rattachent (L'Ancienne France)	410
LOWDERMILK, W. H. History of Cumberland (Md)	1250
Lower Canada Almanack (The) for 1840	1418
Loyalists. Claim of the American—reviewed	1265
LOYSEAU, Jean. Le baton perdu	886
LUBBOCK, Sir J. Nationalities of the United Kingdom	629
LUBORMIRSKI, le prince J. La côte barbaresque et le Sahara	561
LUCAS, C. P. Historical geography of the British Colonies	511
Luther. His life and work, by P. Bayne	36
LYALL, E. Autobiography of a Slander	843
LYON, Lemuel. Military Journal for 1758	1262
Lytton, Rosina, Lady. Life of, by Louisa Devey	494
MACASSEY, L. A. Private Bill legislation	36
MACAULAY, Lord. Life and Letters. By G. O. Trevelyan. New ed	494
MACAULAY, Dr. Victoria, R. J. Her life and reign	396
McCARTHY, J. Prohibitory Legislation in the U. S.	467
McCARTHY, Justin. History of Our Own Times down to end of 1836	596
McCARTHY (J.) and PRAED, Mrs. Campbell. "The Right Honourable"	843
McCARTHY, J. H. Ireland since the Union	40
———— ———— ———— Case for Home Rule	54
McCARTY, Rev. J. M. Two thousand miles through Mexico	1373
McCARTY, L. P. Annual statistician	511
MACLAY, W. Debates in 1st Senate of United States	161
McCLELLAN, C. Memoirs of U. S. Grant vs. the Record of the Army of the Potomac	1268
McDONALD, Capt. Alex. Military Journal, 1775-79	1244

	PAGE
MACDONALD, F. W. Life of William Morley Punshon.	493
MACDONALD, Geo. Home again.	844
MACFARLANE, Thos. Trip to South America.	1353
McGill University Calendar, 1887-88.	86
MCGUIRL, T. H. Perspective and geometrical drawing.	714
MCILWRAIGHT, Thos. The birds of Ontario.	639
MCINTOSH, W. C. Report on Cephalodiscus Dodecalophus (Chall. Exp. Zool. Rep. v. 20).	635
MACKAY, Dr Chs. Through the Long Day; or, Memorials of Half a Century.	494
MCKEEVOR, T. Voyage to Hudson's Bay in 1812.	522
MCKENZIE, G. A. Malcolm: a story of Day Spring.	1410
MCKENZIE, Jno. Austral Africa—losing it or ruling it.	469
MCNEILL, J. G. S. How the Union was carried.	51
MACQUEEN, J. F. Husband and Wife. 3rd ed.	85
MACSWINNEY, R. F. Law of Mines and Minerals.	115
MAES, Rev. C. P. Life of Rev. Charles Nerinckx.	1196
MAGRUDER, Julia. A Magnificent Plebian.	844
MAHAFFY, J. P. Alexander's Empire (Story of the Nations).	304
———— Greek life and thought.	322
———— Principles of the Art of Conversation.	81
MAHALIN, P. Le fils de Porthos.	885
———— Les monstres de Paris.	885
MAHOMED-MISRAH. Journey though Africa.	522
Maine Wills (1640-1760) Edited by W. M. Sargent.	1240
Maine. Superintendent of Common Schols Report for 1886.	86
—— Agricultural Reports for 1884-85-86.	660
—— State Board of Health. Report for 1886.	677
MAINTENON, Mm de—, d'après sa correspondance authentique.	494
MAJENDIE, Lady M. On the Scent.	844
MALOT, H. Une femme d'argent.	879
———— Zyte.	879
MANDAT-GRANCEY, Baron E. de. Paddy at Home.	472
Mandements, Lettres pastorales, des évêques du Canada.	1196
Manitoba Statutes, 1886 (Vol. I).	147
MANN, J. Medical Sketches of the war of 1812-14.	1207
MANNERS, R. R. Pasco: a Cuban tale and other poems.	861
Manufacturers of the United States, 1887.	525
"Maple Leaf," Constance; a lay of the olden Time.	1410
MARGRY, P. Un fils de Colbert. (Marquis d'Ormoy).	425
Marguerite d'Angoulême. By A. Mary F. Robinson (Em. Women Ser.).	478

	PAGE
MARGUERITTE, Paul. Mon Père ; avec les lettres du général Margueritte...	494
MARIE-ANTOINETTE. Correspondance inédite, par le Cte. P. V. d'Hunolstein.	426
MARMOTTAN, P. Les Statues de Paris...	434
Marriage, An Essay on (1829)	464
Marriage indissoluble and divorce unscriptural	465
MARSHALL, J. G. Social condition of the Kingdom	510
MARTEL, Cte. de. Les historiens fantaisistes—M. Thiers.....................	429
MARTEL, J. Z. Résumé du droit canadien...	374
MARTINEAU, H. By Mrs F. F. Miller (*Em. Women Ser.*)	478
MARTINI, C. A. de. Ordo historiæ juris civilis....................................	260
MARY, Queen of Scots. Letters of, translated by W Turnbull.............	397
Massachusetts. Transactions of the Historical Society of...................	1235
————— Index to the above..	1235

MATHEMATICS.
  Principles of Dynamics. **Wormell, R.**
  Traité complet d'arithmétique. **Garnier, Jos.**

MATHESON, Rev. G. The Psalmist and the Scientist	45
MATTHEWS, B. Ballads of Books..	855
MATTINSON (M. W.) and MACASKIE, S. C. Corrupt Practices at Elections...	40
MAULEON, A. J. L. de. Plaidoyers et mémoires	290
MAUPASSANT, G. de. Mont-Oriol	882
MAURICE, C. E. The Revolutions of 1848-9	332
MAXIMILIEN I. Souvenirs de ma vie. Traduits par J. Gaillard.............	495
MAXIMILIAN DE WIED NEWWIED. Travels in Brazil, 1815-17	522
MAY, G. A bibliography of Electricity and Magnetism 1860-1883............	900
MAY, Col. Jno. Journal of the journeys to the Ohio country (1788-89)......	1257
MAYER, S. French Code of Commerce..	7
MAYO, W. S. Kaloolah...	844
Medical Directory for 1887..	666

MEDICAL SCIENCES.
  Auto—intoxications (les) dans les maladies. **Bouchard, Ch.**
  Alcool (l')—physiologie pathologie, etc **Peeters, Dr. J. A.**
  Boston Board of Health. Report for 1886.
  Cholera (le) n'est ni transmissible ni contagieux. Par un Rationaliste.
  Climathéropie. **Weber, le Dr. H.**
  Climatic Treatment of Consumption. **Lindsay, J. A.**
  Cure of hæmorrhoids and prolapsus. **Edgelow, G.**
  Diseases of the Rectum. **Cooper, A.**
  Diseases of the Skin. **Hyde, J. N.**
  Diseases of the Veins. **Burnett, J. C.**
  Duties of Nursing in Private Nursing. **Richardson, W. L.**
  Hydrophobia : M. Pasteur's System. **Suzor, R.**
  Hygiène de la table. **La Porte, J. P. A. de.**
  Leçons de thérapeutique. **Mayem, G.**
  Magnétisme (le) animal. **Binet (A.)** et **Féré, C.**

MEDICAL SCIENCES – *Concluded.*   PAGE
   Maine State Board of Health. Report for 1886.
   Maladies des organes génito-urinaires. **Moreau-Wolf.**
   Maladies du système nerveux. **Vulpian, A.**
   Medical Directory for 1887.
   Montreal, Rapport sur l'état sanitaire de. Par le **Dr. Laberge.**
   Nivrose (la). Etude chimique et thérapeutique. **Levin, Dr. M.**
   Obstinate Diseases of the Skin. **Logan, D. D.**
   Pulmonary Consumption. **Williams, C. J. B.** and **C. T.**
   On Cancer, its Allies and other Tumours. **Purcell, F. A.**
   On Surgical Operations. **Barker, A. E. J.**
   Reference Handbook of the Medical Sciences. Vols. 4, 5. **Buck, A. H.**
   Science and Practice of Medicine. 7th ed. **Aitken, W.**
   Traité de l'art des accouchements. Vol. I. **Tarnier (S.)** and **Chantreuil, G.**
   ———————— Vol II. **Tarnier (S.)** and **Budin, P.**
   Year Book of Treatment for 1886.

MEILHAC, H. La duchesse Martin, comédie 878
MEISENDORF, B. de. La France sous les armes. Traduit par Hennebert.... 682
MEMER, Andreas. L'Allemagne nouvelle (1863-67).............................. 391
Mémoire sur les biens des Jésuites en Canada........................... 1190
Mémoire concernant les grèves du Sault au Matelot................... 1190
MENDENHALL, T. C. A Century of Electricity................................. 590
MÉRIMÉE, Prosper. Carmen, (Translation) 885
——————— Théâtre de Clara Gazul. La Jaquerie, etc......... 885
Mérode, F. F. X. de. Life and Works, by Mgr Besson........................ 495
MEROUVEL, Chs. Dos à dos.. 885
MERSENNE, R. de. Voyages imaginaires de Chateaubriand en Amérique.... 1367
Merveilles de la Nature. Brehm, A. E...
MESANGE, le P. Pierre de. Voyage au Grœnland................................ 532
Methodist Church of Canada. Minutes of Annual Conferences........... 1198
MICHAILOW. Adventures among the Kalmucs.................................. 522
Michigan. Horticultural Society Report for 1886 660
————— Supt. of Public Instruction Rep. for 1886................. 85
MIERS, E. J. Report on Brachyura (Chall. Exp. Zool. Rep. v. 17)............ 635
Military Monitor and American Register, 1812-14............................. 1266

MILITARY AND NAUTICAL SCIENCES.
   American Nautical Almanac for 1890.
   Armée (l') et la démocratie.
   Armée (l') de John Bull. **France, H.**
   Australian Defences. From papers of Sir P. Scratchley. **Cooke, C. K.**
   Cesar. Opérations militaires. Par **Heuzey, Leon.**
   Coming (The) Franco-German War. **Koettschau, C.**
   Dictionnaire de marine. **Bonnefoux et Paris.**
   Forces (les) respectives de la France et de l'Allemagne. **Koettschau, C.**
   France (la) sous les armes. **Meisendorff, B. de.**
   Guerre (la) prochaine. **Sequin, L.**
   Memento de connaissances militaires **Pinel, H.**
   Military Collections and Remarks **Donkin, Major.**
   Militia of Canada Standing Orders for 1887.
   Mobilisation (la) et la préparation à la guerre. **Froment, A.**

MILITARY AND NAUTICAL SCIENCES—*Concluded.*   PAGE

    Naval Evolutions,—Papers on, 1886.
    Naval Subjects Pamphlets on, by **Bowles, Vice-Adm.**
    Nautical Almanac and Astronomical Ephemeris for 1890.
    Rank and Badges. Precedence, in H M.'s Army and Navy. **Perry, O. L.**
    Rifle Association, Dominion of Canada, Reports.
    Submarine Mines for the U. S. **Abbott, H. L.**

Militia of Canada. Standing Orders for 1887	683
MILL, J. S. Political Economy	484
MILLAUD, Alb. La Comédie du jour	885
MILLS, H. V. Poverty and the State	471
Millennial Dawn	53
MILLER, F. Glass-Painting	704
—— —— Pottery-Painting	704
MILLER, Mrs F. F. Harriet Martineau (*Em. Women Ser.*)	478
MILTON, Rev. Mr. Conversion of Fitzgerald and Clark executed at St. John's, N. B., 1789	1404
Minuets and Gavottes. Music and Costumes	722
Miramon, le Gén. M. Etude historique par V. Daran	1216
MIRBEAU, Oct. Le Calvaire	882
—— —— Lettres de ma chaumière	882
Miss Bayle's Romance ; a story of to-day	844
Modern Man. By a Modern Maid	845
Mohl, Julius and Mary. Letters and Recollections. By M. C. M. Simpson	495
M[ohl], Madame. Madame Recamier	498
MOISY, H. Dictionnaire de patois normand	789
MOLINARI, G. de. Lois naturelles de l'économie politique	403
MONSELET. Encore Un !	885
MONTEGUT, Em. Mélanges critiques	801
—— —— Nos morts contemporains. 2e série	479
—— —— Choses du Nord et du Midi	883
Montesquieu. By Alb. Sorel (Gt. French Writers)	800
Montreal. The first Catholic cemeteries of,—and a Guide	1196
—— —— Rapport sur l'état sanitaire de. Par le Dr Laberge	677
Montreal Law Reports. Q. B. (1. 2.)	223
MONTULÉ, E. de. Travels in Egypt, 1818-19	522
—— —— Voyage to N. America and the West Indies	522
MOON, C. E. The Poetic Globe	1410
MOORE, Emily J. Life and reign of Victoria, Queen and Empress	396
MOORE, Geo. A Mummer's Wife	845
—— —— Terre d'Irlande	538
—— —— Parnell and his Island	472

	PAGE
MOORE, S. Poems	1410
Moralité nouvelle du mauvais Riche et du Ladre	867
MORE, Sir Thomas. A dialogue of Comfort against Tribulation	32
MOREAU, l'abbé G. Le monde des prisons	414
MOREAU, Hegésippe. Œuvres complètes	879
MOREAU-WOLF. Maladies des organes génito-urinaires	672
MORGAN, L. H. Systems of Consanguinity and Affinity of the Human Family	629
MORGAN, Mary. Poems and translations	1410
MORGAN. W. Freemasonry exposed	469
MORIN, L. Le Cabaret du Puits-sans-vin	882
MORISON, J. C. The Service of Man	52
MORLEY, H. English Writers. New ed	803
Morley, S. Life of, by E. Hodder	496
MORRIS, Chs. Half-hours with American history	1219
MORRIS, J. Life and Martyrdom of St. Thomas à Becket	35
MORRIS, W. The Odyssey done into English verse	813
Mortimer, Rev. G. Life and Letters of—By Rev. J. Armstrong	1286
MORTON, Mrs. G. E. Jubilee Echoes	397
MOSS, S. English Land Laws	90
MOUEZY, A. Mal assortis	883
MOURAVIEW, Capt. Journey to Turcomania and China	522
MOUROT, l'abbé V. Jeanne d'Arc en face de l'église romaine	492
MOUTON, Eug. Chimère	882
MUDGE, Z. A. Fur clad adventurers	845
MUIRHEAD, J. Private Roman Law	10
MULHALL, M. G. Dictionary of Satistics	511
———— Fifty years of National Progress	511
MULLER, Dr. C. Greece and the Ionian Islands, 1821	522
MULLER, Max. Science of Thought	62
MUNRO, Surg. Gen. Records of Service and Campaigning	408
MURPHY, Rev. J. J. Henry Grattan and the Irish Volunteers	1410
MURRAY, D. C. A Novelist's Note Book	845
———— Old Blazers Hero	845

MUSIC.

Minuets and Gavottes. Music and Costumes.
Retour (le) d'Arlequin : pantomime. **Najac· R. de.**
Révolutionnaires (les) de la musique. **Fouque, O.**
Traité d'instrumentation et d'orchestration **Berlioz, H.**
Verdi : Anecdotic history of his life and works. **Pougin, A.**
Wagner, Richard, sa vie et ses œuvres. **Jullien, Ad.**

	PAGE
MYERS, T. B. The Tories or Loyalists in America...................................	1265
NAJAC, R. de. Le retour d'Arlequin : pantomime..................................	720
NAPIER, Rt. Hon. Sir J. Life of, from his private correspondence. By A. C. Ewald..	496
Napoléon Bonaparte et ses détracteurs. Par le prince Napoléon (Jérôme)...	430
Nasmith, David. Memoirs of, by John Campbell...................................	496
National Board of Trade (U. S.) Reports, 1887	5-4

NATURAL HISTORY.
    Contributions to the Natural History of Alaska. **Turner, L. M.**
    Evolution des espèces organiques. **Leroy, le P. M, D.**
    Merveilles de la Nature : l'homme et les animaux. **Brehm, A. E.**
    New York Geological Survey : Palæontology, Vol. 6.
    Notes of a Naturalist in South America. **Ball, J.**
    Papers on Natural History and Geology. **Dawson, G. M.**
    Smithsonian Miscellaneous Collections. Vols. 28, 29, 30.

NATURAL PHILOSOPHY.
    Animal Magnetism (Int S. S. 60). **Binet (A.) et Féré, C.**
    Astronomie populaire. **Flammarion, C.**
    British discomycetes and all the species of fungi. **Phillips, W.**
    Century (A) of Electricity. **Mendenhall, T. C.**
    Chemistry for students of Medicine. **Goodwin, W. L.**
    ———— of the Sun. **Lockyer, J. N.**
    Deep-sea Sounding and Dredging. **Sigsbee, C. D.**
    Electric lighting. **Gordon, J. E. H.**
    Electricité, Principales applications de l'. **Hospitalier, E.**
    Electricité : application aux sciences. **Gariel, C. M.**
    Geographical and Geological distribution of animals (Int. S. S. 58). **Heilprin, A.**
    Greenwich Observatory. Astronomical observations, 1885. 4 Vols.
    Histoire du ciel. **Flammarion, C.**
    Merveilles (les) célestes. **Flammarion. C.**
    Mes voyages aériens. **Flammarion, C.**
    Mesure (la) du mètre : dangers des savants qui l'ont déterminée. **Fouvielle, W. de.**
    Mondes (les) imaginaires. **Flammarion, C.**
    Mort de faim—Etude sur les nouveaux jeûneurs. **Fouvielle, W. de.**
    New (The) Astronomy. **Langley, S. P.**
    New (A) basis for Chemistry. **Hunt, T. Sterry.**
    Other Suns than ours. Essays on Whist, &c. **Proctor, R. A.**
    Petroleum : its production and use. **Redwood, B.**
    Sorcellerie, magnétisme, morphinisme, etc. **Regnard, Dr P.**
    Spiritualism. Preliminary Report of the Seybert Commission on.
    Terres (les) du ciel. **Flammarion, C.**
    Traité de cinématique. **Laboulaye, C.**
    Weather : Changes from day to day (Int. S. S. 59). **Abercromby, Hon. R.**

Nautical Almanac and Astronomical Ephemeris for 1890.......................	687
Naval Evolutions,—Papers on, 1886	686
NAZAROFF, P. Expedition to Kokand...	522
NEAL, Jno. Brother Jonathan, or, The New Englanders........................	845
NECKER DE SAUSSURE. Voyage to the Hebrides.....................................	522
——————— Travels in Scotland..	522

	PAGE
NEFF, J. K. Army and Navy of America from the French and Indian War to Florida War (1755-1835).........................	1262
NELSON-SMITH, W. Coins, Moneys, Weights, &c...........................	504
NERINCKX, Rev. C. Life of, by Rev. C. P. Maes............................	1196
NEUMANN-SPALLART, Dr F. X. Uebersichten der Weltwirthschaft............	511
NEVE, Jno. Concordance to the poetical works of Wm. Cowper................	858
New York. Geological Survey : Palæontology Vol. 6..........................	613
—————- Historical Society's Collections Vol. 15........................	1244
—————- State University. Report of Regents for 1886............	86
NEWMAN, Card. Loss and Gain. New ed..................................	845
Nibelungenlied. Traduit de l'allemand, par E. de Laveleye.................	894
———————— Translated by Alfred G. Foster-Barham......................	894
NICOT, L. L'Allemagne à Paris..	396
NIEMEYER, Dr A. H. Travels on the Continent and in England...........	522
NORGATE, Kate. England under the Angevin Kings..................	373
Norris, W. E. Major & Minor..	945
North (The) American (Newspaper) Swanton, Vt..........................	1413
North West Territories Official Gazette...................................	147
Northern (The) Lakes of Canada...	1390
NORTON, Rev. J. Capture and Burning of Fort Massachusetts, (1746).......	1197
Nova Scotia Baronets, and the British American Association...............	1336
OAKLEY, T. W. H. Divorce Practice.....................................	86
O'BRIEN, R. B. Irish Wrongs and English Remedies......................	472
O'CAGNE, M. d' Les grandes écoles de France............................	81
O'CONNOR, E. M. Index to the works of Shakspere.....................	863
O'CONOR, W. A. History of the Irish People.............................	400
OGDEN, Jas. The British Lion Roused...................................	1260
ODGERS, W. B. Digest of Slander and Libel, 2nd ed.......................	78
O'GRADY, Standish. The Emigrant : a poem.............................	1410
O'HAGAN, Thos. A Gate of Flowers and other poems.....................	1410
OHNET, G. Cloud and Sunshine...	879
—————- Noir et rose..	879
OLDCASTLE, J. Life of Leo XIII...	31
OLIPHANT, L. Haifa : or, Life in Modern Palestine........................	549
—————— Episodes in a life of adventure	846
OLIPHANT, Mrs M. O. W. A Country Gentleman and his family..........	846
OLIPHANT, T. L. K. The Old and Middle English.........................	791
OMALIUS D'HALLOY, J. J. d' Des races humaines........................	630
O'MEARA, Kathleen. Narka, the nibilist.................................	497
OMOND, G. W. T. The Arniston Memoirs, 1571-1838.....................	393

	PAGE
O'NEIL, C. A. American electoral system...........	163
Ontario Legislative Assembly. Rules of................	130
Ontario Law Reports. Vols. 11, 12...................	222
OPPENHEIM, E. Phillips. Expiation: a novel of England and our Canadian Dominion................	846
O'REILLY, B. Life of Leo XIII....................	31
Origine Touranionne des Américains Tupis-Caribes............	1181
O'SHEA, J. A. Romantic Spain: a record of personal experiences......	540
O'SULLIVAN, D. A. Manual of Government. (2nd ed.)............	130
OSWALD, F. L'assassinat de la ligne du Havre..............	884
———— André le Justicier...................	884
OTTLEY, E. B. Rational Aspects of some Revealed Truths.........	50
"Ouida." A House Party: a novel.	846
Our American Cousins.....	159
Our Queen............	396
Our Sovereign Lady: a book for Her people............	336
OVID. The Metamorphoses. Translated by H. T. Riley............	823
———— The Fasti, Tristia, &c. Translated by H. T. Riley........	823
Oxford University Calendar............	78
OZANAM, F. La vie et ses œuvres, par P. Chauveau............	497
PADDOCK, Mrs. A. G. The fate of Madame La Tour	1199
PAILLERON. La Souris................	879

PAINTING, ENGRAVING, ETC.

Academy Sketches, 1886.
Art (l') du travestissement; costumes historiques, etc. **Sault, L.**
Art, Masterpieces of Italian.
Art (l') et les artistes français. **Claretie, J.**
Maîtres contemporains. **Jouin, H.**
Painters and Painting. Cyclopedia of, Vol. 4.
Perspective and geometrical drawing. **McGuirl, T. H.**
Photographie (la) sans appareils. **Boudet de Paris, D M.**

PAIRPOINT, Alf. Sketches of America in 1854-55-56............	1382
PALGRAVE, W. G. Ulysses: or, Scenes and Studies in many lands.......	528
PALMER, G. H. The New Education..........	81
Paré, Ambroise. Par le Dr. Le Paulnier..........	497
Parent, Rev. A. Life of............	1198
PARHAM, C. J. Lyrical translations............	1410

PARLIAMENTARY, LEGISLATION, &c.

American Almanac for 1887.
American Electoral System. **O'Neil, C. A.**
Biographical Annals of Politicians. **Lanman.**
Debrett's House of Commons.
Gladstone and his contemporaries.

PARLIAMENTARY, LEGISLATION, ETC.—*Concluded.*   PAGE

    Imperial Hansard. Vol. 310.
    Imperial White Books.
    Justice Dept (U. S.), Register of the.
    Liberal Year Book, 1887.
    Magna Charta. **Wells, J. C.**
    Manual of Government. 2nd Ed. **O'Sullivan, D. A.**
    Manual of Parliamentary Practice. **Thomson, H. C.**
    North West Territories Official Gazette.
    Ontario Legislative Assembly, Rules of.
    Parliamentary Record, 1887. **Ross'.**
    Peel & O'Connell. **Lefevre, Rt. Hon. G Shaw.**
    Postal Guide, 1887, United States.
    Privy Council. **Dicey, A. V.**
    Routledge's Almanac, 1888.
    Statesmen's Year Book, 1887.

PASSY, L. Colonisation et agriculture au Canada 1285
Patents, (American). Official Gazette 740
Patents, (English). Illustrated Journal of Patented Inventions 740
———————— Official Journal of the Patent Office 740
———————— Specifications 740
PATON, W. A. Down the Islands: a voyage to the Caribbees 1349
PATTON, J. H. Natural Resources of U.S. 528
PAYN, J. Holiday Tasks 846
——— Glow Worm tales 846
——— The Heir of the Ages 846
——— A Prince of the Blood 846
PAYSON, DUNTON & SCRIBNER. Manual of penmanship 86
Peabody Institute, Catalogue of Library. Vol. 3 905
PEETERS, Dr. J. A. L'alcool-physiologie, pathologie, etc 669
PELLET, M. Variétés révolutionnaires 423
PELLICIER, Guil. Correspondance diplomatique par J. Zeller 424
PELSENEER, P. Report on Pteropoda (Chall. Exp. Zool. Rep. v. 19) ... 635
PÈNE, H. de. Née Michon 886
Pennsylvania Magazine of History and Biography 1247
PERELAER, M. T. H. Run away from the Dutch: Adventures in Borneo ... 569
PEREY L. Histoire de la princesse Hélène de Ligne 494
——— Memoirs of the Princess de Ligne 494
PEREY (L.) & MAUGRAS, G. La jeunesse de Mme d'Epinay 487
———————— Dernières années de Mme d'Epinay 487
PERKINS, S. History of the late War (1812-14) 1267
PERRAULT, J. Exploration de Québec au Lac St. Jean 1403
PERRET, Paul. Le roi Margot 884
PERRY, Rt. Rev. C. Letter on the Church in the Diocese of Melbourne 40
Perry, C. C. German Elementary Schools and Training Colleges 77
Perry, Comm. M. C. Biographical sketch of, by W. E Griffis 1229

	PAGE
PERRY, O. L. Rank and Badges, Precedence, in H. M.'s Army and Navy.	684
PERTUSIER, Chs. Promenades in Constantinople and on the Bosphorus	522
PESSARD, H. Mes petits papiers (1860-1870)	433
Peterborough, Earl of. Memoir by Col. F. S. Russell............................	497
PETERMANNS Mittheilungen 1886-87	510
PETITOT, R. P. E. Les grands Esquimaux.................................	1190
———————— Monographie des Esquimaux Tchiglet du Mackenzie....	1190
———————— Monographie des Dènè Dindj'é.......................	1190
———————— En route pour la mer glaciale........................	1372
PFEIFFER, E. Women and Work	451
PHELPS, E. S. The Gates between...................................	846
Philadelphia, 1681-1887. By E. P. Allison and B. Pemrose................	1247
Phillips, Cath. Memoirs of the life of	1198
PHILLIPS, J. A. Out of the Snow, and other stories.....................	1410
PHILLIPS Exeter Lectures	81
PHILLIPS, W. British discomycetes and all the species of fungi. (*Int.*, *S.S.* 61.)	578

PHILOLOGY AND LITERARY HISTORY.

Altaic Hieroglyphs and Hittite Inscriptions. **Conder, C. R.**
Ancient Nahuatl Poetry. **Brinton, D. G.**
Annals of the Cakchiquels. **Brinton, D. G.**
Art (l') de dire le monologue. **Coquelin aîné et cadet.**
Art (l') de dire—extraits commentés. **Leloir, L.**
Books which have influenced me.
Cabinet of Irish literature. **Read, C. A.**
Comédie (la) de Molière. **Larroumet, G.**
Contemporains (les)—études et portraits 3e série. **Lemaître, J.**
Dictionnaire de patois normand. **Moisy, H.**
Dictionnaire des doublets ou doubles formes. **Brachet, A.**
Encyclopædic Dictionary. Vols. 11, 12
English Writers. New ed. **Morley, H.**
Essais de critique. **Fuster, Chs.**
Etude sur Beaumarchais. **Lescure, M. de.**
Familiar Studies of Men and Books. **Stevenson, R. L.**
Femmes (les) philosophes. **Lescure, M. de.**
Grammar of the Cakchiquel language. **Brinton, D G.**
——— of the Cree language: the Chippeway dialect. **Howse, J.**
Histoire du romantisme. **Gautier, Theop.**
Impressions littéraires. **Ratisbonne, L.**
Literary success: a guide to practical journalism. **Reade, A. A.**
Look (A) round literature. **Buchanan, R.**
Mélanges critiques. **Montegut, Em.**
Montesquieu. By **Sorel, Alb.** (Gt. French Writers).
Morceaux choisis des écrivains du XVIe siècle. **Brachet, Aug.**
Modern Italian Poets. **Howells, W. D.**
Naturalisme (le). **Bazan, E. P.**
Old and Middle English. **Oliphant, T. L. K.**
Origin of the English people and of the English language. **Roemer, J.**
Parole (la). **Laflitte, P.**
Poe, Edgar Allan (*Am. Men of Letters*). **Woodberry, G. E.**

PHILOLOGY AND LITERARY HISTORY—*Concluded*.

Poésie (la) liturgique au moyen-âge. **Gautier, L.**
Portraits contemporains. **Gautier, Théo.**
Practical Journalism. **Dawson, Jno.**
Rire (le). **Coquelin, cadet.**
Roman (le) russe. **Vogüé, E. M. de.**
Russian Novelists. **Vogüé, E. M. de.**
Scottish Dictionary, Supplement to. **Jamieson.**
Sévigné, Mme de. By **Boissier, Gaston** (*Gt. French writers*).
Sigfred Arminius and other papers. **Vigfuson (G) & Powell. T. Y.**
Sobriquets and Nicknames. **Frey, A. R.**
Souvenirs et études de théâtre. **Regnier, P.**
Story (The) of some famous books. **Saunders, F.**
Temps passé (le) : Mélanges de critique et de morale. **Guizot, M. et Mme.**
Then and now : Fifty years of newspaper work. **Haut, W.**
Vie (la) des mots. **Darmesteter.**
Yesterday with actors. **Winslow, C. M. R.**

PHILOSOPHY.

Histoire de la philosophie en France au XIXe siècle. **Ferraz.**
Pensées sur divers sujets **Bonald, le Vte. de.**
Science of Thought. **Muller, Max.**
Socialisme, naturalisme et positivisme. **Ferraz.**
Spiritualisme et libéralisme. **Ferraz.**
Traditionalisme et ultramontanisme. **Ferraz.**

PICHÉ, Rev. Em. Pour l'Irlande... 396

PIKE, G. Holden. Victoria, Queen and Empress........................ 396

PIKE, Z. M. Voyage au Nouveau Mexique, 1805-07................. 1368

PINDAR. Odes. Translated in prose by D. W. Turner; in verse by A. Moore... 815

PINEL, H. Memento de connaissances militaires...................... 682

PINET, G. Histoire de l'école polytechnique............................. 87

PINGAUD, L. Choiseul-Gouffier. La France en Orient sous Louis XVI...... 391

PITMAN, R. B. A Ship Canal across the Isthmus of America........ 1361

Pocahontas and her descendants. By W. Robertson and R. A. Brock........ 1249

POCOCKE, R. Tours in Scotland, 1747, 1750, 1760..................... 398

Pole, Reg., Card. Abbp. of Canterbury. An historical sketch by F G. Lee. 493

POLITICAL ECONOMY AND ECONOMICS.

Agricultural Labourer. **Kebbel, T. R.**
Arbitration between Capital and Labour. **Ryau, D. J.**
Big wages and how to earn them.
Canadian Economics.
Cobden Club Papers, v. 4.
Fair Trade Papers
Federal Taxes and State Expenses. **Jones. W. H.**
Free Trade **Gill, R.**
Higher Ground. **Jacobson, A.**
Home Rule, speeches on. **Chamberlain, Rt. Hon. J.**
Land, Labour and Liquor. **Burgess, Rev. Wm.**
Pioneers of Poverty. **Campbell, H.**
Political Economy. **Laughlin, J. L.**
Political Economy. **Mill, J. S.**
Political Economy. **Sidgwick, H.**

POLITICAL ECONOMY AND ECONOMICS—*Concluded.*
    Politics of Labour. **Thompson, P.**
    Poverty and the State. **Mills, H. V.**
    State Aid. **Baden-Powell, G.**
    Wealth and Progress. **Gunton, G.**
    Wealth and Welfare. **Berkeley, H.**

POLITICS.
    American Fisheries, Rights and Interests of.
    Case for Home Rule. **McCarthy, J. H.**
    Churchill, Lord R. **Crozier, J. B.**
    Election Campaign Speeches, 1886. **Blake, Hon E.**
    Fisheries and the Mississippi, Letters on. **Adams, J. Q.**
    Fisheries Dispute, a letter. **Jay, J.**
    Fishery Question. **Isham C.**
    Fisheries, Report on Question of the, (1871).
    Hand-book of Dominion Politics. **Roses'.**
    Irish (the) Problem.
    Irish Union. **Ingram.**
    Irish Wrongs and English Remedies. **O'Brien, R. B.**
    Irlande, l'our l'. **Piché, Rev. Em.**
    Jews in England, Status of. **Egan, C.**
    Land in Fetters. **Scrutton, T. E.**
    Letters from Ireland.
    Letters on Unionist Delusions. **Dicey, A. V.**
    Liberty and Liberalism. **Smith, B**
    New South. **Hillyard, M. B.**
    Old and New Republican Parties. **Allen, S. M.**
    Our American Cousins.
    Paddy at Home. **Mandat-Grancey, Baron E. de.**
    Parnell and his Island. **Moore, G.**
    Philadelphia. **Allinson (E. P.), & Penrose, R.**
    Political and other discussions. **Blaine, J. G.**
    Political pamphlets. **Roebuck, J. A.**
    Political Speeches. **White, Hon. T.**
    Present Position of European Politics (1887). **Dilke, Sir C.**
    Primrose League.
    Reciprocity Treaty between Great Britain and United States (1854).
    Spirit of the Metropolitan Conservative Press (1839).
    Tory Policy of Salisbury. **Bagenal, P. H.**

POLITIQUE.
    Allemagne (l') actuelle.
    ————— à Paris **Nicot, L.**
    ————— nouvelle (1863-67). **Memer, Andreas.**
    Chez l'addy. **Mandat-Grancey, Baron E. de.**
    Choiseul-Gouffier. La France en Orient sous Louis XVI. **Pingand, L.**
    Deux républiques. **Portalis, A. E.**
    Droit divin de la démocratie. **Vibert, Theod.**
    France (la) et sa politique extérieure en 1887. **Rothem, G.**
    ————— juive devant l'opinion. **Drumont, E.**
    Histoire de la civilisation française. Vol. 2. **Rambaud, A.**
    ————— sommaire de la civilisation. **Ducoudray, G.**
    Organisation (l') normale du suffrage universel. **Lasserre, H.**
    Pour l'Irlande. **Piche, Rev. Em.**
    Questions d'aujourd'hui et de demain. **Blanc, L.**
    Science (la) politique dans ses rapports avec la morale. **Janet, P.**
    Sentiments (les) moraux au XVIe siècle. **Desjardins, A.**
    Suffrage (le) des femmes aux Etats-Unis. **Destrel, H.**
    Suffrage universel et la manière de voter **Taine, H.**
    Vatican (le) et les Francs-Maçons. **Taxil, L.**

	PAGE
POLLOCK, Sir Fredk. Personal Remembrances.....................	498
POLLOCK, F. Contracts..	108
———.—— Land laws...............	487
POOR's Directory of Railway officials...............................	508
—— Manual of Railroads for 1887.................................	508
POPE, A. M. In and around the Magdalen Islands................	1410
PORTALIS, A. E. Deux républiques.................................	396
[POST, L. M.] Recollections of the American Revolution........	1266
POUGIN A. Verdi: Anecdotic history of his life and works.....	721
POUQUEVILLE. Travels in Greece.................................	522
——————— Travels in Southern Epirus......................	522
POWELL, A. Law of printers, publishers and newspapers......	113
POWNALL, G. H. Bankers' calculations...........................	502
Practice Reports, Ontario. Vol. 11................................	222
PRADEL, G. L'amazone bleue..	885
PRADEZ, Chs. Nouvelles études sur le Brésil.....................	1356
PRADON. Ouvres de...	872
PRAED, Mrs. Campbell. Miss Jacobson's Chance................	846
PRESS, W. H. Victorian Triumphs: a jubilee bead roll........	396
PRESTON, T. Jubilee of George III................................	394
PRICE, E. C. Alexia..	847
Primrose League. History of.......................................	449
Prince Edward Island Laws (1887).................................	147
PRIOR, J. Voyage on the Indian Seas.............................	522
——— Voyage along the Eastern Coast of Africa...............	522
PROCOPIUS. History of the Wars of the Emperor Justinian.....	325
——— Court of the Emperor Justinian...........................	325
PROCTOR, R. A. Chance and Luck................................	724
——————— Other Suns than ours. Essays on Whist, etc....	582
PRUDHOMME, Sully. Le Prisme, poésies diverses................	885
PUNCH's, (Mr.) Victoria Era.......................................	397
Punshon, Rev. W. M. Life of, by F. W. Macdonald.............	493
PURCELL, F. A. On Cancer, its allies and other tumours.......	672
PYLE, H. The Rose of Paradise.....................................	847
QUARANTINE Laws, U. S...	176
QUATREFAGES, A. de. Histoire générale des races humaines...	629
Quebec Law Reports. Vol. 12......................................	223
Queensland Almanac and Directory................................	150
QUINTILIAN. Institutes of Oratory. Translated by J. S. Welby......	824
Quotidienne (la) publiée à Montréal (1837-38)...................	1413

	PAGE
RACINE, Jean. Théâtre complet.	870
RACOT, A. Champagne Cornod.	885
Railway and Corporation Law Journal	C

RAILWAY ECONOMY.
    English and American Railroads. **Dorsey, E. B.**
    Investors Notes on American Railroads. **Swann, J.**
    Manual of Railroads for 1887. **Poor's.**
    Railway Officials, Directory of. **Poor's.**
    State-Purchase of Railways. **Waring, C.**

RAMBAUD, A. Histoire de la civilisation francaise. Vol. 2.	393
RAMON DE LA SAGRA. Cinq mois aux Etats-Unis en 1835	1381
RAMSAY. Appeal Cases	137
RAMSAY, J. R. Win-on-ah: or, the Forest Light and other poems	1410
Ranch life in the North-West.	1388
RAND, E. A. Fighting the Sea.	847
RAND, S. T. History of Micmac Indians in Nova Scotia and P. E. Island	1189
RAND, McNALLY & Co. Overland Guide from Missouri to the Pacific Ocean	1364
RANSOME, C. Short history of England.	333
RAPALJE, S. Law of witnesses.	74
RAPSON, E. J. England and France in India.	458
RATISBONNE, L. Impressions littéraires	800
RAWLINSON, G. Ancient Egypt (Story of the Nations)	304
READ, C. A. Cabinet of Irish literature.	803
READE, A. A. Literary success: a guide to practical journalism	802
Reade, Chs. Memoir by C. L. and Rev. Compton Reade	498
READE, T. M. Origin of Mountain Ranges.	620
REBOUL, Jean. Poésies	879

RECIPROCITY.

UNITED STATES

OFFICIAL DOCUMENTS RELATING TO TRADE AND COMMERCE AND RECIPROCITY WITH CANADA.

Congress.	Session.	Name of Document.	No. of Document.	Volume.	Date of Document.
19th.	2nd.	House Reports....................................	50	1	32nd Jan., 1827
22nd.	1st.	Senate Documents ...., ...	52	1	8th Feb , 1832
26th.	1st.	House Executive Documents..............	14	2	12th Dec., 1839
27th.	2nd.	House Report	835		
31st	1st.	House Executive Documents..	64	8	7th May, 1850
32nd.	1st.	Senate do	112	11	25th Aug., 1852
32nd.	2nd.	Senate Miscellaneous Documents.......	40	1	22nd Nov., 1852
32nd.	2nd.	House Reports............	4	....	11th Feb., 1853
33rd.	1st.	House Miscellaneous Documents	67	1	19th April, 1854
33rd.	2nd.	do	21	1	5th Jan., 1885
34th.	1st.	House Executive Documents........ ..-	2	2	10th Dec., 1855
34th.	1st.	do '	47	10	4th March, 1856
35th.	1st.	Senate Executive Documents............	71	13	11th June, 1859
36th.	1st.	House Miscellaneous Documents	69	6	28th May, 1860
36th.	1st.	House Executive Documents	96	13	18th June, 1860
37th.	2nd.	House Reports	22	3	5th Feb., 1862
37th.	2nd.	Senate Miscellaneous Documents......	74	....	28th March, 1862
37th.	2nd.	House Executive Documents......	146	10	11th July, 1852
37th.	2nd.	do	149	10	12th July, 1862
38th.	1st	do	39	11	16th Feb., 1864
38th.	1st.	House Reports	39	1	1st April, 1864
38th.	2nd.	House Executive Document	28	8	19th Jan., 1885
39th	1st.	House Miscellaneous Documents.	46	2	16th Feb., 1866
39th.	1st.	do	47	2	19th Feb , 1866
39th.	1st.	House Executive Documents.....	128	12	12th June, 1866
39th.	2nd.	do	78	11	6th Feb., 1867
39th.	2nd.	Senate Executive Documents	30	2	19th Feb., 1867
40th.	2nd.	Senate Miscellaneous Documents......	4	1	9th Dec., 1867
40th.	2nd.	do	22	1	31st Jan., 1868
40th.	2nd.	House Executive Documents............	240	15	30th March, 1868
40th.	2nd.	do	Pt. 2, 240	15	14th May, 1868
40th.	2nd.	Senate Miscellaneous Documents	67	1	2nd June, 1868
40th.	3rd.	House do	15	1	6th Jan., 1869
40th.	3rd.	House Executive Documents	36	7	12th Jan., 1869
40th.	3rd.	do	75	9	8th Feb., 1869
41st.	2nd.	Senate Executive Documents..	10	1	22nd Dec., 1869
41st.	2nd.	do	19	1	22nd Dec , 1869
41st.	3rd.	House Executive Documents	94	8	3rd Feb , 1871
41st.	3rd.	Senate Miscellaneous Documents......	51	1	3rd Feb., 1871
42nd.	2nd.	House Executive Documents............	126	10	7th Feb., 1872
43rd.	3rd.	House Miscellaneous Documents	50	2	15th June, 1875
44th.	1st.	House Reports	9	1	18th Jan., 1876
44th.	1st.	do	389	2	11th April, 1876
46th.	2nd.	do	1127	4	33rd April, 1880
46th.	2nd.	do	Pt. 2, 1127	4	7th June, 1880
49th.	1st.	do	3361		

RECLUS, E. Nouvelle géographie universelle. Vol. 12 510
REDWOOD, B. Petroleum : its production and use...... 594
REED (Dr. A) & MATHESON, JAS. Visit to the American Churches in 1834. 1198
REEVES, J. The Rothschilds 499
REGNARD, Dr. P. Sorcellerie, magnétisme, morphinisme, etc 591
REGNAULT, E. Criminal history of the English Government.................. 396

	PAGE
REGNIER, P. Souvenirs et études de théâtre.............	801
REILY, John I. Conewago: a historical sketch. ....,,	1196

RELIGION, THEOLOGY AND HISTORY OF RELIGION.

Abraham, Joseph and Moses in Egypt. **Kellog, A. H.**
Apostolic (The) and Post-Apostolic Times. **Lechler G.**
Autorité (l') de l'evangile. **Wallon, H.**
Becket, St. Thomas à. Life and Martyrdom. By **Morris, Rev. J.**
Bible Salvation and Popular Religion contrasted. **Sims, Rev. A.**
Bossus, (Mathurus). Opera varia.
Bourdaloue. Sermons pour l'Avent.
Catechism of 1552. **Hamilton, Archbp. John.**
Chaire (la) française au moyen-âge. **Lecoy de la Marche, A.**
Christ and Christianity. **Haweis, H. R.**
Christianity, Islam and the Negro Race. **Blyden, A. W.**
Church (The) in the Colonies.
Church Dictionary, 14th ed. **Hook, W. F.**
Church of England. Year book for 1887.
Church (The) and the Roman Empire. **Carr, A.**
Cinquante ans dans l'église de Rome. **Chiniquy, Rév. C.**
Concordantiæ Bibliorum Sacrorum. **Dutripon, F. P.**
Continuity of Christian Thought. **Allen, A. V. G.**
Cranmer, T. (Abbp. of Canterbury). Life of, by **Collette, C. H.**
Crockford's Clerical Directory.
Défense (la). Solutions courtes des principales objections contre la religion.
Dialogue (A) of Comfort against Tribulation **More, Sir Thomas.**
Dictionary of the Church of England. **Cutts, A. L.**
———— of Religion. **Benham, Rev. W.**
Diocese of Melbourne. Letter on the Church in the. **Perry, Rt. Rev. C.**
Doctrine of the Methodist Church of Canada **Ryckman, Rev. E. B.**
English (The) Church and its bishops, 1700-1800. **Abbey, C. J.**
Epistle (The) of St. Paul to the Romans. **Burwash, N.**
Experiences of a Backwood's preacher. **Hilts, J.H.**
Fifty years in the Church of Rome. **Chiniquy, Rev. C.**
Guiding (The) Hand. **Stafford, Rev. E A.**
Handbook of biblical difficulties. **Tuck, Rev. R.**
Histoire du Concile du Vatican. **Cecconi, Mgr. Eug.**
History of the Catholic Church. **Brueck, H.**
———- of the Catholic Church of Scotland. **Bellesheim, Rev. A.**
———- of the Christian Church. **Fisher, G. P.**
———- of the Inquisition of the Middle Ages. **Lea, H. C.**
Journal of a Visitation in Newfoundland (1849). **Feild, Bhp. E.**
Loving Counsels : Sermons and Addresses. **Garrett, Rev. C.**
Luther. His life and work, by **Bayne, P.**
Millennial Dawn.
Nos missionnaires : La Société des Missions étrangères. **Launay, A.**
Leo XIII. Life, by **Oldcastle, John.**
———— Life of, by **O'Reilly, Rev. B.**
Pie VII, Le Pape, à Savone. **Chotard, H**
Psalmist (The) and the Scientist. **Matheson, Rev. G.**
Rational Aspects of some Revealed Truths. **Ottley, E. B.**
Reasons for being a Churchman **Little, A.W.**
Reformed Church of Ireland (1537-1886). **Ball, Rt. Hon. J. T.**
Religion of the Ancient Babylonians (Hibbert Lectures, 1887). **Sayce, A. H.**
Religious Houses of the United Kingdom.
Religious sentiment : its source and aim. **Brinton, D. G.**
Rise and Growth of the Anglican Schism. **Sander, N.**

RELIGION, THEOLOGY AND HISTORY OF RELIGIONS—*Continued*.   PAGE
   Russian (The) Church and Russian Dissent. **Heard, A. F.**
   Sabbath (The) for man. **Crafts, W F.**
   Saints (les) Evangiles, traduction nouvelle. **Lasserre, H.**
   Sainte Catherine de Sienne. Histoire de, par le **P. Capecelatro, A.**
   Scottish Pulpit from the Reformation to the present day. **Taylor, W. M.**
   Self-Revelation (The) of God. **Harris, S.**
   Service (The) of Man. **Morison, J. C.**
   Social aspects of Christianity. **Westcott, B. F.**
   Suarez, R. P. Francisci. Opera omnia.
   Sundays at Balmoral : Sermons. **Tulloch, J.**
   Tactics of Infidels. **Lambert, L. A.**
   Talks for the times. **Wild, Rev. J.**
   Thomas à Kempis—scenes in which his life was spent. **Cruise, F. R.**
   Throne (The) of the Fisherman. **Allies, T. W.**
   Victorian Hymns. English Sacred Songs of fifty years.
   Voyage in a Convict Ship to Tasmania. **Forster, T. H.**
   Was Moses Wrong ? **Denovan, J.**
   Welsh (The) Pulpit of to day. **Jones, Rev. C.**
   Wish (The) to believe. **Ward, W.**
Religious Houses of the United Kingdom 33
REMUSAT, M. de. Correspondance pendant les premières années de la Restauration. Vol. 5, 6 431
Representative Poems of Living Poets 855
REVILLON, T. L'agent provocateur 882
———— Les Marquis de Saint-Lys 882
REY, Captain. Voyage from France to Cochin-China 522
REY, J. A. Ferments et fermentation 734
REYBAUD, L. Le fer et la houille 426
———— La laine 426
———— La soie 426
Rhode Island. Genealogical Dictionary of, by J. O. Austin 1226
RICE, A. T. Reminiscences of Abraham Lincoln 1229
RICHARDSON, R. Story of the Niger 563
RICHARDSON, W. L. Duties of Nursing in Private Nursing 678
RIDDELL, Mrs. J. H. Miss Gascoigne 847
RIDLEY (S. O.) & DENDY, A. Report on the Monaxonida (Chall. Exp. Zool. Rep. v. 20) 635
Rifle Association, Dominion of Canada, Reports 683
Rights and Interests of American Fisheries 526
RILEY, A. Athos : or the Mountain of the Monks 545
RIS-PAQUOT. La peinture sur faïence et porcelaine 734
RITCHIE, A. F. Her Majesty, Her Ancestors and Her Family 396
Rivals (The) of Acadia, a novel 1404
RIVOT, L. E. Voyage au Lac Supérieur 1394
ROBERT (MANNING) of BRUNNE. The Story of England (*Rolls' Chron.*) 337
ROBERTS, C. G. D. In divers tones 1410

	PAGE
ROBERTS, Dorothea. Two Royal Lives: The Crown Prince and Princess of Germany	442
ROBERTS, Morley. The Western Avernus	1372
ROBERTSON, E. Law of Legitimacy	86
ROCHET, Chs. Traité d'anatomie appliquée aux beaux-arts	689
ROE, E. P. The Earth trembled	847
ROEBUCK, J. A. Political pamphlets	22
ROEMER, J. Origins of the English people and of the English language	791
Rogers, S. Early life of: by P. W. Clayden	499
ROGERS, J. E. T. Bank of England	498
ROLAND, W. Algoma West; its mines and industrial resources	1396
Rolls' Chronicles. Roger de Wendover. Vol. 1	337
———————— Historians of the Church of York	337
———————— Reigns of Stephen, Henry II and Richard I	337
ROQUEFEUIL, C. de. Voyages round the World, 1816-1819	522
ROSCOE, E. S. Digest of building cases	88
ROSE. Handbook of Dominion politics	130
ROOSEVELT, Theo. Hunting trip of a Ranchman	725
Ross. Parliamentary Record	51
ROSIER. Relation of Waymouth's Voyage to the Coast of Maine, 1605	1240
ROTHAM, G. La France et sa politique extérieure en 1887	391
ROTHWELL, Annie. " Loved I not Honour more ! "	499
Rothschilds (The). The Financial Rulers of Nations. By J. Reeves	1410
Roussel, T. Lois sur la protection de l'enfance. Rapport sur	411
———— Loi (la) sur les aliénés. Rapport sur	341
ROUSSET, C. Le Cte. de Gisors (1732-1758)	426
———— Les Volontaires, 1791-1794	427
———— Histoire de la guerre de Crimée, 2° édition	448
ROUTLEDGE'S Almanac, 1888	546
ROWE, Lizzie. An Old Woman's Story	1410
ROWELL. Newspaper Directory for 1886	861
ROWELL, Mrs. J. H. Julia Campbell	1410
Royal Kalendar and Court Register for 1887	914
Rules of Law Courts in Canada and United States	132
RUSKIN, J. Hortus inclusus: messages from the Wood to the Garden	848
RUSSELL, Jno. The Schools of Greater Britain	83
RUSSELL, F. S. Memoir of Chas. Mordaunt, Earl of Peterborough	497
RYAN, D. J. Arbitration between Capital and Labour	489
RYCKMAN, Rev. E. B. Doctrine of the Methodist Church of Canada	39
SABIN. Bibliotheca Americana. Vol. 16	904
SACHS, J. von. Lectures on the physiology of plants	647

	PAGE
Saint Sulpice. Memoirs in behalf of the Seminary of, at Montreal............	1190
Sainte Catherine de Sienne. Histoire de, par le P. A. Capecelatro	25
SANDER, N. Rise and Growth of the Anglican Schism.............................	37
SANSOM, JOS. Travels in Lower Canada..	522
SAPPHO. Memoir, text and a literal translation. By H. T. Wharton.	817
SARGENT, W. Life and Career of Major John André	1265
SARS, G. O. Report on Cumacea (Chall. Exp. Zool. Rep. v. 19)	635
————— Report on Phyllocarida (Chall. Exp. Zool. Rep. v. 19)..........	635
SAULT, L. L'art du travestissement : costumes historiques, etc................	719
SAUNDERS, F. The story of some famous books...............................	804
————— Salad for the solitary and the social...................................	848
SAUVAL, H. Histoire des Antiquités de la ville de Paris	433
SAYCE, A. H. Religion of the Ancient Babylonians (Hibbert Lectures, 1887)	53
SCHARF, J. T. The Chronicles of Baltimore.................................	1250
————— History of the Confederate States Navy	1269
SCHERER, Edm. Melchior Grimm	490
SCHOLZ. Travels in Egypt and the Lybian desert........	522
SCHOOLCRAFT, H. R. Journal of a tour into Missouri and Arkansaw	522
SCHULZE, Dr. F. E. Report on Hexactinellida (Chall. Exp. Zool. Rep. v. 21)	635
SCHURZ, Carl. Life of Henry Clay (Amer. Statesmen Ser.)	1229
Science and Art Department of Great Britain Directory......................	80
SCOTT, Alex. Captivity of, among the Arabs of Africa...........................	522
SCOTT, Rev. W. The Teetotaler's Hand-book.......................................	466
SCRIBNER, C. H. Law of Dower. 2nd ed..................................	87
SCRUTTON, T. E. Contract of Affreightment in charter parties................	112
————— Land in fetters..........	438
SÉCHÉ, L. Jules Simon, sa vie et son œuvre................................	501
SEELEY, J. R. Courte histoire de Napoleon I...............................	429
SELLAR, R. History of the County of Huntingdon up to 1838.....	1397
SEMMES, Capt. R. Service Afloat : or, the Career of the "Sumpter" and the "Alabama"..	1269
SEQUIN, L. La prochaine guerre...	682
"Seranus." Canadian Birthday Book..	1410
————— Crowded out : and other sketches	1410
SÉVIGNÉ, Mme. de. By Gaston Boissier (Gt. French writers)................	800
SHAFFNER, T. P. History of the United States of America.....................	1219
SHAIRP, J. C. Sketches in history and poetry	849
SHAKESPEARE, W. Works of. Victoria edition.............................	863
————— Index to the Works of, by E. M. O'Connor...................	863
SHAND, A. J. Half a century ; or, changes in Men and Manners	849
SHAW, Jno. Rambles through the United States and Canada	1371

	PAGE
SHEARMAN, M. Athletics and Football. (*Badminton Lib.*)	724
Sherman, Gen. W. T. and his Campaigns: a biography. By Cols. S. M. Bowman and Irwin	1269
SHERWOOD, H. A Welcome to Albert, Prince of Wales, and other poems	1285
Shiloh, or the Tennessee Campaign of 1862	1268
SHIPP, B. History of Hernando de Soto and Florida	1255
Shipping World Year Book, 1887	519
SHORTT, J. Informations, Mandamus and *quo warranto*	79
Siddons, Mrs. By Mrs. A. Kennard (*Em. Women Ser.*)	478
SIDGWICK, H. Political Economy	487
SIGSBEE, C. D. Deep-sea Sounding and Dredging	579
Sillery, Vie de l'illustre serviteur de Dieu, Noel Brulart de	1192
SILLIMAN, B. A tour to Quebec in 1819	52_2
SILVAGNI, D. Rome, its princes and people. Vol. 3	436
SIMMONDS, P. L. British Roll cf Honour: Orders of Chivalry	507
Simon, Jules. Sa vie et son œuvre, par L. Séché	501
SIMOND, L. Travels in Switzerland	522
SIMPSON, M. C. L. Letters and Recollections of Julius and Mary Mohl	495
SIMS, Rev. A. Bible Salvation and Popular religion contrasted	17
SMART, H. The Outsider	849
SMART, W. The Sugar bounties	514
SMEE, A. Mon Jardin: géologie, botanique, culture	663
SMET, R. S. de. Indian tribes of the Rocky Mountains	1391
SMITH, B. Liberty and Liberalism	443
SMITH, D. M. L. Manual of Engineers' Calculations	745
SMITH, J. W. Common Law. 10th edition	63
SMITH, W. W. Poems	1410
SMITH, Z. F. History of Kentucky	1251
Smithsonian Miscellaneous Collections. Vols. 28, 29, 30	614
SNOW, J. A. Map of the City of Ottawa (1887)	1400

SOCIAL SCIENCE.
    Freemasonry Exposed. **Morgan, W.**
    Freemasonry, History of. **Gould, R. F.**
    Lunacy in Many Lands. **Tucker, G. A.**
    Marriage, An Essay on, (1829).
    Marriage of Near Kin. **Huth, A. H.**
    Social Condition of **U.** Kingdom. **Marshall, J. G.**
    Social Problems. **Graham, Wm**.
    Teetotalers' Hand-Book. **Scott, Rev. W.**
    Women and Work. **Pfeiffer, E.**

SOMMIERES, L. C. V. de. Travels in Montenegro	522
SONNENSCHEIN, W. S. The Best Books	900
SOREL, A. Chute de la Royauté	330

	PAGE
SOULATGES, J. A. L'ordonnance de 1737 concernant le France........	295
Spanish Settlements in America, 1762...	1176
SPENCER, TRASK & Co. Bond investment tables................................	502
SPENS, (W. C) and YOUNGER, R. T. Law of Employers and Employed.....	98
Spirit of the Metropolitan Conservative Press (1839)............:...............	449
Spiritualism. Preliminary Report of the Seybert Commission on............	592

SPORTS AND GAMES.
    Athletics and Football. (*Badminton Lib.*) **Shearman, M.**
    Chance and Luck. **Proctor, R. A.**
    Cycling (*Badminton Lib.*) **Bury, (Viset). and Hellier, G. L.**
    Hunting trip of a Ranchman. **Roosevelt, Theo.**
    Jeu (le) de l'épée. **Jacob, Jules.**
    Portraits of celebrated Race Horses. **Taunton, T. H.**
    Sportsman's (The) Paradise : The Lake lands of Canada. **Watson, B. A.**
    Tiger-shooting in the Doon and Ulwar. **Cookson, Lt. Col.**

SPRAGGE, Mrs. A. From Ontario to the Pacific, by the C. P.R...............	1406
SPRINGER, J. S. Forest life and forest trees of Maine..........................	1240
STAEL, Mme de. Corinne ou l'Italie...	876
—————— By Bella Duffy. (*Em. Women Ser.*)..	478
STAFFORD, Rev. E. A. The Guiding Hand.......................................	50
STANTON, H. B. Random Recollections...	1229
Statistical Society. Catalogue of the Library of the (1884)....................	900
—— ————— Index to subject-matter of the Catalogue (1886).........	900
——— —— ——— Journal. Vol. 49	512

STATISTICS.
    Annual Statistician. **McCarthy, J. D.**
    British Almanac, 1888.
    Dictionary of Statistics. **Mulhall, M. G,**
    Fifty Years of National Progress. **Mulhall, M. G.**
    Statistical Abstract for 1878 to 1882. United States.
    Statistical Atlas. **Hastings, E. J.**
    Statistical Society Journal, v. 49.
    Nebersichten der Weltwirthschaft. **Neumann-Spallart, Dr. F. X.**

Steamboat Inspection—United States plans on.....................................	112
STEBBING, W. Some verdicts of history reviewed................................	851
STEPHEN, Sir J. F. Digest of Criminal Law.......................................	76
—————— Digest Law of Evidence....................................	74
STEPHEN, L. Dictionary of national biography. Vol. 10, 11, 12...............	473
STEPHEN, W. Educational list and directory of the United Kingdom........	79
STEPNIAK. La Russie sous les tzars.............	446
STEVENSON, R. L. The Merry Men and other tales	851
—————— Familiar Studies of Men and Books...........................	803
—————— Underwoods......	864
STEWART, D. Law of Mariage and Divorce.......................................	85
STEWART, Jr., G. Evenings in the Library..	1410

	PAGE
STEWART, Phillips. Poems	1409
STILLMAN, W. J. On the track of Ulysses	322
STIMSON, Rev. E. R. Church and State	252
STINDE, J. The Buchholz family; Sketches of German life	895
———— Frau Wilhelmine	895
STOCKTON, F. R. The Hundredth Man	851
———————— The Bee Man of Orn	851
STONE, Rev. J. S. The Heart of Merrie England.	536
STOKES, W. The Anglo-Indian Codes	153
STONE, O. M. Tenerife and its six satellites	560
STORRS, J. W. The "Twentieth Connecticut" a regimental history	1268
STRONG, J. Our Country	157
SUAREZ, R. P. Francisci. Opera omnia	26
SULLIVAN, Maj. Gen. Jno. Campaigns against the Six Nations of Indians (1779)	1265
SULLIVAN, J. T. Interoceanic Communication by way of the American Isthmus	1361
SULLIVAN, W. The Public Men of the Revolution	1223
Surgeon General's Office Library, U.S. Index catalogue. Vol. 8	905
Sutro Tunnel Company	166
SUZOR, R. Hydrophobia; M. Pasteur's system	675
SWAIN, J. Investors' Notes on American railroads	508
SWINBURNE, A. C. Locrine, a tragedy	864
"SYLVANECTE." Profils vendéens	428
TACITUS. Works. Vol. 2	825
TAILLANDIER, A. Loi de la procédure civile de Genève	382
TAINE, H. Suffrage universel et de la manière de voter	282
Tales before Supper. Translated from Gautier and Merimée	85³
TANNEYHILL, R. H. The Leatherwood God	1257
TARBÉ, E. Le roman d'un crime	883
TARDIVEL, J. P. Etudes religieuses, sociales, politiques et littéraires	1411
TARNIER, (S.) & CHANTREUIL, G. Traité de l'art des accouchements. Vol. I.	672
———————— & BUDIN, P. do do do Vol. II.	672
Taschereau, Mgr. Le Premier Cardinal Canadien, par le Rev. T. E. Hamel.	1196
TAUNTON, T. H. Portraits of celebrated Race Horses	724
TAXIL, L. Le Vatican et les Francs-Macons	393
TAYLOR, J. Great historic families of Scotland	507
TAYLOR, W. H. Four years with General Lee	1229
TAYLOR, W. M. Scottish Pulpit from the Reformation to the present day.	59
TEGAKOUITA, La B. Cath. Sa vie, par le P. Cl. Chauchetière	1193

	PAGE
TEMPLE, G. Britta, a Shetland romance	853
Test Act Reporter	22
TESTE, L. Notes sur Rome et l'Italie	541
TÉTU, l'abbé H. Monseigneur de Laval; esquisse biographique	1192
THACKERAY, W. M. Collection of Letters, 1847-1855	853
THEAL, G. Mc. History of the Boers in South Africa	469
Théatre (le) et la Musique jusqu'en 1789 (L'Ancienne France)	410
THEURIET, A. Au Paradis des Enfants	882
———— L'affaire Froideville	882
THICKNESSE, R. Law of Husband and Wife	85
THIERRY, E. La Comédie française pendant les deux siéges (1870 71)	434
THOMAS, G. Révolutions politiques de Florence 1177-1530	437
THOMPSON, P. The Politics of Labour	471
THOMSON, H. C. Manual of Parliamentary Practice	38
THORNTON, P. M. The Brunswick Accession	392
TICKELL, R. Anticipation; a political pamphlet (1778)	1261
TICKNOR & Co. Handbook of the Maritime Provinces	1364
———— Handbook of New England	1364
TIKHOMIROV, L. Conspirateurs et policiers	898
TIMBERLAKE, Lieut. H. Memoirs of	1187
TISSANDIER, G. Recettes et procédés utiles	735
TOLSTOI, Cte. L. Poulikouchka	898
———— Ma Confession	898
———— The Invaders and other stories	898
———— What to do?	898
———— La puissance des ténèbres; drame	898
TOPELIUS, Z. The Surgeon's Stories (From the Swedish)	896
Toronto University. Fasti from 1850 to 1887. Compiled by W. J. Loudon and W. F. Maclean	87
Toronto University. Year Book of the	87
TORR, C. Rhodes in ancient times	322
TORRIANO, W. H. William the Third	390
TOURGEE, A. W. Button's Inn	854
Tower, Capt. W. Trial of	133
TOWNLEY, Rev. J. Sermon preached at St. Paul's, London, on the taking of Quebec	1278
Trade Guilds of Europe	524

TRAVELS IN AMERICA.
    A travers l'Amérique du Sud. **Dabadie, F.**
    Algoma West; its mines and industrial resources. **Roland, W.**
    Ancient (The) Cities of the New World. **Charnay, D.**
    Aventures et scènes du Nouveau Monde. **Vinl, A. A.**

TRAVELS IN AMERICA—*Continued.*
    Barrow, Point. International Polar Expedition to.
    Brazil, Travels in, in 1817-20. **Von Spix, J. B.**
    Brésil, Nouvelles études sur le. **Pradez, Chs.**
    Canada and the States: Recollections 1851-1886. **Watkin, Sir E. W.**
    Chateaubriand, Vte. de. Lettres sur les voyages imaginaires de—, en Amérique. By **Mersennes, M. de.**
    Cinq mois aux Etats-Unis en 1835. **Ramon de la Sagra.**
    Columbia, New Grenada, Equatorial South America. **Leay, W.**
    De Paris à San Francisco. **Lambert de Sainte-Croix, Alex.**
    Down the Islands: a voyage to the Caribees. **Paton, W. A.**
    Durret, le Sieur. Voyage à Lima et aux Indes Occidentales (1707).
    English (The) in the West Indies. **Froude, J. A.**
    En route pour la mer glaciale. **Petitot, R. P. E.**
    Exploration de Québec au Lac St. Jean. **Perrault, J.**
    Chatellux. Examen critique de ses voyages. Par **Brissot de Warville.**
    Four months in North America. **Charlton, W. H.**
    From Ontario to the Pacific, by the C.P.R. **Spragge, Mrs. A.**
    Giants (The) of Patagonia. **Bourne, B. F.**
    Guatemala, the land of the Quetzal. **Brigham, W. F.**
    Guatemala in 1827-28. **Dunn, H.**
    Histoire du canal de Panama. **Garcon, A.**
    History of the County of Huntingdon up to 1838. **Sellar, R.**
    Holiday (A) in Brazil and on the River Plate. **Edgcumbe, E. R. P.**
    Huron District, map of (1845), by **McDonald, D.**
    "Inchiquin," The Jesuits letters during a late residence in the United States.
    Indian tribes of the Rocky Mountains **Smet, R. S. de.**
    Interoceanic Communication by way of the American Isthmus. **Sullivan, J. T.**
    Isthmus of America. A Ship Canal across the. **Pitman, R. B.**
    Life and Services of Gen John A. Logan. **Dawson, G. F.**
    Map of the City of Ottawa (1887). **Snow, J. A.**
    Map of the Dominion of Canada. **Tuuison, H. C.**
    Maritime Provinces. Handbook of the. **Ticknor & Co.**
    Metlakahtla, The story of. **Wellcome, H. S.**
    Mexique et Californie. **Castets, Em**
    New England. Handbook of **Ticknor & Co.**
    Northern (The) Lakes of Canada.
    Notes of a tour of America, 1832 and 1833. **Davis, S.**
    Notes on the Saguenay **Kelso, S. J.**
    Nova Scotia, New Brunswick, Newfoundland, etc.
    Overland Guide from Missouri to the Pacific Ocean. **Rand, McNally & Co.**
    Pélerinage (un) au pays d'Evangeline. **Casgrain, l'abbé H. R.**
    Rambles through the United States and Canada. **Shaw, Jno.**
    Ranch life in the North-West.
    Ride from Quebec to Lake St. John. **Davenport, Mrs.**
    Rivals (The) of Acadia: a novel.
    Rocky Mountains and Oregon. Life and Adventures on the. **Victor, Mrs. F. F.**
    St. Louis' Isle, or Texiana. **Hooton, C.**
    Scamper (A) through America **Hudson, T. S.**
    Shores and Alps of Alaska. **Kerr, W. H. S.**
    Sketches of America in 1854-55-56. **Pairpoint, Alf.**
    Through the West Indies. **Layard, Mrs. G**
    Tour in Virginia. **Cornelius, Rev. E.**
    Transatlantic Sketches. **Caester, G. J.**
    Traveller's Guide through the States and Canada. **Danison, G. M.**
    Travels in Bolivia. **Bonelli, L H de.**
    Travels through North and South Carolina, Georgia, etc. **Bartram, W.**

TRAVELS IN AMERICA—*Concluded*. PAGE

   Trip to Canada and the Far North-West, 1887. **Elliott, Chs.**
   Trip to South America. **Macfarlane, Thos.**
   Two thousand miles through Mexico. **McCarty, Rev. J. M.**
   Ulloa, Don J. et A. de—Memoires concernant la découverte de l'Amérique.
   Views of Louisiana and the Missouri in 1811. **Brackenridge, H. M.**
   Voyage au Lac Supérieur. **Rivot, L. E.**
   ———— au Nouveau-Mexique, 1805-07. **Pike, Z. M.**
   ———— au pays de pétrole **Clerc, Alexis**
   ———— d'un Suisse dans différentes colonies d'Amérique.
   ———— to California. **Chappe d'Auteroche, Jean.**
   ———— to Newfoundland and Sallee. **Cassini, M. de.**
   Voyages and Discoveries in South America. **Acuna, le P. C. d'.**
   Western (The) Avernus. **Roberts, Morley.**
   Year (A) in the Great Republic. **Bates, E. C.**
   Young Emigrants (The); or, Picture of Canada.

Treasury Decisions, (U.S). Synopsis of... 178
Trois Rivières Noces d'argent du Séminaire des (1885)................... 86
TROLLOPE, T. A. What I remember.. 503
TROTTER, J. G Appeals from Justices.. 29
TRUAN, H. Les grands écrivains français....................................... 76
TRUDELLE, l'abbé C. Histoire de la paroisse de Charlesbourg......... 1411
Trueman's New Brunswick Reports. Vol. 24.................................. 223
TUCK, Rev. R. Handbook of biblical difficulties............................. 10
TUCKER, G. A. Lunacy in many lands.. 118
TUDOR, O. D. Mercantile and maritime law.................................. 110
TUER, (A. W.) and FAGAN, C. F. First Year of a Silken Reign. (1837-8).. 396
TULLOCH, J. Sundays at Balmoral. Sermons................................. 50
TULLOCH, W. W. Story of the life of Queen Victoria..................... 396
TUNISON, H. C. Map of the Dominion of Canada........................... 1399
TUPPER, M. F. Jubilate. An offering for 1887............................... 396
TURGENIEFF, J. Annals of a Sportsman... 898
———————— Dimitia Roudine.. 898
———————— Fathers and Sons.. 898
———————— Liza.. 898
———————— Mumu and the Diary of a Superfluous man................. 898
———————— On the Eve... 898
———————— Smoke... 898
———————— Virgin Soil... 898
———————— Spring Floods and a Lear of the Steppe....................... 898
———————— An unfortunate Woman and Ass'ya............................. 898
TURNER, L. M. Contributions to the Natural History of Alaska...... 612
TWISS, Travers. Droit des gens en temps de paix............................ 268
Tytler, Sarah. Buried Diamonds (Picc. Nov. 176)............................ 847
———————— Disappeared (*Picc. Nov.* 178).................................... 847

	PAGE
ULLOA, Don J. & A. de—Memoires concernant la découverte de l'Amérique.	1352
United States. Irrigation in the, Report by H. J. Hinton..................................	757
——————. Secret service during the Civil War..............................	1268
——————— Commercial relations, 1880-1887..................................	522
——————— Postal Guide, 1887...	161
——————— Statistical Abstract, 1678 to 1882................................	520
——————— Statutes at Large. Vol. 24	169
Universal History compiled from original authors............................	305
Universalism in America	1198

USEFUL ARTS.
    Beer (The) of the Bible. **Death, Js.**
    Cuisine (la) moderne.
    Dictionnaire des arts et manufactures. **Laboulaye, C.**
    Dictionnaire de l'industrie. **Lami, E. O.** Vols. 6 et 7.
    Economie des machines et des manufactures **Laboulaye, C.**
    Electric (The) Light popularly explained. **Holmes, A. B.**
    Elements of construction for Electro-Magnets. **Dumoncel, Th.**
    Encyclopédie des ouvrages de dames. **Dillmont, Thérèse de.**
    Ferments et fermentation. **Rey, J. A.**
    Guide du fabricant d'alcools et du distillateur. **Basset, N.**
    Guide du fabricant de sucre.   do
    Guide du Verrier. **Bontemps, G**
    Manual of type-writing. **Humphrey, F. S.**
    Patents, (American) Official Gazette.
    ——— (English). Illustrated Journal of Patented Inventions.
    ——— Official Journal.
    ——— Specifications.
    Peinture (la) sur faïence et porcelaine. **Ris-Paquot**.
    Recettes et procédés utiles. **Tissandier, G.**

VALENTINE, L. The Queen, her early life and reign............................	396
VALLÉE, O. de. Les manieurs d'argent..	416
VASILI, Cte P. La Société de Rome..	541
——————— La Société de Paris..	539
——————— La Société de Londres..	396
——————— La Société de Vienne...	396
VEITCH, S. F. F. James Hepburn, Free Church Minister........................	854
Verdi. History of his life and work's, by A. Pougin............................	721
VERMONT, E. de. America Heraldica : Arms, Crests, and Mottoes............	508
Verne, Jules. The Clipper of the Clouds.	882
——————— Famous travels and travellers....................................	521
——————— Great Navigators of the 18th Century........................	521
——————— Great Explorers of the 19th Century	521
——————— North against South	882
——————— Nord contre Sud...	882
Vetromille, Eug. A tour in both hemispheres.....................................	·527
VEUILLOT, P. L'imposture des Naundorff	427

	PAGE
VIAL, A. A. Aventures et scènes du Nouveau Monde.....................	1351
VIBERT, Theod. Droit divin de la démocratie.	395
VICTOR, Mrs. F. F. Life and adventures on the Rocky Mountains and Oregon	1389
VICTORIA, Queen, Jubilee of. Celebration at St-John's, N. B............	397
Victorian Hymns. English Sacred Songs of fifty years.................	51
VIGFUSSON (G) & POWELL, T. Y., Sigfred Arminius and other papers. ...	797
VIRMAITRE, Chs., Paris Police	434
VITZTHUM VON ECKSTADT, Ct. C. F. St. Petersburg and London in the years 1852-64	332
VOGUE, E. M. DE. Le roman russe....................................	798
—— —— Russian Novelists............................	798
—— —— Souvenirs et visions.........................	881
VON SPIX, J. B. Travels in Brazil in 1817-20........................	1355
VOSE, G. L. Bridge disasters in America.............................	761
Voyage d'un Suisse dans différentes colonies d'Amérique..............	1359
Voyages autour du monde depuis Christophe Colomb.................	523
Vue de la Colonie espagnole du Mississipi (1803).....................	1254
VULPIAN A. Maladies du système nerveux...........................	668
WALFORD, E. Jubilee Memoir of Her Majesty Queen Victoria.........	396
WALKER, J. D. On Banking law.....................................	106
WALKER, Rev. W. C. History of the 18th Regiment, Connecticut Volunteers.	1263
WALLER, J. A. Voyage in the West Indies...........................	522
WALLON, H. L'autorité de l'évangile................................	11
WALPOLE, F. G. Lord Floysham. A novel...........................	854
WALTON, Mrs O. F. "Our Gracious Queen.".........................	396
WALTZEMULLER, M. H. Ses ouvrages et ses collaborateurs............	899
WAPLES, R. Proceeding *In Rem*.	70
WARD, T. H. Reign of Queen Victoria. A survey of fifty years........	397
WARD, W. The Wish to Believe	45
WARBURTON, E. The Crescent and the Cross........................	549
WARING, C. State purchase of railways.............................	508
WARNER, C. D. My Winter on the Nile..............................	560
WASHBURN, C. A. From poverty to competence. Graduated taxation......	493
WASHBURNE, E. B. Recollections of a minister to France (1869-1877)......	433
WATKIN, Sir E. W. Canada and the States : Recollections 1851-1886........	1372
WATSON, B. A. The Sportsman's Paradise : The Lake lands of Canada......	725
Waverley Anecdotes..	848
Waymouth's Voyage to the Coast of Maine, 1605.....................	1240
Wayne (Fort). History of. By W. A. Bryce..........................	1258
WEBER, le Dr H. Climathéropie	669

	PAGE
Weed, Thurlow, Life of, by T. W. Barnes........	1229
WEIGHTMAN, H. Law of Marriage and Legitimacy......	86
WEIR, A. Historical basis of modern Europe (1760-1815)......	330
WEIR, Arthur. Fleur-de-Lys and other poems......	1410
WEISS, J. J. Au pays du Rhin	544
WELLOOME, H. S. The story of Metlakahtla......	406
WELLS, J. C. Magna Charta	156
WERTHEIMER, J. Law relating to Clubs......	78
Wesley, Susanna. By Eliza Clarke (*Em. Woman Ser.*.)......	478
Wesleyan Methodist Church of Canada. Annual conferences of......	1198
WEST, Mary. Allegra......	854
WESTALL, W. The Phantom City. A volcanic romance......	854
———— Captain Trafalgar......	854
WESTCOTT, B. F. Social aspects of Christianity......	48
Westminster Magazine (1781)......	915
WETHERAL, Mabel. Two North country maids......	854
WHARTON, H. T. Sappho : Memoir, text and translation......	817
WHEATLEY, H. B. Handbook of pottery and the precious metals......	692
WHEELER, C. G. The course of empire......	305
WHEELHOUSE, Sir W. Corrupt Practices Prevention Act, 1883......	40
WHIPPLE, E. P. Recollections of eminent men......	1229
WHITE, (F. T) and TUDOR, O. D. Leading Cases in Equity......	62
WHITE, Hon. Thos. Political Speeches......	130
WILD, Rev. J. Talks for the times......	52
WILDE, Lady (Speranza). Legends and Superstitions of Ireland......	310
WILDENBRUCH, E. von. The Master of Tanagra......	895
WILLIAMS, C. J. B. and C. T. Pulmonary Consumption......	672
WILLIAMS, Rev. E. Life of Thomas Williams, chief of the Caughnawaga Indians......	1188
WILLIAMS, G. W. History of the Negro troops in the American Rebellion (1861-65)......	1269
WILLIAMS, Capt. G. Newfoundland, its trade and fishery......	1337
WILLIAMS, S. W. Biographical memoir of Rev. Jno. Williams......	1197
WILSON, J. H. China : travels and investigations in the " Middle Kingdom "......	557
WILSON, R. Life and times of Queen Victoria......	397
WILSON's Business Directory of New-York City......	525
WINSLOW, C. M. R. Yesterdays with actors......	802
WINSOR, J. Narrative and Critical history of America. Vols 5 & 6......	1179
WINTER, J. S. Garrison gossip gathered in Blankhampton......	855

	PAGE
WOOD, H. Natural law in the business world	486
WOOD, H. G. Mandamus	79
Wool and Manufacturers of Wool	513
WOODBERRY, G. E. Edgar Allan Poe. (*Am. Men of Letters*)	803
WORMELL, R. Principles of dynamics	600
WYNKOOP, R. Vessels and Voyages as regulated by Federal Statutes	178
YEAR BOOK of Scientific and learned Societies for 1887	911
YEAR BOOK of treatment for 1886	666
YEATS, J. Growth of Commerce	517
——— Recent and existing commerce	517
YONGE, C. M. Victorian half century. A Jubilee Book	396
York Deeds, Maine (1642-76). Edited by H. W. Richardson	1240
YOUNG, Hon. J. Letters of Canadian trade, etc.	524
Young Emigrants (The); or, Picture of Canada,	1369
YOUNGER, R. R. Counting-House Guide	503
YRIARTE, Ch. Autour du Concile: croquis et souvenirs	541
ZELLER, J. Diplomatie française du XVIe siècle	424
ZOLA, Em. L'œuvre	887
Zollverein Papers 1838-85	520

The following is a list of the ENGLISH, CANADIAN and AMERICAN Pamphlets collected during the past year:—

ENGLISH PAMPHLETS.

VOL. 633.

1. Manning, Cardinal. The Vatican Decrees and Civil Allegiance. New York, 1875.
2. Ullathorne, Bishop. Gladstone's expostulation unravelled. New York, 1875.
3. Vaughan, Rt. Rev. Herbert, (Bishop of Salford). Submission to a Divine Teacher, neither Disloyalty, nor the surrender of Mental and Moral Freedom. New York 1875.

VOL. 634.

1. Newman, Cardinal. Letter to the Duke of Norfolk on Mr. Gladstone's recent Expostulation, with Postscript. New York, 1875.
2. Vatican Council. Decrees and Canons of. New York, 1875.
3. Fessler, Dr. Joseph. The True and False Infallibility of the Popes. New York, 1875.

VOL. 635.

1. Fessler, Dr. Joseph. The True and False Infallibility of the Popes. New York, 1875.
2. Manning, Cardinal. Vatican Decrees and Civil Allegiance. New York, 1875.
3. The Syllabus for the People. By a Monk of St. Augustine, Ramsgate. New York, 1875.

VOL. 636.

1. "Chasuble," Archdeacon. Comedy of Convocation in the English Church. New York, 1875.
2. Oxenham, Rev. T. N. Everlasting Punishment. Is the popular Doctrine *de fide*? And if not, is it True? Toronto, 1875.
3. Is " Eternal" Punishment endless? By an Orthodox Minister of the Gospel. Boston, 1879.

VOL. 637.

1. A Brief Historical Account of the Behaviour of the Jesuits and their faction for the first twenty-five years of Queen Elizabeth's Reign. London, 1689.
2. Considerations which ought to move all True and Sound Catholics who are not wholly Jesuited. London, 1688.
3. Colton, C. Church and State in America, part I. London, 1834.
4. ——— do part. II. London, 1834.'
5. British Guiana. Memorial to Queen Victoria on the condition of the Catholic Church in. London, 1841.
6. ——— ——— The Catholic Church in. Letter to the Archbishop of Vienna in Austria. London, 1841.
7. Nassau. The Disendowment Question in. London, 1868.
8. Preston, Rev. Thomas S. The Church and the World. An Address. New York, 1871.
9. Gladstone, Rt. Hon. W. E. Italy and the Church, with an Introduction by H. M. Thompson. New York, 1875.
10. English, (The) Religion. Letters addressed to an Irish Gentleman. Dublin, 1876.

VOL. 638.

1. Our Constitution and the Elective Franchise. London, 1866.
2. Smith, Augustus. Constitutional reflections on the present aspects of Parliamentary Government. London, 1866.

3. "KÚKLOS." National Debts and the Funding of the National Wealth. London, 1876.
4. ———— Free Trade—Its Failure as an Economical Policy. London, 1879.
5. ———— The present Depression in Trade—Its Cause and Remedy. London, 1876.
6. ———— Standards of Value, and the depreciation in the value of Gold. London, 1876.
7. GLADSTONE, Rt. Hon. W. E. Bulgarian Horrors and the Question of the East. Montreal, 1876.
8. PARKES, Henry. Intercolonial Agreement, s. l., 1881.
9. McEWEN, Alexander. The Need of Protection. London, 1880.
10. TORRENS, W. M., Imperial and Colonial Partnership in Emigration. London, 1881.

CANADIAN PAMPHLETS.

VOL. 552.
MÉDECINE.

1. DANSEREAU, P. Le délire tremblant (thèse). Montréal, 1835.
2. PAINCHAUD, le Dr. Le choléra asiatique (conférence). Québec, 1849.
3. (Bois, l'Abbé). Michel Sarrasin, médecin du roi à Québec. Etude. Québec, 1856.
4. GUÉRIN, Dr. H. De l'hydrothérapie. Montréal, 1863.
5. GRENIER, George. Contagion de la variole. Montréal, 1872.
6. Collége vétérinaire de Montréal. Annuaire pour 1875-76. Montréal, 1875.
7. Examens pour l'admission à l'étude de la médecine. 1885, s. l.
8. CREVIER, Dr. J. A. Le choléra. Montréal, 1885.
9. HAMON, A. L'hygiène en Europe. Montréal, s. d.

VOL. 553.
GOUVERNEMENT ECCLÉSIASTIQUE DES PAROISSES.

1. CHABOILLEZ, Rév. M. Gouvernement ecclésiastique du district de Montréal. 1823.
2. Questions du refus de la sépulture ecclésiastique. Limoges, 1840.
3. La Fabrique de Sainte-Famille vs. Moyse Poulin. Québec, 1858.
4. Cause en appel : Philippe N. Pacaud vs. le Rév. Pierre Roy. Québec, 1867.
5. BEAUDRY, J. U. Mémoire au soutien de l'appel de la fabrique de N.-D. de Montréal. Rome, 1867.
6. Réponse à l'appel de la Fabrique de N.-D. de Montréal. Rome, 1867.
7. BEAUDRY, J. U. Réplique des Marguilliers de N.-D. de Montréal à la réponse à l'appel de la même Fabrique. Montréal, 1867.
8. Droit de tenir les registres civils dans les paroisses canoniques de Montréal. Paris, 1869.
9. Considérations sur les réponses aux questions proposées par Mgr. de Montréal et Mgr. de Rimouski. Montréal, 1876.
10. Décrets concernant l'érection canonique de certaines paroisses. Montréal, 1875.
11. LARUE, Hubert. Les corporations religieuses de Québec, et les nouvelles taxes. Québec, 1876.

VOL. 554.
RELIGION.

1. Vie de Saint-Hermas. Montréal, 1863.
2. PERNIN, l'Abbé. Le doigt de Dieu est là. Montréal, 1874.
3. LEROY, P. Gage de la victoire. s. l. 1878.

4. Sainte-Marguerite. Pélerinage à—Montréal. 1880.
5. TARTE, J. Isr. Le clergé, ses droits, nos devoirs. Québec, 1880.
6. CHABERT, l'Abbé J. La guerre au Canada. Montréal, 1881.

VOL. 555.
RELIGION.

1. BOURGET, Mgr. Lettres pastorales contre les erreurs du temps, etc. Montréal, 1858.
2. MOREAU, Mgr. L. Z. Mandement d'entrée dans son diocèse. Saint-Hyacinthe, 1876.
3. RAYMOND, M. (V. G.) Devoirs envers le pape, (discours). Montréal, 1861.
4. Canonisation des martyrs japonais à Rome en 1862. Québec, 1862.
5. PROULX, F.-H. Histoire populaire de Pie IX. Sainte-Anne de la Pocatière, 1867.
6. Fête de Pie IX à N.-D. de Montréal (50e anniversaire). Montréal, 1869.
7. CHAUVEAU, P. J. O. Noces d'Or de Pie IX (discours). Québec, 1869.
8. RAYMOND, Mgr. Dissertation sur le Pape. Montréal, 1870.
9. RACINE, l'abbé Ant. Vingt-cinquième anniversaire du couronnement de Pie IX. Québec, 1871.
10. PINSONNEAULT, Mgr. Discussion sur le *Syllabus*. Montréal, 1876.
11. PIE IX. Allocution aux cardinaux, le 12 mars 1877. Montréal, 1877.
12. De la Souveraineté temporelle du pape. Montréal, 1878.

VOL. 556.

1. RACINE, l'abbé Ant. Eloge de la Vénérable Mère Marie de l'Incarnation. Blois, 1870.
2. Notice biographique sur la Révérende Mère Barat, fondatrice de l'Institut du Sacré-Cœur de Jésus. Montréal, 1874.
3. GIROUX, Henri. La Communauté du Bon-Pasteur, à Montréal, Montréal, 1879.
4. ——————— Mme Gamelin et ses œuvres. Montréal, 1885.
5. BOIES, A. Le chemin de fer du lac Saint-Jean (Conférence). Québec, 1886.
6. Le métier de ministre (Sir Hector Langevin). Montréal, 1886.
7. RIEL, Louis "David." Poésies religieuses et politiques. Montréal, 1886.
8. "BEAUREGARD, Geo."—Le 9e Bataillon au Nord-Ouest. Québec, 1886.

VOL. 557.
EDUCATION.

1. PERRAULT, J. F. Manuel pratique de l'école élémentaire françoise. Québec, 1829.
2. ——————— Tableau alphabétique de mots de trois syllabes. Québec, 1830.
3. JACOTOT, Emile. Comment se fait l'inspection primaire. Québec, 1876.
4. Notre-Dame de Liesse : translation de sa statue au Gésu de Montréal. Montréal. s.d.

VOL. 558.
EDUCATION.

1. MONDELET, Chs. Elementary and Practical Education. Montreal, 1841.
2. ——————— Lettres sur l'Education élémentaire et pratique. Montréal, 1841.
3. Le dépôt de livres et la pétition des libraires. s.l.n.d.
4. Observations sur la dernière loi de l'instruction publique, dans la province de Québec. Québec, 1877.
5. Lois sur l'instruction publique, province de Québec. Québec, 1877.

6. ROUSSELOT, l'abbé V. Réponses aux attaques de l'*Evening Post*. (Question des écoles catholiques de Montréal.) s.l. 1879-81.

VOL. 559.
EDUCATION.

1. LANCASTER, Jos. Improved system of Education for Lower Canada. Quebec, 1815.
2. PERRAULT, J. Frs. Plan raisonné d'Education générale permanente. s.l. 1830.
3. SAUVAGEAU, Chs. Notions élémentaires de musique. Québec, 1844.
4. Traité d'élocution. Montréal, 1870.
5. VERBIST, l'abbé P. J. Projet d'organisation d'une académie des beaux-arts à Montréal. Conférence. Montréal, 1873.
6. LIPPENS. B. Pierre Leroy, son système, sa marotte, etc. Québec, 1874.
7. Pédagogie : son but, etc. Québec, 1877.
8. PAQUIN, Rév. L. P. Conférences sur l'instruction obligatoire. Québec, 1880.

VOL. 560.
ENQUÊTES.

1. TASSÉ, D. Réponse aux correspondances, etc , d'Alex. Dufresne. s. l. 1863.
2. Dismissal of Dr Russell from the Commission of the Peace. s. l. 1858-59.
3. Dismissal of P. M. Partridge, Superintendent of Woods and Forests. Quebec, 1867.
4. Documents au sujet de la démission de M. Bréhaut. Montréal, 1864.
5. Documents au sujet de la conduite de C. E. Belle, agent d'immigration. Québec, 1864.
6. Le Major L. N. Voyer et la charge de chef de la police provinciale. Québec, 1874.

VOL. 561.
JOURNAUX.

1. DARVEAU, L. M. Histoire de *La Tribune*. Québec, 1863.
2. GÉRIN, E. *La Gazette de Québec*. Québec, 1864.
3. By-laws, etc. of the Dominion Editors and Reporters Association, 1874-75. Ottawa.
4. TÊTU, H. Historique des journaux de Québec. Québec, 1875.
5. BUIES, A. La presse canadienne française et les améliorations de Québec. (Conférence.) Québec, 1875.
6. BUIES, A. Même conférence, en anglais.
7. Célébration du quatrième centenaire de l'imprimerie en Angleterre par Caxton. Montréal, 1877.
8. DUQUET, J. N. Une fête à l'imprimerie du *Canadien*. Québec, 1878.
9. TÊTU, H. Journaux et revues de Québec par ordre chronologique. Québec, 1881.
10. Prospectus de *La Revue Canadienne* : nouvelle série. Montréal, 1881.
11. Troisième anniversaire de *La Patrie*. Montréal, 1882.
12. PROULX, F. H. *La Gazette des Campagnes* : sa 19me année (1881-82). Sainte-Anne de la Pocatière, 1884.

VOL. 562.
AFFAIRES MUNICIPALES.

1. L'éclairage au gaz de la ville de Québec : contrat à ce sujet, le 29 oct. 1847. s. l. n. d.
2. LANGELIER, F. Les affaires municipales de la cité de Québec. Québec, 1868.
3. L'administration actuelle de la Corporation de Québec. Québec, 1869.

4. The Case of the Butchers selling in the Public Markets. Montréal, 1879.
5. La même brochure en français. X.
6. Le passé, le présent, l'avenir ! (Par X* * * *). Montréal, 1875.
7. Les scandales. La Corporation. (Par Poligraphe). Montréal, 1875.
8. Les Infâmes ! La Corporation. (Par Poligraphe). Montréal, 1875.
9. Les Buses. La Corporation. (Par Poligraphe). Montréal, 1875.
10. Les Bourreaux. La Corporation. (Par Poligraphe). Montréal, 1875.
11. Baillargé, Chs. The Municipal Situation. Quebec, 1878.
12. Grain Elevating in the Harbor of Montreal, s.l. 1879.
13. FYSHE, Thos. Municipal Taxation. Halifax, N. S., 1880.
14. BALCER, Geo. Three Rivers as a Sea Port. Three Rivers, 1880.
15. Harbour Commissioners of Three Rivers (By-laws, etc.) Three Rivers, 1883.
16. Le même ouvrage en français.
17. PATTERSON, Wm. J. Canadian Inland Commerce. Montreal, 1882.
18. Hydraulic Power of the Lachine Rapids. Montreal, 1880.
19. ROBERTSON, And. Business of the Port of Montreal for 1883, s. l. n. d.

VOL. 563.

1. KINGSFORD, Wm. A Canadian Political Coin. Ottawa, 1874.
2. STEVENSON, Jas. The Card Currency of Canada during the French Domination. Quebec, 1875.
3. HINCKS, Sir Fr. The Political History of Canada, between 1840 and 1855. (A lecture). Montreal, 1877.
4. Questions in Canadian History and the answers of "Hermes." Montreal, 1880.
5. McCORD, Fred. A. Errors in Canadian History culled from "Prize Answers." Montreal, 1880.
6. DAWSON, Sir J. W. British Association for the Advancement of Science. (An Address). London, 1886.
7. Canadian Numismatic Bibliography. Montreal, 1886.

VOL. 564.

RELIGIOUS PAMPHLETS.

1. SHREVE, R. R. Lenten Addresses on the Seven Words of Jesus. St. John, N.-B., 1882.
2. SPRAGUE, D. D. H. St. Paul's doctrine of the Atonement. St. John, N. B., 1883.
3. EVENS, Rev. E. The Origin of the Organization and Government in the early Church. St. John, N. B , 1884.
4. GAYNOR, Rev. Wm. C. Papal Infallibility. Letters of " Cleophas " in defence of the Vatican Dogma. St. John, N. B., 1885.
5. DAVENPORT, Rev. John M. Papal Infallibility. "Catholic's " Reply to " Cleophas " refuting the Vatican Dogma. St. John, N. B., 1885.
6. Low, George, L. The first miracle of Christ and prohibition. Toronto, 1886.
7. The Baptist Year Book of the Maritime Provinces. Halifax, N. S., 1887.

VOL. 565.

1. Trinity House. (Lower Canada). By-Laws and Regulations. Quebec, 1819.
2. Postes de la Province du Bas-Canada. Rapport sur. Québec, 1831.
3. Petition of the House of Assembly of Lower Canada to the King. London, 1836.

4. ROEBUCK, J. A. Existing difficulties in the Government of the Canadas. London, 1836
5. WRIGHT, Joseph. Protection of Canadian Industry. Dundas, 1864.
6. Canadian "Guerilla." Notes on the Road. Toronto, 1868.
7. NORRIS, William. The Canadian Question. Montreal, 1875.

VOL. 566.

1. Nouvelle-Ecosse. Procédés de l'Assemblée sur la convention conclue entre Sa Majesté et les Etats-Unis de l'Amérique. Québec, 1823.
2. GRAY, Hon. J. H. Speech on the Vote of want of confidence, delivered in the House of Assembly. Fredericton, 1856.
3. Seat (The) of Government of Canada ; and "Double Majority Question." Quebec, 1843-56.
4. RAMSAY, T. K. Government Commission of Inquiry. Montreal, 1863.
5. Nouvelle-Ecosse. Correspondance et négociations relatives aux affaires de la. Ottawa, 1869.
6. New Brunswick. Report of the "Better-Terms" Delegation of— (1871). St. John, N.B., 1872.
7. Le siège du gouvernement provincial. Québec, 1856.
8. Marine marchande anglaise ; dépêches échangées entre le gouvernement du Canada et le gouvernement impérial. Ottawa, 1875.
9. Manufactures and other Articles exchanged between Canada and Australian Colonies, together with copies of the Tariffs. Ottawa, 1878.
10. Factories in England and upon the Continent of Europe. Report. Ottawa, 1883.
11. BLACKEBY, A. H. Report of the System of laws regulating Labour in the State of Massachusetts. Ottawa, 1883.
12. Interprovincial Trade. Report of Select Committee on. Ottawa, 1883.
13. Interprovincial Trade. Evidence taken before Select Committee on. Ottawa, 1882.

VOL. 567.

1. Society for Promoting Christian Knowledge. Report of the York Committee. York, 1833.
2. Aubrey, Bp. George. The Church of God (a sermon), St. John's Newfoundland, 1842.
3. Toronto General Hospital. Report of the Trustees of. Toronto, 1855.
4. Salaries of the Clergy. Letter Commendatory from Right Reverend Bishop of Toronto. Toronto, 1858.
5. Trinity College. Judgments on the Theological Teaching of. Toronto. 1863.
6. Montréal, City of. Report of Protestant Board of School Commissioners for. Montreal, 1872.
7. McGill University. Statement of Royal Institution for the advancement of Learning, addressed to Friends and Benefactors of. Montreal, 1874.
8. SANGSTER, Dr. John H. Reply to the "Globe's" Slanderous Attack on his private character. Toronto, 1874.
9. Montreal. Report of Protestant Board of School Commissioners for. Montreal, 1877.
10. MACLAREN, William. Premillenialism in relation to Revelation. Toronto, 1882.

VOL. 568.

1. DAWSON, J. W. Air Breathers of the Coal Period. Montreal, 1863.
2. Lower Canada. Land and Fresh Water Mollusks of. 1863.

3. Eastern Canada. Notes on gold of. Montreal, 1864.
4. HUNT, T. Sterry. Petroleum; its Geological Relations in Gaspé. Quebec, 1865.
5. Prince Edward Island. Report on the Geological Structure and Mineral Resources of. By Sir J. W. Dawson. Montreal, 1871.
6. FLETCHER, Col. The Defence of Canada. A Lecture. Ottawa, 1875.
7. DAWSON, Sir J. W. Origin and History of life on our Planet. An Address. Montreal 1875.
8. DAWSON, Sir J. W. Geological development of the Atlantic. AN ADDRESS. London, 1886.
9. Geological and Natural History Survey of Canada. List of Publications. Ottawa, 1884.
10. SELWYN, A. R. C., & DAWSON, G. M. Physical geography and geology of Canada. Montreal, 1884.

VOL. 569.

Règlements et constitutions de clubs et sociétés Canadiennes:—Société Française; Club de Verchères, 1871; Union de Montréal, 1872; Union Typographique de Québec 1873; Club Cartier, 1874; Ottawa Snowshoe Club, 1876; Club Gas Company of Montreal, 1878; St. James' Club, Montreal, 1880; Ottawa Rowing Club, 1881-85; Ottawa Rifle Club, 1881; Dominion Trav. Association, Montreal, 1882; Ottawa Foot Ball Club, 1882; Ottawa Lawn Tennis Club, 1882; Ottawa Literary Society 1887.

VOL. 570.

1. McCULL, G. S. Travels and Adventures, with introduction by John B. McGann. Toronto, 1862.
2. PELTIER, Louis. Voyage par terre et par mer. Québec, 1862.
3. GÉRIN, E. Le Saint-Maurice. Notes de voyage. s. l. 1871.
4. TACHÉ, J. C. Remarks on Mr. Harvey's paper on census of 1871. s. l. n. d.
5. The third Volume of the Census of 1871 and its critics. Ottawa, 1883.
6. CLAPIN, Sylva. Londres et Paris, (lecture). St. Hyacinthe, 1880.
7. GLACKMEYER, E. C. Almanac containing Alphabetical List of Cities, Towns, Villages, &c. of the Province of Quebec. Lévis, 1880.
8. Dominion of Canada. Historical sketches of the various provinces of. Montreal, s. d.
9. CAMPBELLS. Address of the Canadian—to the Marquess of Lorne. Ottawa, 1882.

VOL. 571.

1. HILL, Rev. George W. "The School of the Prophets," (a sermon). Halifax, 1860.
2. Allan Gray and his doubts. By a lover of Truth. Halifax, 1871.
3. BLAND, H. T. "Soul Winning," A course of four lectures delivered at Cobourg University. Toronto, 1883.
4. HENDERSON, W. Reply to Archdeacon Farrar's Excursus in Eternal Hope. Montreal, 1884.
5. DICKSON, Rev. James A. Working for the children in the Home and Sunday school. Toronto, 1885.

VOL. 572.

1. Montreal. Panoramic View of the City of. Montreal, 1860.
2. BURR, WM. Pictorial Voyage to Canada. New York, 1850.
3. GIROUX, HENRI. Histoire et statistique des institutions catholiques de Montréal. Montréal, 1869.

INDEX.

4. MARCHAND, N. Guide de la ville de Longueuil pour 1874-75. 1874.
5. Montreal. (City of). The Hotel Guest's Guide. Montreal, 1875.
6. Montreal. Handbook and Guide of, with illustrated Map of the City. Montreal, 1876.
7. Northern Lakes. Guide to the. Toronto, 1876.
8. MARTEL, J. Z. Guide de l'Assomption. L'Assomption, 1883.
9. BUIES, A. Sur le parcours du chemin de fer du Lac Saint-Jean. Québec, 1886.

VOL. 573.

1. BURK, Luke. Phrenological Enquiries by. Quebec, 1840.
2. GOLDIE, T. W. The Mosaic Account of the Creation of the World and Noachian Deluge. Quebec, 1856.
3. Shape of the Earth. Controversy between a Newtonian Astronomer and a Poet. Weston-Super-Mare, 1872.
4. KENDALL, Rev. C. H. Theory and Experiment. A Lecture. Montreal, 1859.
5. MACDONALD, Dougald. The Heavenly Bodies. How they move and what moves them. Montreal, 1877.
6. MARSHALL, J. G. Fictions and Errors in J. W. Dawson's "Origin of the World." Halifax, N.S., 1877.
7. BAYMES, GEO. A. Disposal of the Dead. By land, by water, or by fire, which ? Montreal, 1875.
8. Electric Lighting in Canada. Its future. Montreal, 1882.

VOL 574.

1. MORTON, D. C. Rapport sur les explorations du chemin de fer de Québec à Richmond. Québec, 1881.
2. Sommes payées par le Gouvernement et correspondance relativement à certains chemins de fer dans la province de Québec. Québec, 1853.
3. Grand-Tronc. Liste des actionnaires de la compagnie du. Québec, 1855.
4. ―――――― Remises de débentures provinciales. Toronto, 1856.
5. Montreal in 1856. A Sketch for the opening of the G.T.R. of Canada. Montreal, 1856.
6. Grand Trunk. Statements, Reports, and Accounts of the. Toronto, 1857.
7. HESELTINE, Edward. Reply to Mr. Watkins, Chairman of the Grand Trunk Railway London, 1863.
8. "Investor." Letter addressed to the Proprietors of the G.T.R. of Canada, 1873.
9. Grand Trunk Railway. Its very latest Scheme. London, 1873.

VOL. 575.
PAMPHLETS ON RAILWAYS.

1. Toronto. Report of the select Committee for the Esplanade. Toronto, 1855.
2. HEWSON, M. Butt. The Grand Trunk Railway of Canada. Toronto, 1876.
3. Grand Trunk Railway. Correspondence between the Great Western and the. London, 1876.
4. ―――――――― Deed for the union of the, and Great Western Railway Company, London, 1882.
5. ―――――――― Its Position and Prospect. London, 1842.
6. HICKSON, J. Letters to Sir John A. Macdonald, and other members of the House of Commons. Montreal, 1884.

7. Toronto. Memorandum re Esplanade Improvements. Toronto, 1883.
8. ———— The Esplanade Difficulty. The disputed Entrance to Harbour of. Toronto, 1880.
9. ———— Report of the Credit Valley Railway Application for Right of Way and Crossings at the City of Ottawa, 1879.
10. ———— The Credit Valley Railway Application and Reports of Railway Managers. Toronto, 1880.
11. Same as N° 8. In French. Ottawa, 1880.

VOL. 576.

CANADIAN RAILWAYS,

1. St. Lawrence and Atlantic Railway. Letter from A. T. Galt to the Chairman of the Northern American Colonial Association. London, 1867.
2. ———————————————— Its position as a private undertaking. Montreal, 1849.
3. BARTON, James L. Commerce of the Lakes and Erie Canal. Buffalo, 1851.
4. KEEFER, Thos. C. Report on survey for Railway Bridge over St. Lawrence at Montreal, Montreal, 1853.
5. Quebec and Saguenay Railway—Report on the survey of. Quebec, 1854.
6. Ontario, Simcoe and Huron Railway—Report of Chief Engineer to the Directors of. Toronto, 1853.
7. Toronto and Owen-Sound Central Route. Engineer's Report on. Toronto, 1857.
8. Ontario, Simcoe and Huron Railway Union Company, Present position of the., Toronto, 1858.
9. Wellington, Grey and Bruce Railway. Prospectus of. Hamilton, 1868.
10. Huron and Ontario Ship Canal—Summary Report on the. Toronto, 1868.

VOL. 577.

CANADIAN RAILWAYS.

1. ALLAN, Sir Hugh. The " Times " and Canadian Railways. London, 1875.
2. Northern Railway Company of Canada; Campbell vs. the. Ottawa, 1880.
3. HOLMES, Hon. S. A. Speech on Railway Consolidation. Halifax, 1832.
4. THOMSON, Wm. Examination of Railway Employés, as to Color Blindness. Philadelphia, 1883.
5. American Railroad Superintendents. Eight meetings of the, in Boston. Chicago, 1884.
6. The Ontario and Quebec Railway. Lease of the,—to the C. P. R. Co. Montreal, 1884.
7. Pontiac Pacific Junction Railway. Acts of Parliament respecting the. Montreal, 1884.
8. ———————————————— Contract and Specification relating to. Montreal, 1884.
9. Toronto, Grey, and Bruce Railway. Lease of, to the Ontario and Quebec Railway Co. Ottawa, 1883.
10. MACFARLANE, James. American Guide. New York, 1885.
11. Quebec Railway and Harbour Works, No. 1. W. Pilkington. Quebec, 1879.
12. Quebec Harbour and Dock Works, No. 2. W. Pilkington. Quebec, 1879.
13. LIGHT, A. L. Report upon the shortest line from Montreal to Halifax, with map. Quebec. 1885.

INDEX.

VOL. 578.
CANADIAN RAILWAYS.

1. Canada Southern Railway. Prospectus, Reports and Documents of the. With map. New York, 1871.
2. GOUDIE, D. R. Perpetual Sleigh Road ; or, From the Atlantic to the Pacific in 40 to 45 hours. Toronto, 1874.
3. LEGGE, Chas. Exploration report from Deep River to Georgian Bay. Montreal, 1874.
4. TATE, J. W. Report on the Toronto and Owen Sound Central Railway Route. With map. Peterborough.
5. SWINYARD, Thomas. Reports on the Prince Edward Island Railway. Ottawa, 1875.

VOL. 579.
CANADIAN RAILWAYS.

1. Saint Lawrence and Atlantic Railway. Report on its influence upon the Trade of the St. Lawrence. Montreal, 1849.
2. Plattsburg and Montreal Railway Co. Counter statement of. Montreal, 1855.
3. Stanstead, Shefford and Chambly Railway Co. Report of Directors. Waterloo, 1857.
4. Millbrook and Peterborough Branch Line Railway. Copies of papers connected with. Peterborough, 1862.
5. Brockville and Ottawa Railway Co. Second annual report of the. Montreal, 1866.
6. ———————————— Third annual report of the. Brockville, 1867.
7. Montreal and Ottawa City Junction Railway. Report of the Survey of. Montreal, 1871.
8. Phillipsburgh, Farnham & Yamaska Railway. Report to the Directors of. St. Hyacinthe, 1872.
9. Portland and Ogdensburg Railway. Sixth annual Report of its President and Directors. Portland, Me., 1875.
10. Toronto and Ottawa Railway. Facts for the consideration of Hon. Members. s.l.n.d.
11. Railway Companies' Authorized Grants. Detailed statements of. Quebec, 1883.
12. Grand Occidental. Remises de droits faites à la Compagnie du. Ottawa, 1875.
13. Northern, North-Western and Sault Ste. Mary Railway Co. An Act to incorporate the. s.l.n.d.
14. Canada Central Railway. Repayment of Pembroke subsidy to. Ottawa, 1883.
15. Grand Trunk Railway Co. Returns of correspondence between the—and the Government of Canada. Ottawa, 1883.

VOL. 580.

1. KEEFER, Thos. C. The philosophy of Railroads. 4th Edition. Montreal, 1853.
2. ——————— Le même en français. Montreal, 1853.
3. ——————— Rapport sur le chemin de fer du St-Laurent et de l'Outaouais. Montréal, 1853.
4. Levis and Kennebec Railway. Prospectus of. Quebec, 1873.
5. ——————————— Its difficulties. By Charles A. Scott. Quebec, 1877.
6. Réfutation de la brochure de C. A. Scott, par L. N. Larochelle. Quebec, 1877.

VOL. 581.

1. Quebec and Saguenay Railway. Report of Survey and By-laws for the Company of. Quebec, 1854.

2. Chemin de fer de Québec au Lac Saint-Jean. Nécessité et possibilité d'un. Par J. C. Langelier. Québec, 1873.
3. ——————————————————.—— Lettre sur. Québec, 1882.
4. Lake St. John and The Great North-East. Soil, Forests and climate of. Quebec, 1883.
5. Quebec and Lake St. John Railway Co. Copies of correspondence between the—and Provincial Government. Quebec, 1879.
6. Chemin de fer de Saint-Laurent, Basses-Laurentides et Saguenay. Rapport de l'exploration du. Trois-Rivières, 1880.
7. Quebec, Montmorency et Charlevoix Railway. Sketch of the Scheme of. Three-Rivers, 1881.
8. Quebec and Lake St. John Railway. Report on the 3rd section of. By Charles Baillairgé. Quebec, 1885.

VOL. 582.
INTERCOLONIAL RAILWAY.

1. Intercolonial Railway. The best Route through the Provinces of Quebec, New Brunswick. Which? By W. M. Buck. St. John, N.B., 1867.
2. ———————— A letter on the. By J. W. Laurence. St. John, N.B., 1867.
3. ———————— Route of the. In a national, commercial and economical point of view. 1867.
4. ———————— Analysis of the Frontier, Central and Bay Chaleurs Routes of. By J. O'Hanley. Ottawa, 1868.
5. ———————— Rapport du major W. Robinson sur la ligne projetée du. Ottawa, 1868.
6. ———————— Rapport sur l'exploration préliminaire du. Par Sandford Fleming. Ottawa, 1868.
7. Observations de M. Wilkinson sur le rapport du major Robinson. Ottawa, 1868.

VOL. 583.
INTERCOLONIAL RAILWAY.

1. Intercolonial Railway. Same as No. 2 Vol. 582.
2. ———————— No. 3. Volume 582.
3. ———————— Appeal to the Privy Council, Senators and Members of the House of Commons on. s. l. n. d.
4. ———————— No. 5. Vol. 582. Ottawa, 1868.
5. ———————— Harbour at Rimouski. Rimouski, 1869.
6. ———————— Description of the Route of. Toronto, 1869.
7. ———————— Rapport des Commissaires du. Ottawa, 1870.
8. ———————— Addenda to the Report of the Commissioners of. Ottawa, 1870.
9. ———————— A Trip over the. By Fred. J. Hamilton. Montreal, 1876.
10. ———————— Embranchement projeté du. Québec, 1882.

VOL. 584.
CAN. PACIFIC RAILWAY.

1. SMYTH, Major R. Carmichael. British Colonial Railway, Communication between the Atlantic and Pacific. Letter to the Author of the "Clockmaker." London, 1849.
2. FLEMING, Sandford. Overland Route to British Columbia. Toronto, 1862.
3. KINGSTON, H. G. The great Highway between Canada and Pacific, 1863.

4. WADDINGTON, Alfred. Overland Route through British America, with Map. London, 1868.
5. FORSTER, John. Railway from Lake Superior to Red River Settlement. Montreal, 1869.
6. Canada Pacific Railway. Exploratory Survey of. Ottawa, 1871.
7. WADDINGTON, Alfred. Overland Railroad. 2nd Ed. of No. 4. Ottawa, 1871.
8. TASSÉ, Joseph. Le chemin de fer Canadien du Pacifique. Montreal, 1872.
9. Pacific Railway Branch. Terminus of the, on North Shore of Lake Superior. Ottawa, 1874.
10. CRAWFORD, Robert. Answer to "The Questions of the Terminus." Collingwood, 1874.
11. MACLEOD, M. Pacific Railway Routes by. Montreal, 1874.
12. The Pacific Railway. Its Eastern Connections. A Speech by Louis Beaubien, M.P.P. Montreal, 1875.
13. ―――――――― Same as above in French. Quebec, 1875.
14. ―――――――― Britannicus' Letters, &c., thereon. By M. McLeod (1869-75). Ottawa, 1875.

VOL. 585.

CAN. PACIFIC RAILWAY.

1. Canadian Railways. Review of Potter's letter on. By C. J. Brydges. Ottawa, 1875.
2. ―――――――― "The Times" and Mr. Potter. By Edward Jenkins, M.P. London, 1875.
3. Canada Pacific Railway. Extra tax for it, not necessary. Ottawa, 1876.
4. ―――――――― Speech on the. By Hon. Dr. Tupper. Ottawa, 1877.
5. ―――――――― Terminus. Prince Arthur's Landing. Toronto, 1878.
6. ―――――――― Brittannicus' letter, &c., thereon. By M. McLeod. Ottawa, 1875.
7. ―――――――― Telegraph Monopoly. Montreal, 1884.
8. ―――――――― By General M. Butt-Hewson. Toronto, 1880.
9. ―――――――― Remarks by Acton Burrows. Ottawa, 1880.
10. ―――――――― Speeches by Sir Charles Tupper, Hon. H. L. Langevin, J. B. Plumb, and Thomas White, M.P. Montreal, 1880.
11. ―――――――― and The North West. Startling Facts!! By C. Horetzky. Ottawa, 1880.

VOL. 586.

CANAD. PAC. RAILWAY.

1. MACLEOD, Malcolm. Problem of Canada. Ottawa, 1880.
2. Sir John and Sir Charles; or the Secrets of the Syndicate. Montreal, 1881.
3. Canada Pacific Railway Terminus. [Reply to "Old Settler," by a British North American. London, 1881.
4. ―――――――― Assaillants. Letter from "Mohawk." London, 1882.
5. ―――――――― Schemes of the Syndicate. By "Diogenes." London, 1882.
6. ―――――――― Annual Statement of the Minister of Railways, for 1883. Montreal, 1883.
7. ―――――――― Sir Charles Tupper's Speech on the. Ottawa, 1882.
8. ―――――――― Annual Statement of the Minister of Railways, for 1884. Ottawa, 1884.
9. ―――――――― Resolutions. Hon. Mr. Blake's Speech on the. Ottawa, 1884.
10. ―――――――― Sessional papers relating to, (1883-84). Ottawa, 1884.

VOL. 587.

CANAD. PAC. RAILWAY.

1. Canada Pacific Railway Co. Lease of the Ontario and Quebec Railway Co, to the. Montreal. 1884.
2. —————— Company's Methods of Financing, &c. Montreal, 1884.
3. —————— Speeches on, by the Hon. Thos, White, M. P. Montreal, 1884.
4. —————— Efforts to secure Portland for its Winter Port. Montreal, 1884.
5. Northern Pacific Railway Co. Statement of Henry Veillard to the Stockholders of. New York, 1884.
6. Canada Pacific Railway. Report of Shareholders (1885). Montreal, 1885.
7. —————— The Syndicate. What is it? Ottawa. s. d.
8. —————— Appeal against the Selkirk Range Pass. By " Philo Veritas." Montreal, 1885.
9. —————— Statement of Affairs to the Shareholders of. Montreal, 1885.
10. —————— Resolutions. Speech of Hon. Mr. Chapleau on. Ottawa. 1885.
11. Grand Trunk Railroad. Letters to Right Hon. Sir John Macdonald and others. By J. Hickson. Toronto, 1884.

VOL. 588.

NORTH SHORE RAILWAY.

1. Chemin de fer de Montréal et By-town. Prospectus du. Montréal, 1853.
2. Chemin de fer de la Rive Nord. Rapport sur les ressources probables du. Québec, 1854.
3. —————— Report on the Survey and Resources of the same. Québec, 1854.
4. —————— Past history, present condition, and future prospects of. By Silas Seymour. Quebec, 1872.
5. —————— Report on location and construction of. By Silas Seymour. Quebec, 1872.
6. —————— Value of the Land Grant of—with appendices. Québec, 1872.

VOL. 589.

NORTH SHORE RAILWAY.

1. North Shore Railway. Statutes referring to. Quebec, 1872.
2. —————— Report to the Directors of. By Silas Seymour. Quebec, 1873.
3. —————— Contracts for construction of. Quebec, 1872.
4. —————— Supplemental contract for construction of. Quebec, 1873.
5. —————— Traffic and Earnings of. By Silas Seymour. Quebec, 1873.
6. —————— Supplemental contract of. Quebec, 1874.

VOL. 590.

NORTH SHORE RAILWAY.

1. —————— Supplementary Report on. Quebec, 1875.
2. —————— Report on Situation of—with appendices. By Silas Seymour. Quebec, 1875.
3. —————— Historical Review of the Government Standard. By Silas Seymour. Quebec, 1875.

4. North Shore Railway. The Chief Engineer (S. Seymour) against the President. Quebec, 1875.
5. ————————— Reply of Chief Engineer (S. Seymour) to the Board of Directors of. Quebec, 1875.
6. ————————— Reasons why the Railway Co. has been unable to complete the road. By Silas Seymour. Quebec, 1875.
7. ————————— Grand Trunk Railway Co's Protest against the Construction of the. Quebec, 1875.
8. ————————— Foundations in deep water. By Silas Seymour. Québec, 1877.
9. ————————— Three letters published in 1876 in refutation of Wm. Light's statements. By Silas Seymour. Quebec, 1877.
10. ————————— Further statement of facts, with a supplement. By Silas Seymour. Quebec, 1877.
11. ————————— A complaint to the Council of the Quebec Bar. By Silas Seymour. Quebec, 1877.

VOL. 591.
NORTH SHORE RAILWAY.

1. Montreal and Bytown Railway Co. Report of the—By M. Loranger. Toronto, 1856.
2. Montreal Northern Colonization Railway. Report on Hochelaga and St. Jerome Section of. Montreal, 1869.
3. ————————————————— Rapport de Chs. Legge et Duncan Macdonald sur. Montréal, 1871.
4. ————————————————— Yea or Nay? s. l. n. d.
5. ————————————————— Visit to St. Jerome. Montreal, 1872.
6. Montreal. Railway interests of the City of Montreal, 1872.
7. Chemin de Colonisation du Nord. Rapport sur le—Par Chs. Legge—avec carte. Montréal, 1872.
8. ————————————— Mémoire à l'appui de la ratification du règlement de Montréal. Montréal, 1872.
9. ————————————— Legge's Report vs. Mr. Mackenzie's Air Line Road. Montreal, 1874.
10. ————————————— Administration de M. L. A. Sénécal—Discours par Chas. Langelier, M.P.P. Québec,
11. ————————————— Discours de M. Chapleau sur la vente du. Québec, 1882
12. ————————————— Discours de M. L. J. Desjardins sur la vente de la partie Ouest du. Québec, 1882.
13. ————————————— Discours de M. Wurtele sur les résolutions concernant le. Québec, 1882.
14. ————————————— Quelques notes sur la vente du. Québec, 1882.
15. JOSEPH REYNAR. Chemin de fer Trois-Rivières et Nord-Ouest. Trois-Rivières, 1885.

VOL. 592.

1. Montreal Colonization Railway. Preliminary Survey from St. Lin to Montreal. Montreal, 1874.
2. ————————————— Bemister's Reports on proposed routes from Montreal Montreal, 1875.

3. Montreal Colonization Railway. Rapport sur les difficultés entre l'ingénieur en chef et l'entrepreneur du—Par Sanford Fleming. Québec, 1875.
4. ―――――――――― Remarks on the "Statement of Facts" of the Eastern Division of the—By A. L. Light, with appendices. Montreal, 1877.
5. ―――――――――― Report on the Rival Routes between Maskinonge and Hochelaga—by Walter Shanly. Quebec, 1878.
6. ―――――――――― Le même, en français. Quebec, 1878.
7. ―――――――――― between Three Rivers and Montreal. Reports of Messrs. A. L. Light, P. A. Peterson and Sannford Fleming on the. Quebec, 1878.
8. ―――――――――― Réponse au rapport de M. P. A. Peterson (1877). Québec, 1878.
9. ―――――――――― Western Division—Six months' report on. Quebec, 1879.
10. ―――――――――― Rapport au sujet de l'affaire Duncan Macdonald—par N. Shanly. Québec, 1879.
11. ―――――――――― Réponse à une Adresse à l'Assemblée Législative concernant le tracé du. Québec, 1880.
12. ―――――――――― Réponse à une Adresse de l'Assemblée Législative au sujet de l'affermage, etc. du. Québec, 1880.
13. ―――――――――― Mortgage Deed of Trust of, To Alfred Brown and Robert Wright. Montreal, 1883.
14. ―――――――――― Correspondence of the Grand Trunk in the matter of the. Montreal, 1884.

VOL 593.
Chemin du Pacifique.

1. Chemin de fer du Pacifique. Discours prononcés au sujet du. Par Sir Charles Tupper, Sir H. L. Langevin et J. B. Plumb. Ottawa, 1880.
2. ―――――――――― Historique de la question du. Par l'hon F. Langelier, M.P. Québec, 1881.
3. ―――――――――― Discours de Sir Charles Tupper et Sir Hector Langevin, sur le. Ottawa, 1881.
4. ―――――――――― Histoire d'un contrat. s. l. 1882.
5. ―――――――――― Correspondance entre la compagnie du Grand-Tronc et le gouvernement au sujet du. Montréal, 1884.
6. ―――――――――― Correspondance entre Sir Hector Langevin et M. L. A. Sénécal. Montréal, 1884.
7. ―――――――――― Discours de Sir Charles Tupper sur les Résolutions du. Ottawa, 1884.
8. ―――――――――― Discours de l'Hon. M. Chapleau sur les Résolutions du. Ottawa, 1885.

VOL 594.
Chemins de Fer.

1. Chemin de Fer du St. Laurent et de l'Outaouais. Rapport sur. Par Thos. C. Keefer. Montréal, 1853.
2. Chemin de Fer de Phillisburg, Farnham et Yamaska. Rapport sur. Par John Foster. St. Hyacinthe, 1872.

3. Chemin de Fer de Colonisation du Nord de Montréal. Rapport de l'exploration à la Baie Georgienne. Montréal, 1874.
4. Les Chemins de Fer. Nos communications avec l'Ouest. Discours de M. Louis Beaubien, M. P. P. Québec, 1875.
5. Chemin de Fer des Cantons du Nord. St. Jérôme, 1884.
6. Chemin de Colonisation du Nord de Montréal. Tracé par St. Eustache. Montréal, 1878.
7. Chemin du Pacifique. Mémoire sur une ligne par le Nord Intérieur. s. l. n. d.
8. ——————— Les Comédies du. (Extrait du " Monde"). 1884.

VOL. 595.

Mines du Canada.

1. Mines d'Or du Bas-Canada. Québec, 1864.
2. Rapport les Terrains Aurifères du Bas-Canada. Québec, 1865.
3. Mines d'Or du Canada. Extraits du Rapport du Commissaire des Terres de la Couronne. Québec, 1865.
4. Chaudière Gold Mines. Report on. Canada, 1863.
5. Gold in Canada. The Chaudière Valley and its Mineral wealth. Quebec, 1880.
6. Acte général des Mines de la Province de Québec. Quebec, 1880.
7. Mines d'Or de la Beauce. Par W. Chapman. Lévis, 1881.
8. Mémoire sur les gisements aurifères du comté de Beauce. Paris, 1882.

VOL. 596.

1. Keefer, Thos. C. L'avenir des Canaux du Canada. (Essai). Toronto, 1850.
2. The St. Maurice Bridges. Sale of--by the Government to T. H. Pacaud, Esq. Montreal, 1853.
3. ——————— Le même, en français. Montréal, 1853.
4. Lacs Supérieur et Huron. Second Rapport sur l'Exploration des. Par le Comte de Rottermund. Toronto, 1857.
5. Legge, Chas. A glance at the Victoria Bridge. Montreal, 1860.
6. Canal de Beauharnois. La question du. Montreal, 1873.
7. Canal des Cèdres. Etude par J. P. Lantier. Ottawa, 1873.
8. Victoria Bridge. Origin of the. . By the Hon. John Young. Montreal, 1876.

VOL. 597.

Tempérance.

1. Chiniquy, le P. Adresse des habitants de Longueuil au. Montréal, 1843.
2. Intempérance. Rapport sur les remèdes aux maux de l'. Montréal, 1849.
3. Tempérance. Annales de la, (janvier et avril 1854). Montréal, 1854.
4. Tempérance et Intempérance. Montreal, 1854.
5. ——————— Second Rapport du Comité Spécial au sujet de la vente des liqueurs. Ottawa, 1873.
6. ——————— Troisième Rapport sur. Ottawa, 1874.
7. Paquin, Rév. L. P. Conférence sur les propriétés délétères des Liqueurs Spiritueuses. Québec, 1879.
8. Abbott, S. A. L'Acool. Voilà l'Ennemi. Montréal, 1883.
9. La prohibition et la compensation. s. l. n. d.

VOL. 598.

1. British Columbia, Gold Fields of. London, 1862.
2. Douglas, Rev. James. The Gold Fields of Canada. Quebec, 1863.
3. Hunt, T. Sterry. Petroleum, its Geological relations and its occurrence in Gaspé. Quebec, 1865.
4. A Geographical, Agricultural and Mineralogical Sketch of Canada. Quebec, 1865.
5. Montreal Apatite Co. Report on the. By Charles Robb. Montreal, 1865.
6. De Léry Gold Mining Co. Statement of the. New York, 1866.
7. Gold Regions of Canada. Explorer's Guide by Henry White. Toronto, 1867.
8. Canadian Phosphates. Report on the. By Gordon Broome. (Part. I). Montreal, 1870.
9. Silver Plume Mining Co. Prosecution against the. Montreal, 1881.
10. Leeds, (P. Q.) Iron Mine. Description of its Ore and its quality. Quebec, 1883.
11. Dobson, G. H. Coal Industry of the Dominion. Ottawa, 1879.
12. Svenkerud, Hans. Guide to Phosphate Miners. Ottawa, 1879.
13. Silver Islet Mine. History of its developement by Thomas Farlane. Montreal, 1879.

VOL. 599.

1. Timber duties. Proposed Reduction of the. London, 1851.
2. Perry, Geo. H. The Staple Trade of Canada. Ottawa, 1862.
3. Commerce de Bois. Rapport sur le. Par Wm. Quinn. Québec 1864.
4. Charlton, John. Objections to export duty on Timber. Lynedock, 1869.
5. Tassé, Joseph. Philemon Wright. Etude. Montreal, 1871.
6. Lumber Trade of the Ottawa Valley, (4th edition.) Montreal, 1871.
7. Wood and Sawdust deposits in the Hudson and Ottawa Rivers. Ottawa, 1873.
8. Ottawa River Sawdust Nuisance. Memorandum by R. J. Wicksteed. Ottawa, 1886.
9. Forest protection. Public Opinion on. New York, 1883.
10. Small, H. B. Canadian Forests and Forest trees. Montreal, 1884.

VOL. 600.
Canad. Canals.

1. Mines and Minerals of Nova Scotia. Report of Chief Commissioner, (for 1868). Halifax, N.S., 1869.
2. ——————————————— Report of Chief Commissioner (for 1869). Halifax, N.S., 1870.
3. ——————————————— Report of Chief Commissioner, (for 1877). Halifax, N.S., 1871.
4. ——————————————— The Cumberland Coal Fields. Report on. By J. Campbell. Halifax, N.S., 1871.
5. Rutherford, John. Coal Fields of Nova Scotia. Newcastle upon Tyne, 1871.
6. Heatherington, A. Mining Industries of Nova Scotia. London, 1874.

VOL. 601.
Canadian Canals.

1. Chambly Canal. Minute Statement of the Works of the. Montreal, 1836.
2. New Castle District Canal. Report upon the navigation of. By N. H. Baird. Belleville, 1855.
3. Georgian Bay Canal. Reports on. By Col. A. B. Mason and K. Tully. Chicago, 1858.

INDEX.

4. Georgian Bay and Lake Ontario Ship Canal. Report on. Quebec, 1864.
5. Lachine Canal. Harbour Improvements at foot of. Report by Charles Legge. Montreal, 1864.
6. Ontario and Erie Ship Canal Co. Charter of the. Niagara, 1869.
7. St. Jérome, (P.Q.) Report on Water Power at. By William Malsburg. Montreal, 1870.
8. Ingersoll, J. H. Answers to questions about Canal Enlargements. St. Catherines, 1871.
9. Beauharnois Canal. The question of the, —By D. Girouard, M. P. Montréal, 1873.
10. Cascade and Coteau-Landing Canal. The question of the,—By J. P. Lantier, M. P. Montreal, 1874.
11. Proposed Baie Verte Canal. Report on. By J. W. Lawrence. St. John, N. B., 1876.

VOL. 602.

PAMP. ON TEMPERANCE.

1. CARPENTER, W. B. Use and Abuse of Alcoholic Liquors. Hamilton, 1852.
2. Sons of Temperance. Proceedings of the Grand division of the,—At annual meeting, Bytown (1854). Kingston, 1854.
3. LINDSAY, Chas. Prohibition Liquor Laws and their operation. Montreal, 1855.
4. EMRA, J. N. The Question of the day. Temperance Lecture. Montreal, 1873.
5. BUCKE, R. M. Alcohol in health and disease. London, Ont., 1880.
6. ANDREW, John A. The Errors of Prohibition. A lecture delivered in Boston, 1867. Boston, 1880.
7. SMITH, Goldwin. An Address on the Scott Act. Toronto. n. d.
8. PATTERSON, George. How to promote Temperance. Hamilton, 1881.
9. WHITE, (M. P) Thomas. Speeches on Dominion License Act. Montreal, 1885.
10. LUCAS, Rev. D. V. A reply to the Anti-Scott Act Address of Mr. Goldwin Smith, Toronto, 1886.
11. Low, George, J. Prohibition. A Sermon. Montreal, 1885.
12. Scott Act. Ought I to vote for the—? 1884.

VOL. 603.

1. Division of the Debts and Assets of Quebec and Ontario. Opinion of the Arbitrators of the Government of Quebec. Montreal, 1870.
2. Partage de la dette entre Québec et Ontario. Correspondance relative au—. Québec, 1870.
3. —————————— Hon. E. B. Wood's Arguments before Arbitrators of the—, with copy of the Award. Toronto, 1870.
4. Quebec Subsidy. Documents relating to the readjustement of the. Quebec, 1883.
5. DESJARDINS, M. L. G. Discours sur les Finances de la Province de Québec. Québec, 1885.

VOL. 604.

1. Courts of Justice. Reports on language of the writs and summons in. Quebec, 1886.
2. PALMER, John. Practice on appeals from the Colonies to the Privy Council. London, 1831.
3. Cour Supérieure de Montréal. Règles de Pratique. s. l. n. d.
4. Justice. Report on administration of. Montreal, 1842.
5. SNELLING, Richard. Land Debentures. Toronto, 1862.
6. McCORD, T. Synopsis of the changes in the Law. Ottawa, 1886.

7. RIMMER, Alfred. The great defect in the law of Evidence. Montreal, 1867.
8. TORRANCE, T. W. Letter on the administration of justice. Montreal, 1873.
9. Harbour Commissioners of Montreal. The Raft Cases. Ottawa, 1873.
10. CAMPBELL vs. The North and North Western Railway Company, in Chancery. Ottawa, 1880.
11. JARVIS, H. M. Statement of the case of. Ottawa, 1880.
12. FORGET, David. Analytical Table of the Municipal Code of the Province of Quebec. Montreal, 1882.
13. ARMSTRONG, Q. C. J. Laws of Intestacy in the Dominion of Canada. Montreal, 1885.

VOL. 605.

1. Registry Ordinance and Proclamations relating thereto. Montreal, 1842.
2. BONNER, John. Essay on the Registry Law of Canada. Quebec, 1852.
3. HERVIEUX, J. A. Analyse des lois d'Enregistrement avec un appendice. Montréal, 1864.
4. L'Enregistrement de la Quittance. Opinion sur la nécessité de. Marie-Ville, 1879.
5. WILLIAM, J. H. Manual of the Criminal Law of Canada. Quebec, 1861.
6. HIBBARD, ASHLEY. Evil of secret Indictment by Grand Juries. Montreal, 1862.
7. WILLIAM, J. H. Improvement of the Criminal Law. Quebec, 1867.
8. GIROUARD, D. Considération sur les lois civiles du mariage. Montréal, 1868.
9. Quebec Advocates' Library. Statutes for the corporation of the. Quebec, 1845.
10. Barreau du Bas-Canada. Assemblée annuelle du. Québec, 1867.
11. Notariat. Admission à l'Etude et à la Pratique du. s.l. 1883.
12. Chambre des Notaires. Rapport et compte-rendu de la. Par F. J. Durand. Montréal 1880.
13. Barreau de Montréal. Rapport sur l'administration de la justice par le comité du. Montréal, 1881.
14. Barreau de la Province de Québec. Rapport du Conseil du—pour l'année 1884-85. Montréal, 1885.

VOL. 606.

1. Navigation between Quebec and St. Catharine's. Survey of the—with a Map. Quebec 1834.
2. Canada. State of Political Parties. Toronto, 1851.
3. River Richelieu. Observations on bridging the. By A. M. Delisle. Toronto, 1851.
4. ——————— and Lake Champlain. Application of the Champlain and St. Lawrence Railroad Co. to bridge the. Toronto, 1851.
5. Ocean Steamers. Establishment of the Line of,—between Liverpool and Canada. Quebec, 1855.
6. Havre de Refuge. Rimouski vs. Bic. Par James Smith. Québec, 1866.
7. ——————— Dissertation sur la question d'un. Par J. B. E. Chamberland. Québec, 1857.
8. Compagnie de navigation d'Yamaska. Premier rapport annuel de la,—(pour 1858). Montréal, 1859.
9. ——————————— de Richelieu. Acte d'incorporation de la. Montréal, 1882.
10. ——————————— de Beauharnois, Chateauguay, et de Huntingdon. Act of Incorporation of the. Montreal, 1866.
11. River St. Lawrence. Hydrology of the Basin of the. By T. E. Blackwell. Montreal, 1874.

VOL. 607.
Canad. Trials.

1. Trial and Acquittal of Robert Randall. By Francis Collins. York, 1825.
2. —— of Alexander McLeod, for murder during the Rebellion of 1837-38. New-York, 1841.
3. ——- of Dr. King, for the murder of his wife. Toronto, 1859.
4. —————— His life, confession and execution. Brighton, 1859.
5. ——- of S. S. Halliday—The Maitland distillery case, by William Coldwell. Toronto, 1866.
6. -—— and Inquest of Mary Boyd, at Lunatic Asylum, Toronto. Toronto, 1868.
7. —— and Defence of Dr. E. B. Sporham—A Medico-Legal Inquiry. Brockville, 1876.

VOL. 608.

1. La Faillite (1864). Etude sur l'Acte de—Par Désiré Girouard. Montréal, 1864.
2. ————— (1869). Tableau des délais fixes—Par E. Lareau. Montréal, 1870.
3. The Silver Question and the Insolvent Act (1869). Montréal, 1870.
4. Insolvent Act (1875). Synopsis and Index of the—By William Wilson. Ottawa, 1875.
5. ——————— (En français). Par C. Beausoleil. Montréal, 1877.
6. Insolvent Act (1875). Reprint of. Toronto, 1875.
7. ——————— Amendments proposed to—by the Toronto Board of Trade. Toronto, 1883.
8. Insolvency Laws. Fallacy and baneful effects of the. Belleville, 1885.
9. Bankruptcy Legislation. Address by E. R. C. Clarkson. Toronto, 1885.
10. Cession de Biens. La Loi de la—Edité par J. Monier. Montréal, 1885.

VOL. 609.
N. B. School Law.

1. Parish School Law in New Brunswick in 1858. Fredericton, 1858.
2. Common Schools of New Brunswick. Report of the Superintendent of the (for 1870). Fredericton, 1870.
3. Ecoles Communes du Nouveau-Brunswick. Réponses au sujet de l'Acte des (1871). Ottawa, 1873.
4. ——————————————— et le Cardinal de Angelis—consultation. Montréal, 1872.
5. ——————————————— Manual of the. Fredericton, 1873.
6. ——————————————— Manual and revised regulations of the (for 1877). Fredericton, 1877.

VOL. 610.
Canad. Fisheries.

1. Canadian Fisheries and the Navigation of the St. Lawrence. Return of all Licenses granted to American Fishermen in 1867-68. Ottawa, 1869.
2. ———————————————————— Review of President Grant's message to U.S. Congress relative to the—By P. Mitchell, M.P. s.l.n.d.
3. ———————————————————— Correspondance entre le Gouvernement du Canada et le Gouvernement Impérial au sujet des. Ottawa, 1871.
4. Traité de Washington. Discours de Sir John A. Macdonald sur le. Ottawa, 1872.
5. ——————————— The same as above in English. Ottawa, 1872.

6. Traité de Washington. Documents du Conseil Privé au sujet du. Ottawa, 1872.
7. ———————— Return of correspondence with the Colonial Office or the United States' Government with regard to the United States' canals in accordance with the. Ottawa, 1876.
8. ———————— Correspondence between the Government of the Dominion and the Government of Prince Edward Island respecting claims to Fishery Award. Ottawa, 1880.
9. ———————— Rights of American fishermen in British North American waters. Message from the President. Washigton, 1886.

VOL. 611.

1. Newfoundland Fishery. Considerations on the. London, 1805.
2. Gaspé District Fishery. A bill for the better regulation of the. Quebec, 1823.
3. New Brunswick Fisheries. Reports on the. By M. H. Perly. Fredericton, 1852.
4. Newfoundland Fishery Question. Report of the Council of the Royal Colonial Institute on the. London, 1875.
5. The Fishery Question. Letters from the New York Herald's special Commissioners. s.l.n.d.
6. Washington Treaty (1872). Balance sheet of the. By Rt. Hon. Viscount Bury, M.P. London, 1873.
7. Newfoundland Fishery Question. Report of the. London, 1875.
8. Treaty of Washington. A review of. By D. Girouard, M.P. Montreal, 1871.
9. Fisheries Exhibition, London, 1883. Canada at the. Ottawa, 1884.
10. The Fisheries of Canada. By L Z. Joncas. Ottawa, 1885.

VOL. 612.
Personal Claims.

1. Case of Lieut. Col Bouchette. Exposition of the, before House of Assembly of Lower Canada. Quebec, 1816.
2. —— of Ryland. Documents relative to. Montreal, 1848.
3. —— of William Power (Circuit Judge). Factum of the. Quebec, 1853.
4. —— of James Reeve, owner of Schooner " Mazeppa," seized by Americans. Chatham C.W., 1854.
5. —— of W. L. Mackenzie, M.P.P. The Mackenzie Homestead. Toronto, 1856.
6. —— of Robert F. Gourly. Statement of the. Speech delivered before the Legislature (1858). Toronto, 1858.
7. —— of Captain T. Wm. Jones. Statement of the, vindication of his character. Toronto, 1859.
8. —— of John George Bowes vs. The City of Toronto. Appeal to the Privy Council. London, 1858.
9. —— of Rev. A. Adamson. Letters and Addresses to. Quebec, 1861.
10. —— of A. Gugy. " How I lost my money." Montreal, 1847.
11. —— of A. Gugy. Une explication. Adresse à mes concitoyens. Québec, 1871.
12. —— of John MacAuley. Letters addressed to the people of Canada. Ottawa, 1871.
13. —— of A. Gugy vs. Brown. Quebec, 1871.

VOL. 613.
PERSONAL CLAIMS.

1. Claim of Edward Quinn against the Government for losses sustained. Quebec, 1858.
2. —— of J. L. Beaudry *vs.* Mayor, &c., of the City of Montreal, before the Privy Council. Montreal, 1857.
3. —— of Hon. Hector Langevin. Jugement dans la contestation de Charlevoix. Québec, 1857.
4. —— of J. H. Smith *vs.* J. B. Smith. Statement of facts relative to. New York, 1857.
5. —— of Wm. Kingsford *vs.* Sir Hector Langevin. Toronto, 1882.

VOL. 614.

1. RAMSAY, T. R. Government Commissions of Inquiry. Montreal, 1863.
2. Imperial Statutes affecting British North America. Ottawa, 1869.
3. GIROUARD, D. The Royal Commission. Montreal, 1863.
4. Prorogation du Parlement, le 13 août 1873. Documents concernant la. Ottawa, 1873.
5. Royal Instructions. Correspondence between the Government of Canada and the Government of the United Kingdom, prior to the 5th of October 1878, upon the subject of the. Ottawa, 1879.
6. Instructions Royales. Privilèges et Préséance du Parlement Fédéral. s. l. n. d.
7. MACDOUGALL, Hon. W. Argument in the Mercer Escheat case. Ottawa, 1871.
8. Great Seal Question. Eleven papers relating to the—1870-77.

VOL. 615.
TRADE AND NAVIGATION.

1. Canadian Trade and Navigation. A Letter on—By Hon. John Young. Montreal, 1855.
2. —— —— —— —— —— —— The same as above, in French. Montreal, 1855.
3. —— —— —— —— —— —— Rival routes from the West to the Ocean and Docks at Montreal - By John Young. Montreal, 1859.
4. —— —— —— —— —— —— Harbour improvements and construction of Docks at Montreal—By John C. Trautwine. Montreal, 1859.
5. —— —— —— —— —— —— Hydraulic Docks at Montreal—By Charles Legge. Montreal, 1861.
6. —— —— —— —— —— —— Harbour of Montreal. Report on improvements of—By R. Forsyth, C.E., with a memorandum on the same subject by Charles Legge, C.E., Montreal, 1861.
7. —— —— —— —— —— —— Improvements at the Foot of Canal—By Charles Legge, C.E., Montreal, 1864.
8. —— —— —— —— —— Deepening of the Ship Channel between Quebec and Montreal—By A. G. Nish. Montreal, 1872.
9. PATTERSON, Wm. J. Two Trade Letters. Montreal, 1876.
10. —— —— —— —— Our trade relations with the West Indies and South America— Another Trade Letter. Montreal, 1876.
11. Harbour of Montreal. Extension of Commissioners Street and the Revetment wall. Montreal, 1876.

VOL. 616.

1. Emigration. An Act for the relief of Indigent sick Emigrants. Quebec, 1823.
2. —— —— —— From Lower Canada to the United States. Report on. Montreal, 1849.

3. Emigration du Canada aux Etats-Unis. Rapport sur l'. Toronto, 1857.
4. U.S. Penitentiaries. Report of Canadian Commissioners on the. Quebec, 1835.
5. JOHN M. GALT, M.D. Asylums for persons of unsound mind. Essays on. Richmond, Va., 1853.
6. TACHE, J. C. Answer to accusations against the Board of Prisons and Hospitals—A letter. Quebec, 1864.
7. FEGIN, A. Observations sur le rapport des Directeurs de l'Asile de Beauport (1872-73). Montreal, 1874.

VOL. 617.

1. Quebec Harbour Commission. A letter from a member of the Board of Trade on the subject of the. Quebec, 1861.
2. —————— Remarks on the—By an observer. Quebec, 1861.
3. —————— Abstracts from the Act providing for the improvement of the. Quebec, 1873.
4. —————— Graving Dock Question—By E. W. Plunket. Montreal, 1874.
5. —————— Proposed improvements in the—By Alexander Sewell. Quebec, 1875.
6. Havre de Québec. Rapports des Commissaires du—pour l'année 1879. Québec, 1880.
7. —————— Address of Jos. Shehyn, M.P.P., before the Board of Trade (1880). Quebec, 1879.
8. Quebec Harbour and Dock Works (the). Quebec, 1880.
9. —————— Commissioners' report for the year 1882. Quebec, 1883.
10. —————— The same as above, in French. Quebec, 1884.
11. —————— Railway vs. Water conrses—a lecture by Jos. Shehyn, M.P.P. Quebec, 1884.

VOL. 618.

1. Navigation du Golfe et du Fleuve St Laurent. Rapport sur la. Québec, 1875.
2. Ocean Mail Steamers and the Northern Route—By Hon. John Young. Montreal, 1877.
3. Halifax Harbour Port. Correspondence and telegrams relating to the. Ottawa, 1881.
4. Steam communication between Prince Edward Island and the mainland. Report relating to. Ottawa, 1883.
5. Navigation of the Hudson Bay. Report on the question of the. Ottawa, 1884.
6. SMITH, William. Lighthouse System of Canada by. Montreal, 1884.
7. Richelieu and Ontario Navigation Co. Report of the Directors and Shareholders of the. Montreal, 1886.
8. ————————————— Consolidation of the Act of Incorporation of the (1857). Montreal, 1886.

VOL. 619.
CAN. SERMONS.

1. SMART, Rev. Wm. Death and Victory—A Sermon. Montreal, 1812.
2. BOSWORTH, Rev. N. The influence of Christianity upon the commercial character. Montreal, 1837.
3. MACCAUL, Rev. John. Love of God and our Neighbour—Toronto, 1840.
4. CRAMP, Dr. J. M. Memoir of the Rev. Wm. Knibb. Montreal, 1846.
5. FISK, Joel. Filial respect—Montreal, 1847.
6. RICHARD, Rev. Matthew. A sermon on the occasion of the death of Rev. Wm. Croscombe, Halifax, N.S, 1859.

7. Lewis, Rt. Rev. Bishop of Ontario. Free Seats in our Churches.—Montreal, 1870.
8. Fuller, Rev. T. B. A sermon preached in Toronto. Toronto, 1872.
9. Presbyterian Union. The question of—By an Elder. Toronto, 1872.
10. White, Jr., Thomas. The Protestant Minority in Quebec—A letter. Montreal, 1876.
11. Ingersoll, Col. R. G. Refutation of—By a Rationalist. Toronto, 1880.
12. "Cyrus the Elamite." The Position—A Thesis. Louisville, 1879.

VOL. 620.

1. Hall, M.D., Arch. Midwifery—with a Sketch of the life of the late A. T. Holmes, M.D. Montreal, 1860.
2. Canadian Medical Association. Code of Ethics of the. s.l. 1868.
3. College of Physicians and Surgeons of Lower Canada. By-laws of the. Montreal, 1871.
4. Osler, Wm., M.D. Lecture on the opening of the McGill Medical Faculty. Montreal, 1877.
5. Howard, Henry, M.D. Hysterical Mania. Montreal, 1878.
6. Prevost, L. C., M.D. The use of Alcohol in Pneumonia. Ottawa, 1880.
7. Nichol, Thomas, M.D. Diphtheria and its management, by. Montreal, 1884.
8. ———————— Small Pox and its preventive. Montreal, 1885.
9. The "Anti Vaccinator." Montreal, 1886.

VOL. 621.
Boundaries.

1. Canada and New Brunswick Boundary. Toronto "Globe," 1851.
2. Yule, Major P. Remarks on the disputed Boundary between New Brunswick and Maine. London, 1838.
3. Commission of Expertise. Disputed Boundary between New Brunswick and Quebec. Ottawa, 1880.
4. Kewaydin, Province of. Report upon the boundaries of the adjoining Province of Ontario—with map by N. Sanson d'Abbeville. Winnipeg, 1884.
5. Hincks, Sir Francis. The Northerly and Westerly boundary of Ontario. Toronto, 1881.
6. Farnham, Thomas J. Oregon Territory and the United States' title to it. New York, 1844.

VOL. 622.

1. Hincks, Hon. Francis. His different views on the commercial Policy of Canada. Montreal, 1883.
2. MacLean, John. Protection and Free Trade, by. Montreal, 1867.
3. Beausoleil, C. La nécessité d'une réforme du Tarif. Montréal, 1871.
4. MacKelcan, F. F. Labour and Capital. Montreal, 1872.
5. Langelier, J. C. Revision of the Canadian Tariff. Montreal, 1872.
6. The Comedy of Trade—By a "Spiritual Medium." Montreal, 1876.
7. Mousseau, J. A. Protection et Libre-Echange. Montréal, 1876.
8. Colby, C. C. Speech on Tariff revision in the House of Commons. Ottawa, 1878.
9. Protection (la) combattue et refusée par le Gouvernement Libéral. Extrait du "Courrier de St. Hyacinthe."
10. Free Trade and Protection. Political facts for the consideration of the Freeholders of Canada. s. l. n. d.
11. Charlton, John, M.P. Speech on the Question of Protection. Ottawa, 1878.

12. Protection et Libre-Echange. **Montréal, 1879.**
13. White, Thomas. Speeches on Dominion Finances and the National Policy. Montreal, 1883.

VOL. 623.

1. Laflèche, Mgr. L. R. Discours à l'occasion des Cérémonies funèbres en l'honneur des soldats pontificaux. Trois-Rivières, 1861.
2. Rameau, E. Situation religieuse de l'Amérique Anglaise. Paris, 1866.
3. Zouaves Pontificaux. Démonstration à Montréal à l'occasion de leur départ pour Rome. Montréal, 1868.
4. Dupanloup, Mgr. Lettre sur le futur Concile Œcuménique. Québec, 1868.
5. Colin, (S. S.) le P. Le Pape Honorius. Réponse au Révérend Père Gratry. Montréal, 1870.
6. ——————— Les Zouaves Pontificaux Canadiens à leurs compagnons de France Montréal, 1871.
7. Raymond, Rév. M. Action de Marie dans la Société. Discours par. Québec, 1873.
8. Provancher, l'Abbé, L. Le Mois de Marie des familles. Québec, 1877.
9. Guerard, J. La France Canadienne. Extrait. Paris, 1877.
10. Paquin, Rév. L. P. La Souveraineté Temporelle du Pape. Montréal, 1878.

VOL. 624.

1. Expressions vicieuses. Anglicismes. Recueil des. Québec, 1860.
2. ——————— Manuel des. Par J. F. Gingras. Ottawa, 1880.
3. Manseau, J. M. Dictionnaire des locutions mauvaises du Canada. Québec, 1881.
4. Pennée, Mrs. G. M. Guide to French Genders. Quebec, 1871.
5. Langue Française. Le sons et les articulations de l'. Québec, 1874.
6. Tardivel, J. P. L'Anglicisme. Voilà l'ennemi. Québec, 1880.
7. Tremblay, L. H. The pronunciation of the French Language. Quebec, 1881.

VOL. 625.

1. Strossmayer, Mgr. Discours sur l'Infaillibilité. Montréal, 1872.
2. Souvenir. Beaudry, C. M. J. Montréal, 1872.
3. Grandin, Mgr. Lettre au sujet des Sauvages du Nord-Ouest.
4. Desmazures, S. S. l'abbé. M. E. Picard, prêtre de Saint-Sulpice. Montréal, 1886.
5. Martin, (Le P.) Notice biographique. s. l. n. d.
6. Racine, Mgr. A. Une autre Magdeleine au Bon-Pasteur de Québec. Sherbrooke, 1886.
7. L'investiture du *Pallium* à Mgr. Duhamel. Ottawa, 1886.
8. Cercles agricoles. Premier congrès. Montréal, 1887.
9. Barnard, Ed. A. Le desséchement des terres. Montréal, 1887.
10. Beaugrand, H. De Montréal à Victoria. (Conférence.) Montréal, 1887.
11. Héron, M. A. La perte du Canada. Rouen, 1887.
12. De Celles, A. D. La crise du régime parlementaire. Montréal, 1887.
13. Chauveau, M. Le *Dies iræ*, traduction en vers français. Montréal, 1887.

AMERICAN PAMPHLETS.

VOL. 265.

1. HAWLEY, Chs. Early chapters of Cayuga History, with an Introduction, by J. G. Shea. Auburn, N.Y., 1879.
2. MARSHALL, O. H. The first visit of De la Salle to the Senecas (1669). Buffalo, 1874.
3. DE PEYSTER, J. W. The Bourgoyne Campaign (1777). Philadelphia, 1883.
4. DAVIS, A. Antiquities of Central America, and the Discovery of New England by the North Men, five hundred years before Columbus. Boston, 1842.
5. Du Luth (City), Lake Superior and Mississipi R. R. St. Paul, 1869.
6. SANBORN, J. W. Legends, Customs, and Social Life of the Seneca Indians. Gowanda, N. Y., 1878.
7. HULBURT, H. H. Father Marquette at Mackinaw and Chicago. Chicago, 1878.
8. SHEA, J. G. Bibliography of Hennepin's Works. New York, 1880.
9. WELSH, II. Visit to the Great Sioux Reserve, Dakota, in 1883. Indian Rights Association. Philadelphia, 1883.
10. DE PEYSTER, J. W. Address before the Historical Society of New Brunswick. New York, 1883.
11. ———————— Suworrow. Philadelphia, 1883.
12. GATES, Gen. H. A plea in behalf of, *versus* Burgoyne, with a Rejoiner by J. Watts De Peyster. Saratoga, 1883.

VOL. 266.

1. HILL, H. A. The Detroit Commercial Convention of 1865. An Address. Boston, 1886.
2. HULBURT, H. II. Father Marquette at Mackinaw. Chicago, 1878.
3. MASON, T. B. M. The War between Chile, Peru and Bolivia in 1879-81. Washington, 1886.
4. Indian Tribes. Linguistic families of the—north of Mexico. s. l. n. d.
5. HODGE, W. Early Navigation on the Great Lakes. Buffalo, 1883.
6. MORRIL, Hon. J. S. Unveiling of the Portrait of—at Cornell University. Ithica, N.Y., 1844.
7. Philadelphia. On the Erection of the Public Buildings of. Philadelphia, 1885.
8. SMITH, Wm. H. Charles Hammond and the contest for freedom of Speech. Chicago, 1885.
9. GOULD, Dr. Benj. Apthorp. Addresses at the complimentary dinner to. Boston, 1885.
10. Merchants and Manufacturers' Association. Addresses at the Annual Meeting, Jan. 13, 1886. Baltimore, 1886.

VOL. 267.

1. America known to the Northmen. An Essay by an American Englishman (Sam. Mather) Boston, 1773.
2. DAVIS, A. Discovery of New England by the Northmen. A lecture. Boston, 1844.
3. Slavery in the United State. Its evils, alleviations, and remedies. *Reprint from the N. American Review.* Boston, 1851.
4. WARD, Hon. H. Reconstruction. A Speech delivered in Congress (1866).
5. SUMNER. Hon. Chs. Disfranchisement on account of Color. Speech in the Senate of the United States. Washington, 1866.
6. CAREY, H. C. Letters to Hon. Henry Wilson on Reconstruction. Philadelphia, 1867.
7. Report of the Joint Committee of the two Houses of Congress U. S. on Reconstruction. Washington, 1866.
8. CHANLER, Hon. J. W. Down with the Black Flag of Confiscation. Speech in House of Representatives. Washington, 1867.

INDEX.

9. WALKER, R. J. Letter on the purchase of Alaska. Washington, 1868.
10. SUMNER, Hon. Chs. Speech on the Annexation of the "Island of St. Domingo." Washington, 1871.
11. —————— Speech on the "St. Domingo Resolutions." Washington, 1871.
12. MUNGEN, Hon. W. Foreign policy of the Government as regards Russia. Speech in U. S. Congress (1871). Washington, 1871.
13. DELANO, C. Remarks on the Policy of the Government. Washington, 1871.
14. STEVENSON, Hon. J. E. Speech on the Ku-Klux-Klan, in the House of Representatives, Washington, 1871.
15. BINGHAM, J. A. The Laws of the U. S., and the Rights of the people. Speech in U. S. Congress. Washington, 1871.
16. MITCHELL, Hon. P. Review of President Grant's Message on the Canadian Fisheries and the navigation of the St. Lawrence. Ottawa, 1870.

VOL. 268.

1. SUMNER, Hon. Chs. Speech on the occasion of the Cession of Russian America. Washington, 1867.
2. CURTIS, Geo. Ticknor. The last years of Daniel Webster. New York, 1878.
3. HILL, H. A. Commercial Conventions. An Address. Boston, 1885.
4. HILL, Rev. G. M. A sermon commemorative of the Rev. N. Pettit. Trenton, 1885.
5. —————— A sermon on the occasion of the opening of St. Paul's Cathedral, Syracuse N. Y. Trenton, 1885.
6. The Ramsay Pioneer Association. Its Constitution, etc., etc. St. Paul, Min. 1886.
7. WILLIAM, J. F. Reminiscences of St. Paul's Lodge No. 2, I. O. O. F. An Address. St. Paul, Min., 1886.
8. Bostonian Society. Proceedings at the Annual Meeting of the. Boston, 1886.
9. Report of Commissioners for the erection of the Public Buildings to Hon. W. B. Smith, Mayor of Philadelphia. Philadelphia, 1886.
10. Bar Association of the State of Kansas. Annual Meeting of the—at Topeka. Topeka, Kan., 1886.
11. WINSOR, Justin. Arnold's Expedition against Quebec. Cambrige, Mass., 1886.

VOL. 269.

1. TOWNSHEND, Lord. An Essay on the Character and Conduct of. s. l., 1871.
2. CLINTON, Lieut. Gen. Sir Henry. Letters addressed to the Commissioners of Public Accounts. London, 1874.
3. —————— Authentic Copies of letters sent to Commissioners of Public Accounts. London, 1793.
4. DICKSON, Wm. Hints on the Present Important Crisis. Edinburgh, 1803.
5. Message of President of U. S. to Congress (1809). Washington, 1809.
6. Treaties between Great Britain and the United States (1783-1814). Troy, 1815.
7. Message from the President of the U. S., regarding the capture and destruction of the steamboat "Caroline" (1837). Washington, 1838.

VOL. 270.

1. THOMPSON, Z. Natural History of Vermont. Burlington, 1850.
2. YOUNG, Aug. Report on the Natural History of Vermont. Burlington, 1856.

3. WHITEMAN, James. An Inquiry into the Right of visit or Approach by a Ship of War. New York, 1858.
4. GREELY, H. The Tariff Question. Protection and Free Trade considered. New York. s. d.
5. The United States Internal Revenue and Tariff Law compiled by Horace E. Dresser. New York, 1870.
6. RUGGLES, Samuel, B. Agricultural Property and Products of the United States (1840-70). New York, 1874.
7. SWANK, Jas. M. The American Iron Trade. Philadelphia, 1876.
8. WURTELE, Arth. S. C. Standard Measures of U. S. Great Britain, and France. New York, 1882.

VOL 271.

1. BURR, Aaron. An examination of charges preferred against—and the views of his political Opponents. By " Aristides." Philadelphia, 1803.
2. DE PEYSTER, Fred. The early political History of New York. New York, 1864.
3. CORDNER, Rev. J. The American Conflict. An Address. Montreal, 1865.
4. Catholic Union Circle of New York. Constitution of. New York, 1871.
5. HALIBURTON, R. G. American Legislation and the decline of the U. S. as a Maritime Power. London, 1872.
6. WARD, Hon. El. Commercial relations with the Dominion of Canada. Washington, 1876.
7. BUTLER, James D. Portraits of Columbus. Madison, Wis., 1883.
8. Proceedings of the Modern Language Association of America (1884). Baltimore, 1885.
9. ELLIOTT, A. M. The Nahualt Spanish Dialect Nicaragua. s. l. n. d.
10. ARNOLD, Ben. Regimental Memorandum Book of—at Ticonderoga. Philadelphia, 1881.
11. COLMAN, (Hon. N. J.) and SALMON, Dr. D. E. Address on the subjects of American Beef Supply and the Contagious Diseases of Animals (1885). Washington, 1885.
12. FIELD, David D. Nomenclature of Cities and Towns in the United States—A lecture. New York, 1885.
13. GILMAN, D. C. The benefits which Society derives from Universities—An Address. Baltimore, 1885.

BROCHURES FRANCAISES.

VOL. 7.

1. BARBIÉ DU BOCAGE, M. Essai sur les théories commerciales. Paris, 1883.
2. MAUDUIT, Léon. La vigne et le vin pour tous. Paris, 1882.
3. DUJARDIN-BEAUMETZ, le Dr. Le lavage et le gavage de l'estomac. Paris, 1883.
4. THOMAS, Albert. Manuel de l'alcoométrie. Lille, 1882.
5. AUMALE, Discours de M. le duc d'—à l'Académie Française. Paris, 1881.
6. La question Algérienne, à propos de la lettre de l'empereur au maréchal de MacMahon. Paris, 1866.
7. BRELAY, Ernest. Les associations populaires de consommation et de crédit mutuel en 1882. Paris, 1893.
8. QUANTIN, Max. Les ducs de Bourgogne, comtes de Flandre. (1384-1477). Paris, 1882.
9. LUCAS, Charles. Les temples et les églises circulaires en Angleterre. Paris, 1871.
10. NICOLAY, Fernand. Le divorce, son histoire, ses périls. Quatrième édition. Paris. s.d.
11. BILLIART, Norbert. La royauté sans le roi. Paris, 1883.
12. CUMONT, le vicomte Arthur de. Les Incurables. Angers, 1883.

VOL. 9.

1. Kurth, Godefroid. Caton l'Ancien—Etude biographique. Bruges, 1872.
2. Decoster, Vital. Des antécédents du Néoplatonisme—Mémoire couronné. Bruxelles, 1872.
3. Kleyer, C. Des obligations divisibles et indivisibles—Mémoire couronné. Bruxelles, 1873.
4. Maury, Alfred. Rapport sur les archives nationales, pour les années 1876 et 1877. Paris, 1878.
5. La Biblioteca Leopardiana in Recanati. Recanati, 1882.

VOL. 10.

1. Comettant, Oscar. Le naufrage de l'*Evening Star*, et la colère céleste en Amérique. Paris, 1866.
2. Rouquette, l'abbé G. "Père Hyacinthe, vous vous êtes trompé." Paris, 1869.
3. Alleau, Th. Le roi ; couronnement de Jésus-Christ. Paris, 1881.
4. Gravier, Gabriel. Baptistère et Bain liturgique d'Angers. Rouen, 1881.
5. ————— Rapport sur le prix La Reinty. Rouen, 1883.
6. Renan, Ernest. Qu'est-ce qu'une nation?—Conférence. Deuxième édition. Paris, 1882.
7. ————— Le Judaïsme et le Christianisme—Conférence. Paris, 1883.
8. Congrès de Jurisconsultes catholiques tenu à Reims, en octobre 1882 Compte-rendu. Grenoble, 1883.

VOL. 11.

1. Cassagnac, A. Granier de. Récit des événements de décembre 1851, à Paris et dans les départements. Paris, 1851.
2. Genevay, A. Qu'est-ce que la Maçonnerie?—Lettre à Monsieur Viennet. Paris, 1867.
3. Pelletan, Eugène. Adresse au roi Coton. New-York, 1863.
4. Le Faure, Amédée. L'Ordre. Paris, 1871.
5. Richard, H. L'Arbitrage—Discours à la Chambre des Communes d'Angleterre. Paris, 1873.
6. Grand, S. L'industrie huîtrière à Marennes. Paris, 1882.
7. Moerman, Théophile. Notice sur l'électro-métallurgie. Bruxelles, 1882.
8. Constant, Charles. De l'exécution des jugements étrangers dans les divers pays—Etude. Paris, 1883.
9. Say, Léon. La politique financière de la France. Paris, 1882.
10. Laquière, E. M. Loi des Hasards, appliquée aux sciences expérimentales. Paris, 1882.
11. Muston, M. le docteur. Notices géologiques, avec carte. Montbéliard, 1881.

VOL. 12.

1. Guilmin, A. Petit traité de l'Assurance sur la vie. 2e édition. Paris. s.d.
2. Strauss, Louis. Les Dollars ou les valeurs américaines. Bruxelles, 1866.
3. Parigot, J. M.D. Des asiles d'aliénés au point de vue moral et économique. Genève, 1873.
4. Bourgoint-Lagrange. Bons hypothécaires affectés aux emprunts de l'Etat. Deuxième édition. Bordeaux, 1873.
5. Magnat, M. L'enseignement du premier âge. (Méthode Péreire appliquée à.) Paris, 1876.
6. Lemonnyer, J. Les journaux de Paris pendant la Commune. Paris, 1871.

7. Sainte-Marie, E. de. L'Herzégovine, etude géographique, historique et statistique. Paris, 1875.
8. Folleville, Daniel de. Du paiement du prix par l'acheteur en matière de vente. Paris, 1875.

VOL. 13.

1. Gaume, Mgr. Pie IX et les études classiques. Paris, 1874.
2. Montalembert, M. de. Rapport sur l'observation des dimanches et jours fériés. Paris, 1850.
3. Pététot, L. Post-Scriptum sur Honorius. Paris, 1870.
4. Azais, L'abbé. Missions d'Orient. Rapport sur l'état actuel de l'orphelinat de Bethléem. Rouen, 1869.
5. Guéranger, Le R. P. Dom Prosper. De la définition de l'infaillibilité papale. Paris, 1870.
6. Question de for intérieur relative à une loi de for extérieur. Paris, 1874.
7. Dupanloup, Mgr. Etude sur la Franc-Maçonnerie. Paris, 1875.

VOL. 14.

1. Ni paix ni sécurité pour l'Europe avec la Russie telle qu'elle est. Par A. W.... Paris, 1855.
2. Hamel, M. le comte du. L'Angleterre, la France et la guerre. Paris, 1860.
3. Veuillot, Louis. Le guêpier italien. Paris, 1865.
4. Nux, Eméric de. Rome ou Malte. Paris, 1866.
5. Rome visitée par un Catholique. Paris, 1868.
6. Dupanloup, Mgr. Lettre à M. Minghetti sur la spoliation de l'église à Rome et en Italie. Sixième édition. Paris, 1874.
7. Pradier-Fodéré, M. P. La question de l'*Alabama* et le Droit des Gens. Paris, 1872.
8. Curci, C. M. Considérations sur l'Internationale : trad. du comte de Saint-Aymour. Paris, 1872.

VOL. 15.

1. Villefranche, M. Histoire des dix-neuf martyrs de Gorcum (en Hollande), 1572. Paris, 1865.
2. Margerie, Amédée de. Les Fausses Décrétales et les Pères de l'Eglise. Paris, 1870.
3. ――――― Le pape Honorius et le bréviaire romain. Quatrième édition. Paris, 1870.
4. ――――― Réponse à Mgr Héfélé, pour faire suite aux lettres du R. P. Gratry. Paris, 1870.
5. ――――― Quatrième lettre au R. P. Gratry. Paris, 1870.
6. Dechamps, Mgr. La Franc-Maçonnerie. Deuxième édition. Paris, 1874.

VOL. 16.

1. Cieszkowski, Auguste. Moyens d'améliorer le sort de la population des campagnes (Discours.) Paris, 1846.
2. Penilleau, Le Dr A. Etude sur le café. Paris, 1864.
3. Audiganne, A. La nouvelle loi sur le travail des enfants. Paris, 1874.
4. Dupanloup, Mgr. L'Instruction primaire en Prusse. Paris, 1872.
5. Malarce, A. de. Les caisses d'épargne en Angleterre et en France, après la guerre Paris, 1872.

6. Beaulieu, Ad. le Hardy de. La Question monétaire. Paris, 1874.
7. Laveleye, Emile de. Leçon de Droit public à l'Université de Louvain. Paris, 1874.
8. Benoit, A. et M. Le Crédit légal. Marseille, 1876.
9. Vainberg, S. Le cours forcé des billets de banque, et ses conséquences juridiques. Paris, 1874.
10. La Question monétaire. Bruxelles, 1874.
11. Chevalier, Michel. Adam Smith et la fondation de la science économique. Paris, 1874.
12. Douzième congrès des fabricants de papier de France. Paris, 1876.

VOL. 17.

1. Paix ou Guerre. Aix-les-Bains, 1870.
2. Régnier. Une étrange histoire dévoilée : incident Bourbaki. Bruxelles, 1870.
3. Ni Président, ni Roi. Paris, 1871.
4. Paris ou Versailles capitale de la France ? Paris, 1871.
5. Voir le No 4 du vol. 11.
6. La capitulation de Metz : enquête sur la trahison de Bazaine et de Coffinières. Bruxelles, 1871.
7. La trahison du maréchal Bazaine antérieure à la capitulation de Metz. Bruxelles, 1871.
8. Chambord, Le comte de. Mes idées. Paris, 1872.
9. Regnault, H. République, Empire ou Monarchie ? Paris, 1872.
10. Newmarok, Alfred. Les milliards de la guerre. Paris, 1874.
11. L'Urgence. I. Le Bonapartisme. Le République. Le Septennat. II. Les impossibilités de la Royauté. 2e édition. Paris, 1884.
12. Saint-Genest. J'y suis, j'y reste. Paris, 1875.

VOL. 18.

1. Roques, Edouard, M. D. Traitement de la coqueluche par les émanations des usines à gaz. Paris, 1866.
2. Hamel, L., M. D. Du rash variolique. Paris, 1870.
3. Revilliod, le Dr. Etude sur la variole. Genève, 1872.
4. La variole et la vaccine. Conférence de médecins de Paris. Paris, 1872.
5. Rey, le Dr H. Les maladies transmissibles et sujettes à quarantaine. Paris, 1874.

VOL. 19.

1. Le Pape et le Congrès. Paris, 1859.
2. Gams, le R. P. Année du martyre des saints apôtres Pierre et Paul. Paris, 1867.
3. Le Pape et le Congrès, par l'évêque d'Arras. Paris, 1860.
4. Gerbet, Mgr. De la Papauté. Paris, 1860.
5. La lutte religieuse en Allemagne, par P. F. Paris, 1876.
6. Villemain. La France, l'Empire et la Papauté. Paris, 1860.
7. Martin, l'Abbé P. Le Ritualisme en Angleterre. Paris, 1874.
8. Pélage, l'Abbé. Le Concile Œcuménique et la civilisation moderne. Paris, 1869.

CANADIAN MILITIA.

VOL. 1.

1. Military Excursion of the Montreal Volunteer Militia Rifles to Portland in 1861. Montreal, 1858.
2. Colonial Defences in 1859. Report on. By Imperial Commissioners and a Committee of the House of Commons in 1861. Quebec, 1862.
3. Lysons, Col. D. Parting words on the rejected Militia Bill. Quebec, 1862.
4. Cartwright, R. J. Remarks on the Militia Bill of Canada. Kingston, 1864.
5. Howit, Dr. An Address on the formation of Rifle Associations. Guelph, 1886.
6. Armed Strength of Canada. Observations on the. s. l. n. d.
7. Défenses militaires coloniales. Correspondance entre le Gouvernement Impérial et celui de la Puissance. Ottawa, 1868.
8. Colonial Fortifications and Defences. Correspondance with Her Majesty's Government on the subject of. Ottawa, 1869.
9. Thoughts on Defence from a Canadian point of view. By a Canadian.
10. Smith, Major. Records of the Sixty-ninth Regiment. Quebec, 1870.
11. Davis, Lieut. Col. The Canadian Militia. Caledonia, Ont., 1873.
12. Militiamen of 1812-15. Name, age and residence of. Ottawa, 1876.
13. Canada. As a Military Power. London, 1875.
14. Colomb, Capt. J. R. C. The Naval and Military resources of the Colonies. London, 1879.

VOL. 2.

1. Bacon, Lt. Col. Thomas. Military Review on the Queen's birth day at Montreal in 1879. Montreal, 1879.
2. Royal Military College (of Canada). General regulations. Ottawa, 1862.
3. ——————————————— Syllabus course of Instruction. Kingston, 1885.
4. ——————————————— Artillery practice for the Cadets of the. By Lt. Col. Fairtlough. Kingston, 1877.
5. Oswald, Lt. Col. W. R. Historical Sketch of the Canadian Militia. Montreal, 1886.

HUDSON'S BAY PAMPHLETS.

1. Roche, A. A. A View of Russian America. Montreal, 1855.
2. Kernaghan, W. Hudson's Bay's Territory with Routes to the Red River. London, 1857.
3. Hudson's Bay Company. Monopoly of the. Liverpool, 1858.
4. ——————————— The case of the. By And. Freeport. London, 1857.
5. ——————— Territory. Memorial of Hon. Labouchère on the. s. l. n. d.
6. Synge, Capt. M. H. The Colony of Rupert's Land. England's Interest in it, and the Hudson's Bay Co's Pretension. London, 1863.
7. The Hudson's Bay Co. What is it? London, 1864.
8. ——————————— A few words on the. With a Statement of the Grievances of the Half-Caste Indians. London, s. d.
9. ——————————— Canada West and the Indian Tribes. s. l. n. d.
10. ——————————— Route. Lecture by E. P. Leacock. s. l. n. d.
11. ——————————— Adventures to the. By Rev. Mr. Bryce. London. s. d.
12. The Hudson's Bay Company. The Oregon Treaty and the. s. l. 1869.

NORTH WEST TERRITORIES (1857-69) PAMPHLETS.

1. Hudson's Bay Co. Reports on the Rights of the. With a Sketch of the Soil and Climate. s. l. 1857.
2. ———————— Copies of Charters and Leases of the. Toronto, 1859.
3. North West Transportation and Land Co. Prospectus of the. Toronto, 1858.
4. Memorial du Peuple de la Rivière Rouge aux Gouvernements Anglais et Canadiens. Quebec, 1863.
5. Territoire du N:-O. Rapport sur l'acquisition du. Ottawa, 1869.
6. ——— ·———·—— Rapport du Comité Spécial du Sénat sur le. Ottawa, 1870.
7. ——— ·———·—— Copies des Instructions et Documents relatifs à l'arpentage du. Ottawa, 1870.
8. ——————·—— Documents relatifs aux événements de 1869 dans le. Ottawa, 1870.
9. Red River Expedition of 1870. Report on the. By S. C. Dawson. Ottawa, 1871.
10. North-West Territories. Statements of Claims made in the Dominion Government, consequent upon the Insurrection in the. Ottawa, 1871.

… INDEX.

SELECTED ESSAYS.

A SERIES OF ESSAYS AND REVIEWS FROM LEADING PERIODICALS.

VOL. I.
ECONOMIC QUESTIONS.

1. Fair Trade Fog and Fallacy—GEORGE W. MEDLEY.
2. Schools as Prisons and Prisons as Schools—NORTON.
3. Our Great Competitor—JAMES KEITH.
4. Progress of thrift among the Children—AGNES LAMBERT.
5. The Working of School Banks—H. WHITEHEAD.
6. The Iron and Steel Trade—LOWTHIAN BELL.
7. The State of Our Trade—GEORGE HOWELL.
8. Small Farms—WANTAGE.
9. Wealth and the Working Classes—W. H. MALLOCK.
10. The Case for Free Education—E. N. BUXTON.
11. The British Army, Past and Present—JOHN ADYE, General.
12. Fluctuations in Trade and Wages—GEORGE HOWELL.
13. Wealth and the Working Classes (Part II)—W. H. MALLOCK.
14. Victorian Literature—EDWARD DOWDEN.
15. The Progress of Science from 1836 to 1886—GRANT ALLEN.
16. The Progress of Thought in Our Time—JOHN ADDINGTON SYMONDS.
17. English Music during the Queen's Reign—FRANCIS HUEFFER.
18. The Material Growth of the United Kingdom from 1836 to 1886—LEONE LEVI.
19. Fifty Years of Colonial Development—GEORGE BADEN-POWELL.
20. In Parliament—BY A GLADSTONIAN M.P.
21. The Growth of Co-operation in England—GEORGE JACOB HOLYOAKE.
22. Wealth and the Working Classes (Part III)—W. H. MALLOCK.
23. The Material Progress of Ireland—LEONE LEVI.
24. Trade Unions—TRADE UNIONIST.
25. Wealth and the Working Classes (Part IV)—W. H. MALLOCK.
26. Wealth and Ability—H. M. HYNDMAN.
27. The Sweating System—DAVID F. SCHLOSS.
28. Our National Expenditure—LEONE LEVI.
29. Railway Rates—CHARLES T. D. ACLAND.
30. Remedies for Fluctuations of General Prices—ALFRED MARSHALL.
31. Commercial Museums—K. B. MURRAY.
32. Prohibition in the United States—AXEL. GUSTAFSON.
33. The Great Depression of Trade (Parts I and II)—DAVID A. WELLS.
34. Africa and the Drink Trade—F. W. FARRAR.
35. Fall of Prices (Parts I and II)—DAVID A. WELLS.

36. Bimetallism—DAVID A. WELLS.
37. Schools of Commerce — PHILIP MAGNUS.
38. Cobden's Dream—H. R. FARQUARSON·
39. Our Railway System—L. L. DILLWYN.
40. Our Railway System "State Control"—S. LANG.
41. The Railway Problem (Part II)—JOSEPH PARSLOE.
42. State Purchase of Railways—CHARLES WARING.
43. Railway Traffic and Chorles—ERNEST MOON.
44. State Purchase of Irish Railways—CHARLES WARING.

VOL. 2.

IRISH QUESTIONS.

1. Government of Ireland—JOHN MORLEY.
2. Notes and Queries on the Irish Demand—W. E. GLADSTONE.
3. Mr. Gladstone on "The Irish Demand"—BRABOURNE.
4. The Liberal Unionists and Coercion—COWPER.
5. Up to Easter—MATTHEW ARNOLD.
6. American opinion on the Irish Question—E. L. GODKIN.
7. Ingram's History of the Irish Union—W. E. GLADSTONE.
8. Mr. Gladstone and the Irish Union—T. DUNBAR INGRAM.
9. Irish Land Purchase—H. O. ARNOLD-FOSTER.
10. Ireland Beyond the Pale—ARTHUR D. HAYTER.
11. "A Model Land Law"—ARGYLL.
12. Is a National Party Possible?—R. B. HALDANE.
13. Jubilee Time in Ireland—T. M. HEALY.
14. Ireland, 1782 and 1887—EDMUND FITZ-MAURICE.
15. Home Rule and Imperial Unity—THRING.
16. How we became Home Rulers—JAS. BRYCE.
17. The Liberal Party and Home Rule—R. W. DALE.
18. Ireland's Alternatives—THRING.
19. Experiences of an Irish Landowner—MABEL SHERIDAN CRAWFORD.
20. A Fair Constitution for Ireland—C. GAVIN DUFFY.
21. Ulster—R. T. REID.
22. The Position of the Liberal Unionists—SELBORNE.

VOL. 3.

POLITICAL AND PARLIAMENTARY QUESTIONS.

1. "Locksley Hall" and the Jubilee—W. E. GLADSTONE.
2. The Zenith Conservatism—MATTHEW ARNOLD.
3. Lecky's History of England in the 18th Century—W. E. GLADSTONE.
4. The Coming Anarchy—P. KROPOTKIN.
5. Mr. Lecky and Political Morality—W. E. GLADSTONE.
6. Electoral Facts of 1887—W. E. GLADstone.
7. The Position of the Unionists—EDWARD DICEY.
8. The Parliamentary Breakdown—FRANK H. HILL.
9. The Radical Programme—SELBORNE.
10. True Reform of the House of Lords—BRABAZON.

11. Confession of a Metropolitan Member—J. E. THOROLD ROGERS.
12. The American State and the American Man—ALBERT SHAW.
13. The Real Truth about Tory Democracy—DUNRAVEN.
14. Parliamentary Procedure — SAMUEL PLIMSOLL.
15. Marriage with a Deceased Wife's Sister—BRAMWELL.
16. The Constitutional Question—X.
17. Prisoners as Witnesses—J. F. STEPHENS.
18. A Court of Lunacy — ARTHUR D. HAYTER.
19. Parliamentary Procedure — FORTNIGHTLY REVIEW, Feb., 1886.
20. Oaths: Parliamentary and Judicial—W. C., Bishop of Peterborough.

10. Australian Literature — STEPHEN THOMPSON.
11. The Railway Question in Manitoba—GOLDWIN SMITH.
12. The Colonial Conference and Imperial Defence—WILLIAM GRESWELL.
13. Imperial Migration and Settlement—WILLIAM FIELDING.
14. Notes on New Zealand—E. BRODIE HOARE.
15. Are we Worthy of our Empire?—C. C. PENROSE FITZGERALD.

VOL. 4.

COLONIAL QUESTIONS.

1. A Colonial View of Imperial Federation—ROBERT STOUT.
2. The Closer Union of the Empire—JOHN MERRIMAN.
3. On Well Meant Nonsense about Emigration—G. OSBORNE MORGAN.
4. A New Title for the Crown—GEORGE BADEN POWELL.
5. French Penal Colonies — ARTHUR GRIFFITHS.
6. South Africa as it is—JOHN ROBINSON.
7. The Imperial Institute —KENRICK B. MURRAY.
8. The Canadian Fisheries Dispute—LORNE.
9. The Canadian Constitution—GOLDWIN SMITH.

VOL. 5.

SCIENTIFIC QUESTIONS.

1. Physiological Selection—GEO. R. ROMANES.
2. Scientific and Pseudo-Scientific Realism—P. KROPOTKIN.
3. Professor Huxley on Canon Liddon—ARGYLL.
4. Science and Pseudo-Science—T. H. HUXLEY.
5. Science Falsely So-called—C. F. GORDON-CUMMING.
6. A Great Lesson—ARGYLL.
7. Infection and Disinfection—ROBSON ROOSE.
8. Earthquakes—G. H. DARWIN.
9. The Province of Physics — W. S. LILLY.
10. The Moabite Stone—CH. CLERMONT-GANNEAU.

VOL. 6.

BIOGRAPHICAL AND LITERARY STUDIES.

1. Thomas Dekker — ALGERNON CHAS. SWINBURNE.

2. Cyril Tourneur — ALGERNON CHAS. SWINBURNE.
3. A Friend of God—MATTHEW ARNOLD.
4. A Beggar Poet—THOMAS WOOLNER.
5. Comte's Atheism—H. CARLISLE.
6. Valentine Visconti (Parts 1 and 2)— A. MARY F. ROBINSON.
7. A Roman Matron and the Roman Lady—E. LYNN LINTON.
8. Marie Antoinette's Milliner's Bills— GEORGE AUGUSTUS SALA.
9. Fine Passages in Verse and Prose, Selected by Living Men of Letters (Parts 1, 2, 3 and 4).
10. General Boulanger—W. H. GLEADELL
11. Last Words on Shelley — EDWARD DOWDEN.
12. Pascal the Sceptic—W. L. COURTNEY.
13. The Flight of Piero De Medici—A. MARY F. ROBINSON.
14. A Midland University—J. R. SEELEY.
15. Count Leo Tolstoi—MATTHEW ARNOLD
16. Mademoiselle Aïssé—EDMUND GOSSE.
17. The Call of Savonarola—EMILIO CASTELAR.
18. The Imaginative Art of the Renaissance—VERNON LEE.
19. The Great Olympian Sedition—W. E. GLADSTONE.
20. Count Leo Tolstoi—JULIA WEDGWOOD.
21. The Story of Zebeher Pasha— FLORA L. SHAW.
22. Afghan Life in Afghan Songs—JAMES DARMESTETER.
23. The Life and Letters of Chas. Darwin —ARCH. GEIKIE.
24. "Owen Meredith," Earl of Lytton— ALFRED AUSTIN.
25. Lord Iddesleigh—CRANBROOK.
26. Robert Southey—JOHN DENNIS.

VOL. 7.

CONTEMPORARY LIFE AND THOUGHT.

1. Contemporary Life and Thought in the United States—C. K. ADAMS.
2. Contemporary Life and Thought in Italy—G. BOGLIETTE.
3. Contemporary Life and Thought in France—G. MONOD.
4. Contemporary Life and Thought in Germany—H. GEFFCKEN.
5. Contemporary Life and Thought in China—A RESIDENT OF PEKING.

PERIODICALS.

The following Annuals, Reviews, Magazines and Newspapers are taken as issued and bound when the volumes are complete. The titles of Newspapers and Literary Journals are pointed in Italics.

Académie des sciences, Comptes-rendus.
Academy.
Acadian Recorder.
All the Year Round.
Almanach du clergé—la France ecclésiastique.
Almanach de Gotha.
Almanach national.
American Antiquarian.
Am. Ass. for Adv't of Science, Proceed'gs.
American almanac.
American Catholic Historical Researches.
American Catholic Quarterly.
American Chemical Journal.
American Church Review.
American Entomological Society, Transactions.
American Journal of Archæology.
American Journal of Mathematics.
American Journal of Philology.
American Journal of Science.
American Law Review.
American Naturalist.
American Railroad Journal.
American Society of Civil Engineers,—Transactions and Proceedings.
Analecta Juris Pontificii.
Andover Review.
Annales de l'Association pour la propagation de la foi.
Annales de chimie et de physique.
Annales du Conservatoire des arts et manufactures.
Annales du génie civil.
Annales d'hygiène et de médécine légale.
Annales des mathématiques.

Annales des mines.
Annales de l'Observatoire de Paris.
———————— Observations.
———————— Mémoires.
Annales de la philosophie chrétienne.
Annales des Ponts et Chaussées.
———— - de la science agronomique.
Annales (les) Térésiennes.
Année (l') géographique.
Année (l') militaire.
Année (l') politique.
Année (l') scientifique.
Annuaire de l'administration française.
Annuaire diplomatique et consulaire.
Annuaire des eaux et forêts.
Annuaire de l'économie politique.
Annuaire de l'instruction publique.
Annuaire de législation étrangère.
Annuaire des longitudes.
Annuaire météorologique de France.
Annuaire de la noblesse de France.
Annuaire de la société des agriculteurs.
Archives du Droit international.
Archives Parlementaires.
Argosy.
Army list.
Art (l').
Art Journal.
Artiste (l').
Asiatic Quarterly Review.
Association française pour l'avancement des sciences.
Athenæum.
Atlantic Monthly.
Audubon Magazine.
Auk (The).

INDEX.

Bankers' Almanac and Register.
Bankers' Magazine.
Bibliographie catholique.
Bibliographie de la France.
Bibliothèque de l'Ecole des Chartres.
Bib. Arch. Society.
Blackwood's Magazine.
Board of Trade (London, Eng.) Journal.
Bookbuyer.
Book Lore.
Bookmart.
Bookseller.
Botanical Gazette.
Bradstreet's.
Brandon Blade (The).
Brandon Sun (The).
Brandon Times.
Brevets d'invention, Description.
British Almanac.
Brit. Ass. for Adv't of Science, Proceed'gs.
British Colonist (B.C.)
British Quarterly.
Builder (The)
Bulletin de l'Académie de médécine.
Bulletin des arrêts de la Cour de cassation.
Bulletin des arrêts de la partie civile.
Bulletin des arrêts de la partie criminelle.
Bulletin du Bibliophile.
Bulletin des Lois.
Bulletin de la société d'acclimatation.
Bulletin de la société de géographie.
Bulletin de la société de législation comparée.

Cabinet (le) historique.
Canada (le).
Canada—Français.
Canada Health Journal.
Canada Lancet.
Canada Law Journal.
Canada Medical and Surgical Journal.
Canadian Antiquarian and Numismatic Journal.
Canadian Bee Journal.
Canadian Craftsman.
Canadian Entomologist.
Canadian Horticulturist.
Canadian Institute, Proceedings.
Canadian Journal.
Canadian Law Times.
Canadian Magazine of Science and Patent Office Record.
Canadian Manufacturer.
Canadian Methodist Magazine.
Canadia Militia Gazette.
Canadian Mining Review.
Canadian Poultry Review.
Canadian Trade Review.
Canadien (le)
Cassell's Magazine.
Catholic Presbyterian.
Catholic World.
Causeries scientifiques.
Central Law Journal.
Century Magazine.
Chambers' Journal.
Church Builder.
Church Review.
Church Quarterly.
Colonies and India.
Connaissance des temps (la).
Contemporain (le).
Contemporary Review.
Co-operative Index to Periodicals.
Cornhill Magazine.
Correspondant (le)
Cosmos. Les Mondes.
Country Gentleman.
Courrier des Etats-Unis.
Courrier des Provinces Maritimes.
Courrier du Canada.
Critic.
Daily Manitoban.

INDEX.

Daily Times (Moncton, N. B.)
Daily Transcript (Moncton, N. B.)
Dalhousie College Gazette.
Dalloz—Jurisprudence générale.
Documents inédits—Histoire de France.
Dublin Review.
Duvergier—Collection des lois.

Eclectic Magazine.
Ecole Polytechnique, archives et journal.
Economist.
Economiste (l').
Edinburgh Review.
Educational Journal.
Educational Monthly.
Engineering.
English Historical Review.
English Illustrated Magazine.
Entomologica Americana.
Etendard (l').
Etudes religieuses, littéraires, etc.
Evènement (l')
Evening Journal (Ottawa).
Expositor.

Farmer's Advocate.
Florist and Pomologist.
Fortnightly Review.
Forum (The).
France (la) judiciaire.
Free Press (Ottawa).

Galerie (la) contemporaine.
Gazette (Montreal).
Gazette des Campagnes.
Gazette (la) médicale.
Gazette des Tribunaux.
Génie (le) civil.
Gentleman's Magazine.
Globe (Toronto).
Good Words.
Graphic.

Grip.

Halifax Chronicle.
Halifax Morning Herald.
Harper's Magazine.
Herald (Montreal).

Illustrated London News.
Illustrated Naval and Military Magazine.
Illustration (l')
Intermédiaire (l') des chercheurs et curieux.
Interstate Commerce Commission Reports.
Investor's Monthly.
Irish Law Reports.

Journal d'Agriculture (Québec).
Journal d'agriculture pratique.
Journal asiatique.
Journal of Botany.
Journal of the Chemical Society.
Journal of Commerce.
Journal du droit international privé.
Journal de l'école polytechnique.
Journal d'hygiène populaire (Montréal).
Journal des économistes.
Journal de l'instruction publique (Montréal).
Journal de jurisprudence commerciale.
Journal des mathématiques.
Journal of Morphology.
Journal des notaires.
Journal officiel de la République française.
Journal du Palais.
Journal de Québec.
Journal of the Royal Agricultural Society.
Journal of the Royal United Service Institution.
Journal des savants.
Journal des Tribunaux de Commerce.

Law Magazine and Review.
Law Quarterley Review.
Law Times.

129

Lecture (la).
Legal News.
Lettres et Arts.
Library Journal.
Literary Churchman.
Literary News.
Littell's Living Age.
Livre (le).
London Quarterly Review.
London Society.
Longman's Magazine.
Lower Canada Jurist.

Macmillan's Magazine.
Magasin d'éducation.
Magasin pittoresque.
Magazine of American History.
Magazine of Western History.
Mainland Guardian (B.C).
Manitoba (le).
Manitoba Free Press.
Manitoba Law Journal.
Manufacturer and Builder.
Matériaux et documents.
Medico-Legal Journal.
Mémoires de l'Académie de médecine.
Mémoires de l'Institut.
Mémoires de la société d'anthropologie.
Mémoires de la société géologique de France.
Merry England.
Minerve (la).
Missions catholiques (les).
Monde (le).
Monde (le) Illustré, Montréal.
Monetary Times.
Moniteur Acadien.
Moniteur (le) du commerce.
Month.
Monthly Packet.
Montreal Law Reports.
Morning Chronicle (Halifax).

Murray's Magazine.
Musée des familles.
Nation (The).
Nation (la).
National Quarterly Review.
Nature.
Nature (la).
Nautical Magazine.
Naval and Military Magazine.
Naval List.
New England Historical and Genealogical Register.
New Princeton Review.
New York Academy of Sciences, Proceedings.
New York Herald.
Nineteenth Century.
North American Review.
Notes and Queries (English).
Notes and Queries (American).
Nouvelle Revue.
Nouvelle Revue historique du droit.
Nouvelles Soirées canadiennes.
Outing.
Ottawa Daily Citizen.
Palestine Exploration Fund (Report).
Paris-Canada.
Parish Magazine (B.C.).
Patrie (la).
Patriot and Island Argus (P.E.I.).
Pennsylvania Magazine of History.
Political Science Quarterly.
Polybiblion (Revue bibliographique).
Popular Science Monthly.
Presbyterian Record.
Presbyterian Review.
Psyche.
Public Opinion.
Publishers' Circular.
Publishers' Weekly.

INDEX.

Qu'*Appelle Progress.*
Qu'*Appelle Vidette.*
Quarterly Journal of Economics.
Quarterly Journal of the Geological Society.
Quarterly Journal of Microscopical Sciences.
Quarterly Review.
Queen's College Journal.
Quebec Chronicle.
Quebec Law Reports.
Quebec Mercury.

Réforme sociale (la).
Regina Leader
Revue archéologique.
Revue Britannique.
Revue Canadienne.
Revue Catholique des institutions et du droit.
Revue Critique de législation et de jurisprudence.
Revue des Deux Mondes.
Revue de droit international.
Revue des Eaux et Forêts.
Revue de l'art chrétien.
Revue d'histoire diplomatique.
Revue de Législation ancienne et moderne.
Revue Française.
Revue française de l'étranger et des colonies.
Revue du monde latin.
Revue légale.
Revue littéraire de " l'Univers."
Revue maritime et coloniale.
Revue universelle des mines.
Revue du Monde Catholique.
Revue du notariat.
Revue politique et littéraire.
Revue des questions scientifiques.
Revue des sciences médicales.
Revue scientifique.
Royal Geographical Society, Journal.

St John Daily Sun.
St. John Telegraph.
St. Nicholas Magazine
Sabin's American Bibliography.
Saskatchewan Herald.
Saturday Review.
Science.
Science Gossip.
Science populaire.
Scientific American.
Scientific Canadian.
Scottish Review.
Selkirk Herald.
Selkirk Record.
Semaine (la) religieuse.
Southern Law Review.
Stateman's Year Book.
Statistical Journal.
Statistiques de la France.
Sun, The (Winnipeg).
Sunday Magazine.
Swiss Cross (The)
Sydney Herald (Cape Breton).
Tablet (The).
Temple Bar.
Thémis (la)
Time.
Times (*Daily and Weekly Editions*).
Toronto Mail.
Torrey Botanical Club, Bulletin.
Union (l') Médicale du Canada.
United Service Magazine.
U. S. Catholic Historical Magazine.
U. S. Patent Office Official Gazette.
University Magazine.
Vanity Fair.
Varsity (The).
Vick's Illustrated Monthly Magazine.
Week (*The*).
Weekly Tribune and Marquette Review.
Westminster Review.
Whitaker's Almanac.
Woman's World
Zoological Record.

www.ingramcontent.com/pod-product-compliance
Lightning Source LLC
Chambersburg PA
CBHW030346170426
43202CB00010B/1265